Faith and Creativity

Faith and Creativity

Essays in Honor of Eugene H. Peters

Edited by

George Nordgulen, Eastern Kentucky University

George W. Shields, Kentucky State University

CBP Press
St. Louis, Missouri

Scripture quotations, unless otherwise indicated, are from the Revised Standard Version of the Bible, copyrighted 1946, 1952, © 1971, 1973 by the Division of Christian Education of the National Council of Churches of Christ in the U. S. A. and are used with permission.

Library of Congress Cataloging in Publication Data

Faith and creativity

Contents: Eugene Herbert Peters / Damaris Peters
— A Metaphysic of Universal Freedom / Charles
Hartshorne — From pre-panpsychism to pansubjectivity /
Lewis S. Ford — [etc.]
1. Peters, Eugene H. (Eugene Herbert), 1929-1983.
2. Process philosophy. 3. Process theology. I. Peters,
Eugene H. (Eugene Herbert), 1929-1983. II. Nordgulen,
George. III. Shields, George W.
B945.P464F34   1987   146   87-14100
ISBN 0-8272-1017-5

Printed in the United States of America

Contents

Note on References

Footnotes which enhance the context of discussion, rather than merely document references, have been placed within the body of the text for the reader's convenience. These are marked with asterisks. Other notes have been placed at the end of each chapter and are numbered consecutively.

Acknowledgment

The editors wish to express their gratitude to Sheryl L. Buckley, M.D. for her financial assistance and direction of fund raising efforts among Hiram College Alumni, without which this book would not have been possible.

Introduction

Dr. Eugene Herbert Peters, Professor and Chair of the Department of Philosophy at Hiram College, died in 1983 after a long and quietly heroic battle with leukemia. Eugene touched and shaped many lives with his teaching, lecturing, scholarly writing, and his preaching as an ordained minister of the Christian Church (Disciples of Christ). Some of us in academe have felt his personal impact so strongly that we have been moved to celebrate his life and thought with this memorial *Festschrift*. We believe that the title, *Faith and Creativity*, is peculiarly appropriate, since both were the hallmark of his person and intellectual endeavors. Indeed, "faith" and "creativity" were the two basic components of Eugene's life-long scholarly project: the articulation, defense and criticism of "process philosophy" (which holds "creativity" to be metaphysically ultimate) as a framework for understanding Christian faith and human religious experience.

A few remarks concerning Eugene's intellectual development and achievements seem in order here, although we refer the reader to Mrs. Damaris Peters' contribution for a more extensive account of biographical matters (along with an appended bibliography). Eugene was accepted into the Ph. D. program at The University of Chicago in 1953, where he studied with, among others, Professor Charles Hartshorne in the Department of Philosophy, and philosopher of religion Bernard Loomer, who was then in the Divinity School. Under Loomer's demanding direction, he completed a tightly argued doctoral thesis— "Form, Power and the Unity of the Individual"—in which he compared the philosophical positions of A. N. Whitehead and Paul Tillich. His aim here was to show how a metaphysics of creativity, as developed by Whitehead, was more adequate in its interpretation of the concrete individual than an ontology of being, as developed by Tillich. While he appreciated Tillich's historical insights and existential analyses, he argued that these could be more clearly understood and more adequately expressed in terms of the categories and concepts of process philosophy. In 1960 he was awarded the degree of Doctor of Philosophy by the University of Chicago on the basis of this thesis.

From 1957–1962, he taught Philosophical Theology at the Graduate Theological Seminary of Phillips University at Enid, Oklahoma. In 1962, he accepted a position in philosophy at Hiram College in Hiram, Ohio, where he remained for the rest of his career.

Eugene published two major studies of process thought—*The Creative Advance* (1966, hereafter: CA) and *Hartshorne and Neoclassical Metaphysics: An Interpretation* (1970, hereafter: HNM). The first of these has the distinction of being perhaps the first (commercially published) book to be substantially devoted to the systematic and critical exposition of the philosophy of Charles Hartshorne. Its critical notices were very good ones,[1] and some two decades later Hartshorne scholars (such as contributor Donald Wayne Viney) lament its being out of print. Says Viney in correspondence with the editors: "The CA is still perhaps the best short introduction to process philosophy." HNM is better known and is a veritable model of the systematic exposition of a philosopher's views. Hartshorne himself has expressed his high regard for this work in his contribution to this volume. Surely it will remain one of the standards by which future Hartshorne research will be judged.

In addition to these two major studies, Eugene contributed numerous articles and reviews to such scholarly journals as *Encounter, The Journal of Religion, Process Studies*, and *The Southwestern Journal of Philosophy*. The editors of the last invited him to author the opening feature article in its 1977 symposium on Hartshorne. In 1981, he was Plenary Speaker at the Society of Christian Philosophers' annual conference held at Eastern Kentucky University, an occasion which brought together Eugene and four of the contributors (Professors Nordgulen, Shields, Vitali and Ford). The proceedings of this session of the conference were published collectively in Volume 44 of *Encounter*. It is also of note that Eugene was invited by the editors of The University of Chicago's symposium papers in honor of Charles Hartshorne (published in 1985 as *Existence and Actuality: Conversations with Charles Hartshorne*) to author the opening essay on Hartshorne's methodology.

Several features of Eugene's scholarly work were distinctive and deserve comment. First of all, he was a remarkably lucid and economical writer. He could get at the heart of a philosophical position or problem, without sparing niceties of detail, in elegantly simple and unpretentious sentences. This is an "art" all too rare among philosophical and theological writers. Indeed, such an ability displays a certain kind of intellectual power. Secondly, Eugene was no mere expositor of process thought. He could be counted on to raise penetrating critical questions of crucial assumptions. In particular in this connection, note "Retrospect and Prospect" (the concluding chapter) in CA; "A Critical Look at Some Crucial Axioms" in HNM; "Hartshorne on Actuality" in *Process Studies* Vol. 7, No. 3 (1977); and "Methodology in the Metaphysics of Charles Hartshorne" in *Existence and Actuality*. Thirdly, Eugene was capable of very rigorous treatment of philosophical and theological issues. He was a master of what Paul Weiss once referred to (at a conference attended by the editors) as Hartshorne's massive methodological "machinery." Not only did he write thoroughly systematic and highly illuminating accounts of neoclassical methodology (cf. HNM, Ch. 2), but he also wrote articles bearing on the rigorous and technically sophisticated work of, for instance, Alvin Plantinga and George L. Goodwin. Finally, Eugene displayed a deep knowledge of the history of ideas, especially metaphysics and philosophical theology, which gave a number of his essays an impressive richness of perspective.

Eugene was not only a philosopher specializing in the critical interpretation and adjudication of Hartshorne's philosophy. He was also a committed Christian and Christian theologian. As such, he constantly struggled to come to grips with the modern world. It seemed to him that the person of faith had an *obligation* to bring the resources of faith into both cognitive and existential relation to the perennial issues of theology: reason and revelation, ontology and history, the kingdom of God and the kingdoms of the world, Christ and the church, etc. Note that, for instance, in the CA, he wrestles extensively with the problem of the relation of process thought to the *life* (not only the doctrine) of the church. Here Eugene is very much a man of faith, a theologian reflecting on the church in the service of the church. And this is done, in part, by reflecting on the full sweep of the history of Christian theology from Augustine, Anselm, and Aquinas to Niebuhr, Tillich, and the more recent process theologians such as Ogden, Cobb, and Williams.

Among contemporary Protestant theologians, Eugene was pointedly impressed by Reinhold Niebuhr's doctrine of persons and his social criticism, but, like Paul Tillich, disliked his lack of metaphysical sensitivity. (He was critical of Barth and Brunner for much the same reason.) Above all, he appreciated the attempt of his teacher Daniel Day Williams to bring together coherently the motifs of God's grace and humanity's hope in the light of the process thought of Whitehead and Hartshorne.

Notwithstanding these important forays into specific theologians and theological issues, the bulk of Eugene's interest was concentrated upon the most fundamental of theological problems: the existence and nature of God. Both of his books and most of his articles reflect his concern with this issue. Since Hartshorne had gone further than Whitehead in exploring and reconstructing the theistic idea, Hartshorne eventually became the main focus of attention. In particular, Hartshorne's development of the ontological argument came to occupy a place of high esteem in Eugene's thought. Consequently, he diligently studied logic, including modal logic, like Hartshorne, seeking the assistance that could be found there in refining one's expression of the argument. Perhaps his most important contribution to ontological argument research can be found in his posthumously published, "Charles Hartshorne and the Ontological Argument" (*Process Studies* Vol. 14, No. 1 [1984]), where he argues very effectively against the view (promulgated by R. L. Purtill among others) that there is triviality or superfluity in Hartshorne's reconstruction of the argument. Moreover, Eugene became a most articulate spokesperson for the view that a basically *coherent* doctrine of God, in contrast to that of Augustine, Aquinas, and the classical theistic tradition in general, can be found in the philosophy of Hartshorne.

Although his positive estimation of both Whitehead and Hartshorne was predominant, as we mentioned earlier, he was critical of and puzzled by a number of points. For instance: He held that Whitehead's natural theology in *Process and Reality* was cryptic and needed elaboration and correction in the light of some of Whitehead's own principles. He agreed with Hartshorne that Whitehead's doctrine of eternal objects does not cohere with a philosophy of process. Concerning Hartshorne, he was troubled by the principle that "to be is to be known," and he queried whether an infallible knower can adequately know (or understand) a fallible one, whether definiteness is the meaning of actuality, and whether we can maintain Hartshorne's notion of divine inclusiveness in relation to the problem of evil. Near the close of his life he argued that there are more achievements in Thomistic metaphysics than process thinkers, particularly Hartshorne, had allowed or recognized. One of his last papers, on "Classical and Neo-classical Theology," was an attempt to delineate some of these unrecognized achievements (see *Encounter* Vol. 44, No. 1 [1983]).

*   *   *   *   *

Eugene was not only a scholar but also an exciting teacher. His classes were provocative, inspiring, and disillusioning. His voice was deep and rich, his manner of presentation charismatic and challenging. At times, his classroom presentations were strictly informative; here was his rich and detailed analysis of ideas and thinkers, of historical situations and existential response. At other times, particularly in seminars, his classes were more like Socratic dialogues in which topics were presented and different views were invited, followed by the development of the dialectic of argument and counter-argument. He always had time (or took time) to see students and to study with them. (While he was working on *The Creative Advance*, he and Nordgulen met on Saturday mornings to discuss Whitehead's *Adventures of Ideas* and *Process and Reality*.) This made for exciting educational experiences. The editor mentioned above can personally attest that much of what he thought he "knew" when he reached theological seminary was destroyed by Eugene's dialectical teaching process. But, happily, what was taken away with one hand was restored by the other. Eugene's sermons at the University Chapel services, and his lectures at conferences, especially his illuminating applications of process thought to the lived world, made deep and lasting impressions on his students.

Another student of Eugene's eloquently expresses her appreciation for him as a teacher. Dr. Sheryl Buckley writes, "Eugene's strength as a teacher sprang from two sources: his scholarship and his personal integrity. He had an enormous respect for each individual he met, which enabled him to take his students and their thought seriously, even when it was not well-organized or precisely presented. In fact, Eugene had amazing patience which allowed him to wait graciously as his students struggled to articulate their ideas. His respect for his students was so essentially a part of the man that he could use virtually any utterance offered in class as a springboard for discussion. I still remember one occasion in which he called upon a classmate who said he had not read the assignment, because he had to do laundry in order to have clothes to wear to class. Eugene pointed out how often in life one fails to achieve the large deed or great plan because of the necessity to deal with mundane but essential chores. He cautioned us to guard our priorities so as not to be diverted from our goals, some of the most sound and practical advice I ever received.

"The best of the best were the small seminars Eugene offered, sometimes in his study at home. The students did not want the classes to end, and had to be chased from the room. Especially during these sessions, students had the opportunity to watch Eugene's mind at work as he would explore ideas with us. He never demonstrated impatience with our struggles to understand the significance of some subtlety, and he was particularly brilliant at finding analogies to unlock some difficult point.

13

"He became the idol of his students in the best possible way: not as a distant figure that he wished we might be magically transformed into, but as a very real human being who valued us and inspired us to strive for the levels of scholarship and integrity he had achieved. To meet him once was an engaging experience. To study philosophy with him was an adventure and a joy, perhaps the most rewarding experience I have yet had, and a rare privilege. I count myself lucky to have been so blessed."

* * * * *

The essays in this book do not form an overall view of the "process movement" or Eugene's perception of it. Rather, they seek, in the spirit of the one whom they honor, to express and explore some of the exciting developments going on today in philosophy and religious thought from a process point of view: Hartshorne argues for "universal freedom" at a time when determinism still holds appeal for many in the scientific and philosophic communities. Ford deals with a technical problem in the interpretation of Whitehead's views on mentality and with its importance for future developments in Whitehead scholarship. Cobb argues for the adequacy of process metaphysics in enabling the process theologian to deal with crucial problems of biblical authority, justification by faith, fundamentalism, ecumenism, and some related moral issues. Ogden sets forth his latest thinking concerning belief in God in a secular and secularizing world from the standpoint of process theology. Griffin takes up the problem of creation in relation to the issues of the nature of God's power, nuclear war and the *Imitatio Dei*. Williamson treats competing positions on the authority of scripture since the *Shoah*. Nordgulen examines one conversation in world religions, namely, that between Judaism and Christianity on the resurrection of Jesus in the light of process theology. Viney examines the relation of faith and reason in Kierkegaard and Lequier from a process point of view. Vitali explores the progress of the growing dialogue between proponents of Neo-Thomistic and Whiteheadean modes of thought, and he explores the promise and limitations this holds for the future. Shields maps the complex relationship of Hartshorne to the analytic philosophical tradition.

In what is to follow, a number of the contributors have discussed or referred to various aspects of Eugene's thought. However, *all* of the contributed papers, none of which have been previously published, are concerned with areas which were of vital interest to Eugene. We have adopted the following (albeit unavoidably overlapping) organizational scheme, corresponding to Eugene's main disciplinary and thematic concerns: Essays in Metaphysics, in Process Thought and Christian Faith, in Theology and Philosophy of Religion, and in Philosophic Method. All of the essays, we submit, reflect Eugene's spirit of exploration, criticism, and openness to emerging issues and problems. Those of us who knew Eugene as a teacher, scholar and friend are confident that he would have endorsed, to wax Whiteheadian, such creative adventures in ideas.

G. N.

G. W. S.

---

[1]See for example *Process Philosophy and Christian Thought*, edited by D. Brown, R. E. James, and G. Reeves (Bobbs-Merrill, 1971) pp. 57–59.

Eugene Herbert Peters:

A Biographical Note

by Damaris Peters

Gene grew up in Austin, Texas, because his parents felt that living in a university town would be an advantage for their two children. His father, Emil, whose parents had emigrated from Germany, was born in the Minneapolis-St. Paul area, where he met and married Louise Snider, a Canadian by birth. When her father and brother became ill with tuberculosis, the young couple moved with the Sniders to Florida. It was there that their daughter, Florence, was born in 1927. Emil had been a farmer in Minnesota and struggled to secure employment in Florida. He then moved the little family all the way to San Francisco, where on January 30, 1929, Eugene Herbert Peters was born. The economic situation was no better on the west coast than it had been in Florida and, after a short stay in Denver, Emil found steady employment as a carpenter in the Galveston, Texas, shipyards. While Gene was still a pre-schooler, the family made the carefully considered move to Austin.

Times were hard for the Peters, as they were for many families during the Depression. They had no car, no phone, and Gene recalled watching his father kill rats in houses they rented. (His parents did not own a home until Gene was in college.) Still, Gene had happy memories from childhood: imaginative games Florence devised for the two of them, playing in the neighborhood all day on long, hot, Texas summer days, and sitting on the back steps in the evening as his father told stories—many of them narratives from the Old Testament.

By the eighth grade, when he was at University Junior High School, Gene had settled into the "straight A" pattern which would mark the remainder of his academic career. He already enjoyed writing: he contributed a column to the Austin newspaper each week and began to try his hand at poetry. He attended junior high school with several children of University of Texas professors, and he began friendly competition with them (and other bright youngsters) which would continue through high school. He would smile as he recalled the exhiliration of solving a difficult trigonometry problem faster than the other members of the class. In the 1940s there was one high school in the city, Austin High School; it was large and offered a fine program. Gene was named poet laureate of the school and graduated at the top of his class. The move to Austin had been a good one.

The Peters had been active in the Baptist Church in Minnesota, but they quickly discovered that Baptists in Texas were not the same. Finding their place in the Hyde Park Christian Church, they became staunch members of the Christian Church (Disciples of Christ). The Hyde Park Church, with Chester Crow as minister, offered an active program for youth. He and his lovely wife, Elizabeth, were important to Gene. Crow believed that the talented young people in the church should try preaching, and sent Gene and others to speak in little country churches when they were mere teenagers. Already an able speaker, Gene met with surprising success.

The University of Texas had an honors program called Plan II into which Gene was invited as a freshman. During that year he also took work with Paul Wassenich, Chair of Bible at the University of Texas. Wassenich was a graduate of the University of Chicago, and it was from him that Gene learned about the Chicago Divinity School.

After one year at Texas, Gene transferred to Texas Christian University in Fort Worth, in part because he wanted to live away from home. Advised to major in religion in preparation for seminary, he felt strongly that he should concentrate in other areas. He completed majors in both psychology and sociology; he took four years of Greek—which he dearly loved—and was a grader for the Greek Department. In his junior year he discovered philosophy and crammed into the remaining two years all the philosophy courses he could. (Though his record at TCU. was outstanding, there was no Phi Beta Kappa chapter for him to join. Gene was pleased when in 1971 he was made a charter member of the Hiram College chapter.)

During the three years at TCU Gene served as student minister for small churches, traveling many miles on the Greyhound bus. He spent the summer of 1950, with the B.A. degree in hand, conducting Youth Round-Ups throughout Texas. Round-Ups consisted of a week of leadership training, recreation, and preaching. Though his major responsibility was preaching, Gene was a magnificent director of recreation. As he himself admitted, he never quite got over being ten years old, and he loved to play. A simple game of "Fruit Basket Turnover" was a riot when he directed it.

One stop on the Round-Up circuit was my church, Central Christian in Vernon. Gene spoke at the Sunday morning service, and I had never before heard such a sermon. The content was clear and challenging, the delivery, powerful. Seventeen years old and just out of high school, I went home from church and wrote in my diary that I had just seen (though not met) the man I intended to marry. He was barely aware of my existence during the week that followed!

That fall, Gene headed for Chicago and the only graduate school he had considered. From 1950 to 1954 Gene lived in the Disciples Divinity House, where he found a warm fellowship and an ideal setting for the serious study he wanted to do. He liked to quote the traditional description of the Disciples House: a combination of the best features of a college fraternity house and a medieval monastery.

The Chicago Divinity School of the 1950s was the perfect context for Gene's intellectual development. The generalized Bachelor of Divinity (B.D.) he took included work in religion and art, religion and personality, ethics, world religions, Bible, church history, and his favorite: theology. His professors were among the best in their fields: Joachim Wach, Alvin Pitcher, James Luther Adams, Wilhelm Pauck, Preston Roberts, Bernard Meland, Amos Wilder (brother of Thornton), John Coert Tylersdaam, Daniel Day Williams, and Bernard Loomer. Every quarter he sat in on the history of philosophy sequence with Alan Gewirth and took courses on Plato and Aristotle from Richard McKeon, all in the University of Chicago Philosophy Department.

One professor with dual appointment in the Divinity School and the Philosophy Department was of special interest to Gene. From the first, Gene was drawn to Charles Hartshorne and his way of doing philosophy. Gene's roommate in the Disciples House, Clyde Smith, tells how Gene labored over papers for Hartshorne's courses. House residents eagerly awaited the return of those papers in order to read the extensive comments Professor Hartshorne had scrawled all over the back of Gene's paper. Thus was born an enduring intellectual and personal friendship.

Having passed comprehensive examinations in all seven areas covered in the degree program, Gene received the B.D. degree in May, 1953. The summer which followed found Gene once again involved with Youth Round-Ups. One was scheduled in Wichita Falls, just fifty miles from my home where I was spending the summer before my senior year at Texas Christian as an "adult" leader for the church youth. When the Vernon youth were invited to attend the nearby Round-Up with Gene Peters as leader, I quickly organized an outing for my young charges. In fact, I spent the entire week in Wichita Falls. Gene and I exchanged letters during the remainder of the summer. (I spent hours on my first letter, consulting the dictionary frequently.) Later, he visited me at TCU before returning to Chicago to begin the Ph.D. We had at most three real "dates" when he asked, "Would you rather marry a preacher or a teacher?" "I would rather marry *you*," was my response. For the next twenty-nine years he insisted that his question had been purely rhetorical, but he was too much a gentleman to disappoint me.

When Gene returned to Chicago in the fall of 1953 he became the first Ph.D. student to receive financial support from the Disciples Divinity House. Dean W. Barnett Blakemore named him Resident Scholar. During the winter quarter, Gene spent two weeks in the hospital with infectious mononucleosis. He had been taking German for a quarter and a half and had registered to take the Ph.D. reading exam. He obtained permission to leave the hospital and give the exam a try. He not only passed it, he passed "at high level." (Later, not wishing to waste a course on French, he bought a box of French vocabulary cards, a verb wheel, and a dictionary; after translating all day for seventeen days, he passed the French exam—though not at high level!)

The following quarter Gene left Chicago to become minister of First Christian Church of Kerrville, Texas. We married in July and lived in Kerrville until the year's end. Having learned that Paul Tillich would be teaching at Chicago beginning in the winter quarter, Gene could not stay away. On January 1, 1955, we were in Chicago.

Gene had a seminar with Tillich, and, in addition, he heard Tillich present a series of lectures which constituted *Systematic Theology*, Volume II. Most of Gene's effort, however, was devoted to preparation for the comprehensive examinations, including an oral exam, and then work on the dissertation. He proposed to write on "Form, Unity, and the Individual" in the writings of two philosophers, Whitehead and Royce, and two theologians, Tillich and Weiman. He completed sections on all four thinkers but used only Whitehead and Tillich in the finished product. His adviser was Bernard Loomer, and he was not a "cooperative" adviser. He loved to discuss every idea with Gene and could seldom be pinned down with an official approval. He laughingly complained about how "pig-headed" Gene was because he would not change his interpretation of Tillich (the major focus of their disagreement), and indeed, Gene made very few substantive changes as a result of their lengthy discussions. Somehow Loomer managed to have the oral exam over the dissertation waived, saying that "there couldn't possibly be an oral exam more grueling than what I have put you through, Peters." Bernie Loomer was a beloved mentor.

Our son, David Alan, was born in March 1957. Gene approached this development with the same intellectual vigor he applied to everything else. For nine months, he urged me—only half facetiously—to write my theology of pregnancy. The Sunday following Dave's birth, his sermon for the West Pullman Christian Church where he was minister was titled "On Becoming a Parent."

Though the dissertation was only half done, Gene felt that in order to provide for his expanded family he must leave Chicago and thus ended an era. Almost twenty years later in August 1973 he wrote in the *Disciples Divinity House Bulletin*:

> I doubt that I will ever capture again the sense of glee I felt every fall when I left balmy Texas and the summer behind, and made the slow trip northward. Those were golden days. True enough, the atmosphere changed and stiffened a bit as we came closer to Chicago. It was hazier, the trees were readier for winter, and everyone seemed more preoccupied and busy. But all this meant to me that the time had come to take up *ultimate* things, and I threw my energies into the study and activity of those days with abandon . . .
>
> All that I do and think now is influenced to some extent by my experiences in Chicago. Of course, I stayed there for some years. But the magnitude and intensity of those days has shaped my life.

From Chicago we moved to Enid, Oklahoma, where Gene became Professor of Theology at the Graduate Seminary of Phillips University. In Enid the family expanded even further: Janet Elizabeth was born in January 1959, and Carol Jean (called "Carrie") in February 1961.

The Enid years were busy ones for Gene. The teaching load was heavy; he supplemented our income by supply preaching; and for the first three years he was trying to polish off the Ph.D. (which included extended long distance calls to Loomer and a trip to Chicago for a nonstop, overnight discussion). Despite all the hard work, there were rewards. In each class there were a few students genuinely interested in philosophical theology, several of whom earned Ph.D.s and are now scholars in their own right. Also, Gene began to publish.

When, out of the blue, President Paul Sharp of Hiram College walked into Gene's office to explore the possibility of Gene's teaching philosophy at the Ohio college, Gene did not hesitate to consider the offer. He had always wanted to teach philosophy, and several aspects of the Hiram position appealed to him: an honors program, sabbatical leaves, summer research grants, a lighter teaching load, opportunities for cross-disciplinary conversations, for example. When we arrived in

Hiram on Labor Day, 1962, we planned to stay five years or so (as we had at Phillips) and then move closer to our families in Texas. But it didn't work out that way. Through the years, when offers came from other schools, they were never quite good enough to entice Gene away from Hiram. When his condition forced him to stop teaching and enter the hospital, he was six weeks short of twenty-one years at Hiram College.

The Creative Advance was published in 1963, the year after we moved to Hiram. The college counted Gene's teaching at Phillips toward a sabbatical leave, and we spent 1964–65 at the University of Texas, where Gene began work on *Hartshorne and Neoclassical Metaphysics*. Dorothy Hartshorne arranged a comfortable corner in the Hartshorne home with the "complete works of Charles Hartshorne" where Gene worked daily, reading every word published by Hartshorne—no small feat even twenty years ago. I once heard Hartshorne say that Gene knew more about "what I have written than I do!" And in the Peters Memorial Lecture (October 1983) he called *Hartshorne and Neoclassical Metaphysics* "the first good and in some ways still the best book about me."

Gene tried to make the process thought of Hartshorne and Whitehead accessible to undergraduate students. He once obtained a grant from the Danforth Foundation to take a class to a nearby state park where they immersed themselves in Whitehead for a long weekend. Another seminar met in our home, in Gene's attic study, pouring over *Process and Reality* for an entire quarter. Later, members of the class gave Gene twelve placemats bearing a drawing of Whitehead and a different significant quotation from Whitehead on each of the mats. Once he arranged a visit from Hartshorne. Much of the dialogue was quite naturally between Gene and Charles, but the students became involved, too. The sessions were tape-recorded, and years later, Gene would listen to them.

There were certain constant elements in Gene's personality. First, he was a student. He loved to learn and never for one moment felt that he knew all there was to know about a topic. One thing he liked about Hiram was the presence of colleagues who became a resource for him. Once he sat in on an entire course in calculus simply because he had never had calculus and was interested. He completed all the assignments, often working problems during meals—a pleasure the children and I could not understand. He audited a course on the poetry of John Donne. He learned from his dear friend, Yuksel Ismail, who though not formally trained in philosophy, had such a keen, analytical mind that Gene always thought of him as a philosopher. They team taught a course on existentialism and had the time of their lives. (Barely fifty years old, Yuksel died three years after Gene.) Gene studied constantly. He never read recreationally, saying he "didn't have time." He was a slow, meticulous reader who remembered everything he read. Disdaining a superficial approach, he had no patience with "speed reading." When a subject interested him, he offered a course in it. An interdisciplinary course on Lovejoy's *Great Chain of Being* was popular. Gene offered it because *he* liked the book and wanted to study it in depth. During the last two years of his life, Gene studied Greek over the lunch hour with a colleague from the political science department who wanted to read Plato. They would fill the blackboards with Greek and engage in some serious dialogues of their own. If Gene could design his own personal heaven, I'm sure it would be a school. He was always a student.

Gene was a private person. He did not "blow his own horn." There are stacks of reprints from his publications because he hesitated to impose them on others. There is no comprehensive list of his publications. He wrote for the joy of it and not for recognition. In the same way, he kept his pain to himself. Although few, if any, of his colleagues realized it at the time, the decade of the 1970s was traumatic for him personally. First his beloved sister, Florence, was killed in a senseless automobile collision. Then both parents suffered strokes, his mother living on for several years, paralyzed. She could not leave Austin, and Gene cared for her from a great distance. Finally, in March, 1980, he discovered through a routine blood test that he had chronic leukemia.

Gene was absolutely adamant that information about his illness should not become public knowledge. We were told that the average life-expectancy following diagnosis was four to six years. He planned to live as normally as possible, hoping that he would be an exception who survived until a cure could be found. He never complained. Only two times did he ever discuss the illness with me. Once, at the beginning, he said, "This may be bad." Just before going into the hospital at the end, he said, with tears in his eyes, "I'm so tired of being sick," and immediately changed the subject. Gene Peters was a private person.

And finally, Gene was a person of the greatest integrity. Everything about him fit together in an integrated whole. His life was consistent with his philosophy. Ideas were not something in which he dabbled; the ideas he cherished informed his every attitude, every act.

He believed that human reason is the glory of humanity, and that it must be used. There is nothing—not in science, not in religion—which cannot or should not be questioned. We arrived at truth by raising questions. A former minister of ours told me recently that he used to despair that Gene could question so many aspects of "the faith." He wondered why Gene didn't have more faith. Then, not long ago, the minister came to realize that it was Gene who had real faith because he was not afraid to raise questions, knowing that truth becomes clearer when scrutinized. Gene liked the scriptural injunction to love God with all the mind.

Gene thought that everyone was capable of using reason, and he liked to lure unsuspecting folk into philosophical discussions—my mother, for example. He would raise perplexing questions and leave her exasperated and frustrated. One day, she thought she had him. "I have a question for you," she said. "Just what good is all this philosophy talk anyway? Has it ever made any difference in the world?" "Why, Ila," he quickly replied "you have just raised a very significant philosophical issue!" And he had in one short statement made her a philosopher once again.

Though he chided me about the music "training" which had neglected my mind, he never permitted me to plead ignorance or lack of interest when it came to ideas. From the beginning he took me to hear Tillich, Hartshorne and others. In Chicago I read aloud to him from Royce or Whitehead while he washed dishes or scrubbed the floor. He read to me everything he ever wrote, beginning with the dissertation and ending with the last paper he wrote. He made me a life-long student, too, and I'm grateful.

Like Hartshorne, Gene was a "panpsychist." He believed that the creation is organically related, all genuinely individual parts being alive and feeling. The difference is in degree, human beings possessing a higher degree of "consciousness." He loved this world to which he felt so closely related, and he reveled in the outdoors. When, despite two back operations, he could no longer run, he walked. Every night, no matter what the weather, he "went up the road." For years, he was accompanied by our dog, Wolfie. On their return, Gene would often report what Wolfie had "said."

Not only is all creation organically related, the creator is intimately involved as well. This notion lends dignity to all creatures, and Gene treated with dignity everyone he knew: his slowest students, the finest students, the cleaning ladies, the full professors, persons of any age. In a metaphorical sense, the world is the body of God. Thus, any injury or pain caused to one of the creatures brings pain to the very life of God. God does not send suffering. There are genuine accidents and aberrations in nature (such as disease) which God must also suffer with his creation. Long before he became ill, Gene maintained that there is evil and suffering in the world about which God can do little, given creaturely freedom. He also believed, however, that in spite of very real loss, life goes on, and "The Creative Advance" continues.

Gene was nostalgic about the past, and was troubled intellectually about the apparent loss of an event once it had occurred. He was, therefore, drawn to the doctrine found in both Whitehead and Hartshorne that "each event in the world is destined for immortality in God's memory." (*The Creative Advance*, 99) He also said,

> When we do good for others, we are always partly ignorant of the good we accomplish. Indeed, a man may be long dead before the good he was instrumental in bringing about is realized. But God is deathless, and every beauty and joy he enables us to have becomes an element in his own experience. (101)

Thank God for "every beauty and joy" he enables us to have through Eugene Peters.

Essays in Metaphysics

- Charles Hartshorne
- Lewis S. Ford

A Metaphysics of Universal Freedom

Charles Hartshorne

From my parents I learned to believe in a God of love. My Father, an Episcopal clergyman, thought the divine love respected the freedom of the creatures, who must make their own decisions. (The best nondivine parents, within their limitations, do this with their offspring.) My mother's clergyman father was similar, I think, and my mother did her best to live a religion of love for a freedom-loving God. Many famous theologians have thought rather differently. Our colonial American genius Jonathan Edwards was perhaps an extreme case of this other tradition; but Calvin, Luther, yes, even Augustine, were scarcely better in this respect. Thomas Aquinas was at best ambiguous or contradictory on the topic. Pascal, and I cannot forgive him for this, was like Edwards in insisting that what happens or is done in the world is completely determined by divine power. Our decisions merely enact what God eternally decides for us. Even our most wicked attitudes, for which God may punish us, are divinely decided. This is not what I was taught to believe as a child or young man. For this I have always been grateful.

During the following century and a half after Edwards, some American philosophers, including the great Unitarian preacher Channing and the great statesman Jefferson, rejected the Calvinistic idea. However, the first American writer with a worked-out technical philosophy strongly supportive of freedom was Charles Peirce. A physicist and mathematician, as well as creative logician and philosopher, Peirce thought that the statistical laws of gases were the models of what natural laws in principle really are. The great physicist Clerk Maxwell had already hinted at this. Fifty years later quantum theory gave the idea

The Eugene Peters Memorial Lecture given at Hiram College on October 25, 1983. Professor Hartshorne added a personal note concerning Dr. Peters.

additional support. The Newtonian type of laws, which made no allowance for individual freedom, whether the individuals be atoms, molecules, cells, or vertebrate animals, turned out to be unjustifiable. Not scientific evidence but only philosophical beliefs could any longer support unqualified determinism. And more and more philosophers have come to admit that determinism is a false doctrine. James, Dewey, Montague, Whitehead, and many others can be named under this head. In Europe there were Bergson and others in France, Germany, and Italy.

Whitehead is the greatest of the philosophical defenders of universal freedom, and Peirce is his most outstanding predecessor. Neither of them thought that the theological or ethical objections to determinism were the only important ones. For them both, determinism was not a usable doctrine, whether in science or in practical life. "Probability," as Bishop Butler had said, "is the guide of life;" even before quantum theory it was emerging as the guiding idea of science. As I understand it, the phase rule of the great American chemist Willard Gibbs is an example; the entropy law of thermodynamics is another; Darwinian evolution was implicitly, and is now explicitly, a matter of probability. No known biological laws determine details of evolution. Darwin *believed* there were laws strictly determining what he called chance variations; but he knew that his theory did not require this. Much less plausibly can contemporary biologists claim to know such deterministic laws.

Some of the greatest quantum theorists have suggested that the known limitations on causal determination of the behavior of molecules, atoms, and particles are probably not the only qualifications to which the belief in determinism should be subjected. That we must use statistical methods may be not merely because there are limits to the precision of possible measurements. It may well be because individuals, on no matter what level—particulate, atomic, cellular, vertebrate, human—are in principle partly self-determining from moment to moment. As Plato said of souls, they are "self-moved." Human freedom may be an intensive, high-level case of what individuality is on every level. Bergson's opinion (before the indeterministic phase of quantum theory) that Newtonian physics could not be true, because it misconceived the very nature of becoming and of change, has been cited to his credit by some French physicists.

In any case the asymmetry between a closed, fully settled past and a partly open or unsettled future is the only view of time that our behavior can express belief in. Say what we will, we *act* on the view that tomorrow is being partly made now and was not fully settled yesterday. That your or my present decision was already determined long ago by your or my heredity and environment can do nothing to guide us as we now decide something. We can only decide *as if* not everything was already settled. After deciding we can, if it amuses us, point to our decision and claim that it was the only decision we could have made. But by then it is too late to get any help in making the decision. It must always be too late. Determinism is pragmatically irrelevant. True, in deciding we may take into account probable results of this or that decision. But probability is not a deterministic idea. Newtonian laws do not mention probability.

Another reason that I feel fairly safe in rejecting determinism is that I have found, fifty times over, that determinists fall into the trap of arguing as if the only way to avoid complete determinism is to affirm sheer chaos. A great biologist I know—at least he is a great field naturalist—who believes in determinism represents indeterminism as implying that "anything may happen" in a given situation, ignoring the question of probability altogether. In fact, many things will be impossible in a given situation, according to any reasonable indeterminism. Between absolute causal order and sheer chaos there is vast room for moderate positions. In time science may give a far better idea than it can now of the qualifications, additional to those of quantum physics, necessary to do justice to the individual behavior of organisms.

Freedom need not be a question of a new "vital force" coming into nature. Even particles act as though they too had freedom, as expressed in half-life laws, for example. Vitality in a generalized sense may be present all the way down in nature. This was Peirce's view. And Epicurus (by whom, as Max Fisch has shown, Peirce was influenced) long ago had a similar idea. He attributed freedom to himself and to atoms. So, I believe, should we.

Still another reason why I am unconvinced by deterministic arguments is the way in which these arguments overlook the distinction between abstract and concrete meanings of words like decide, or act. Martin Luther said that his decision to challenge the Church was the only one he could have made. "I can do no other," he said. Luther was a theological determinist, so his testimony is not impartial. But aside from that, for all I know, something very like what he did was the only probable result of his previous history up to the month or week of his nailing the rebellious theses on the wall. However, several times a second a person does this or that; in a minute hundreds of issues are decided (mostly subconsciously), in an hour, thousands; in a month, hundreds of thousands. What Luther called his decision or deed was only an abstract outline of what he had actually done. If there is some slight freedom each tenth of a second or so of waking life, and I would claim no less than this, then heredity and environment may over a lifetime leave quite substantial matters undecided in advance.

I have twice made a purely voluntary decision to move from one university (that wanted to keep me) to another. Could I have decided not to make those two moves? Perhaps not. But I could, for all anyone can know, have reached my decision "yes" in a thousand ways other than the way I did reach it. And neither I nor anyone can know that my affirmative decision was more than highly probable. Determinists beg the question if they hold that whatever happened was all along "going to happen." To "verify" predictions is not to show that they were true when made, but only that they became true later.

Soon after the year 1600 the Socinian sect of Protestants declared that even God knows our precise decisions only as or after we make them, not eternally or in advance. The very idea of truth may take a different form if indeterminism is accepted. Some logicians declare that all truth is timeless, but they cannot prove this by any self-evident logical law, and several great logicians have rejected the idea. Aristotle, the founder of Western logic, was the first of these. Peirce and Whitehead are two recent examples. William James agreed with Peirce on this issue, as did John Dewey.

My religious upbringing taught me that we should love God with all our hearts, minds, souls, and strengths. But, as many have defined God, it is hard to understand how we can love God at all, a being eternally knowing all our actions, and indeed eternally deciding what these actions shall be! In what sense can we love this being, from whom came all our sufferings as well as all our joys? What have we in common with God so defined?

To love as we know love at its best involves at least two aspects: what we love we delight in contemplating, and with those we love we sympathize, rejoicing in their joys and sharing in their sorrows. But God, according to many theologians, has no sorrows. With absolutely untroubled bliss, God contemplates suffering creatures. Or does God have neither joy nor sorrow? Is that the description of a supremely lovable being? Jesus, often called God incarnate, is said to have wept. He suffered on a cross. Is that a reasonable symbol of a God immune to suffering, or immune to feeling of any kind?

A fundamental aspect of the meaning of life for us human beings is what we call beauty, or aesthetic value. Aesthetic experience is experience that is good in itself. We do not listen to beautiful music merely so that later on we will be better off for having done so. We do it because listening to the music is a good experience. The enjoyment of a good joke is value of this kind. Does God enjoy aesthetic value? If not, then how can we love completely a being lacking in a trait we find essential? If the beauty of the cosmos is divinely enjoyed, then God's awareness of the world must be the supreme form of what we know as aesthetic experience.

There is substantial agreement among philosophers and artists that beauty is a kind of unity in diversity, the diversity being as necessary as the unity. Moreover, the diversity is temporal as well as, indeed even more than, it is spatial. Failure to achieve beauty takes two forms: insufficient diversity, resulting in monotony, an aesthetically negative term; or insufficient unity, experienced as discord of, at the limit, mere confusion or chaos. Sufficient unity and variety in temporal terms means the new recognized as a contrasting form of the old. However, if God surveys all things from a purely eternal standpoint, there is for God no novelty. Eternity is a spatial idea; it must spatialize time, as Bergson puts it, thus denaturing the temporal. If for God everything is known together, whether past, present, or future to us, then divine experience has really nothing in common with or analogous to ours. For even spatial order is causal and temporal for us. Relativity physics is relevant here.

The foregoing is only part of the argument for the conclusion that God is to be conceived neither as wholly without a temporal aspect, nor as wholly without feeling, nor even as feeling only joy but not sorrow, but rather as having a divine kind of temporality and as, in some divine sense, rejoicing and sorrowing with our joys and sorrows. The idea of a suffering deity is an old heresy that is beginning to appear as a higher form of orthodoxy. Berdyaev hints at divine suffering and a divine kind of change, implying a divine kind of time; Whitehead calls God "the fellow sufferer who understands." If God enjoys the creatures as beautiful, then God experiences their actions as partly unanticipated novelties. Our successes are occasions of divine joy and our tragedies, occasions of vicarious divine sorrow. We serve God by achieving as much beauty, harmony, intensity and as little ugliness, discord, and tedious monotony as we can manage in ourselves and the other creatures we influence. In a positive sense we benefit and really serve God by enriching the divinely enjoyed creation.

If this is not what it means to serve God, do not ask me what it does mean, for I have no idea. Many have told us that we serve God by obedience, but not many of those who so view the matter tell us how our obedience does God any good; indeed many tell us that God will have all possible good no matter what we do. The sad truth is that there has been a failure to talk sense in much of the vast literature on this subject. Neither God's love for us nor our love for God has been given a reasonable sense in the main stream of classical theism.

Love at its best is a social relation in which value in one individual thereby becomes value in another individual. God does not value us as mere means to some good simply outside us. It is our very own good that contributes to the divine life. Similarly, to the best human parents what children most contribute is their own enjoyed successes. They are interesting because of their own interest in life, their own eagerness. The supreme art is drama: God is the supreme dramatist. But the drama would be nothing if the players had no decision-making power of their own; in subtle ways the actors always ad lib, make up their own speeches. If God's world were merely the exact echo of divine thoughts coming back to God it would be pointless. Poor God, condemned to perpetual boredom, seeing only completely foregone resolutions to even the most otherwise exciting stories!

Allowing God an open future deprives the divine life of no positive value. Any beauty that ever turns up in the world will be fully enjoyed by God. That the enjoyment is not eternal is no privation; for it *is* everlasting, indestructible. God does not forget, as we do. But without an open future, all analogy between what we know as life and what we can mean by the living God vanishes. We no longer know what we are talking about, other than mere words. This is a privation, both for us and for God.

In a philosophy of universal freedom, deity must be conceived, if at all, as the highest conceivable form of freedom. But why, some may wonder, introduce God at all into the scheme? I answer with Whitehead: for one reason, because freedom as universal principle, but without a highest conceivable form, is a program for chaos. It is like a committee with no chairman, a mob with no leader, no directives to prevent unlimited disagreement and conflict. Could the countless creatures making up the world have somehow formed a conspiracy, so to speak, to maintain a cosmic order, in which the various forms of life can coexist? Each creature is partly making its own decisions, what brings it about that these decisions add up to an ongoing cosmic order? How can what we call natural laws result from universal freedom? Perhaps you say that each creature adapts its behavior to that of the others. But one cannot adapt to chaos. Darwinian theory assumes a basic physical order that it does not explain, the laws of physics and chemistry. Without some stability in the climate and in the inanimate order generally, natural selection could do nothing. Mutual adaptation assumes, does not by itself provide, a solution to the basic problem of order. Unless something guides the freedom of the creatures, no reason appears why a viable world order results.

If freedom is the universal principle, the only solution to the problem of order, or of mutual adaptation, is in the idea of a supreme form of freedom that issues directives to all lesser forms, directives that cannot be ignored. They will not completely determine the decisions of the lesser forms; for that is contradictory. No decider can be completely determined by any other decider. In good English we say that *we make* decisions, or "make up our minds." Theologians have told us, that "God has made us and not we ourselves." Yet, is not what we call our character in good part the influence upon us of our past decisions? Thus to a significant extent we do make ourselves if we make our decisions. The theologian's statement, sounding so pious, is a half-truth. It is a dangerous half-truth. For if God simply makes us as we are, then all our wickedness is divine action. How then can it really be wicked?

Read biographies of distinguished people. Over and over one will learn that individuals lost belief in God because they could not see how a highest conceivable form of goodness and power could produce a world of mixed goods and evils such as ours. The trouble arose from the assumption that the highest conceivable form of freedom, power, or decision-making would consist in power to simply make, determine, decide, all that happens. That this would leave nothing for the lesser beings to decide or determine was regarded as one of those mysteries we cannot hope to understand. Alas, if so, then the agnostics or atheists have a wonderfully strong case. For, if we do not know that we genuinely decide some things that no one and nothing else, human or divine, decides, how is it to be claimed that we know at all what we talk about when we talk theologically?

Without supreme freedom, freedom cannot explain how a world is possible. With supreme freedom, but lesser, though genuine, freedom *in all other beings*, we can explain how a basically good cosmos is possible and explain also how in that cosmos there will be a mixture of goods and bads. Even the suffering of nonhuman animals is explicable in these terms. If no conceivable single agent, even though divine, could determine what happens, then there is no contradiction in saying that a wholly good God, whose power is the highest conceivable, will not be able to prevent some conflict and suffering resulting from the decisions of creatures. Suppose I make decision D and you make decision D', what happens must be compatible with the occurrence of the combination D & D'. Who decided upon this combination? Not I and not you. It just happened. Did God decide it? Not if I genuinely made D and you genuinely made D'. If the combination is fortunate, furthers harmony and beauty in my and your experiences, that is partly good luck. Chance is necessary to a sane view of life. Common sense, with its talk of luck, is correct, and all the wise talk about unknown causal necessities is incorrect.

A great genius, Einstein, went straight to the point when he said that he could not believe in a dice-throwing God. He went straight to the point, but it was the wrong point. An inventor I know, Arthur Young, replied to Einstein, "Of course, God throws dice. He takes a chance on what free creatures may do." That, according to my philosophy, is the bottom line. Einstein did not believe in wasting words. He went to his point. Young went to his still better point. Contemporary science and philosophy seem to be moving toward a consensus that Einstein, superlative discoverer that he was, in his philosophy was the last of the great giants of Newtonian science. He was actually one of the principal creators of early quantum theory, that theory which, in its mature form destroys, or shows to be inadequate, the Newtonian model of science. Einstein could not believe in a kind of theory whose triumph he had helped to bring about. It is somewhat sad or pathetic. But such is human wisdom. None of us is divine. We can all make mistakes. Karl Popper said, "Great men make great mistakes."

I had the thrilling experience of being present when a great scientist, the greatest that I have known really well, the geneticist Sewall Wright, one of the chief creators of population genetics, actually said, "There is nothing but freedom." He meant about what I would mean by this, though he came to it by a remarkably different route from the one I took. He meant that spontaneous, and not entirely predetermined, experiencing is the universal form of concrete reality. Even atoms have some kind of feeling or awareness; and nothing is absolutely determined by its causal conditions.

My only difference from Wright is in regard to God, and what has kept him from a theistic belief was not, it seems, the problem of evil but what he takes to be an implication of relativity physics. It is an implication that some regard as incompatible with an implication of quantum theory called Bell's theorem, and the matter is still, I take it controversial. But otherwise my view (or Whitehead's, or Peirce's) and Wright's are essentially similar.

A century and a half ago *not one* scientist, philosopher, or theologian had a philosophy of *universal* freedom. That many can have it now is a profound cultural change. It has theological implications. The classical form of the problem of evil is no longer relevant. It belonged with the classical period of physics, not to the neoclassical period in which we now live. I call my metaphysics neoclassical by analogy with physics. It was the physicists who began using "classical" in the sense of a view that is worthy of respect, but that is no longer sufficient and that we have found it necessary to transcend. The word neoclassical seems to be my invention. I take classical theology seriously enough to argue against it. That is how physicists take Newton.

If partly free experiencing is the universal principle, it should explain how the causal order of the world is possible. Causality has two aspects. One is the apsect of influence. Whether or not the past fully determines the present, there is no doubt that it strongly influences it. How can this be? Logicians distinguish between necessary and sufficient conditions. Given all the necessary conditions for an event it *can* occur. Given a "sufficient" condition it *will* or must occur. Determinism abolishes the distinction between necessary and sufficient, or between possible and necessary. The necessary causal conditions taken together make up the real possibility for an event. However, not all possibility could be actualized. Logicians are largely agreed upon that. The sufficient condition, then, is something in addition to the totality of necessary conditions. Indeterminism says that the only sufficient conditions for concrete events are the acts of freedom that constitute the events. Your or my present decision is the only sufficient condition for itself. In the past there are necessary but never sufficient conditions for the subsequent concrete acts or singular events. In process metaphysics every singular is an "experient occasion," an instance of subjectivity and of decision in the most concrete sense, for which there were in the past only necessary, never sufficient, conditions. Bergson, Peirce, and Whitehead all say this.

How could so many for so long have been confused about the elementary logic of the causal idea? How could possibility be confused with necessity? How could it be overlooked that the past makes present events possible, while only these events, which are really acts, make themselves actual? We know the history of this matter well enough to answer the question. Exact science began with astronomy and physics, just those parts of nature in which the individual agents that are doing what is done are concealed from our direct sense perceptions. The ancient atomists shrewdly guessed that the agents, other than animals, are so tiny that we cannot see them distinctly or one by one. The impression that so-called inanimate matter is entirely predictable and lacking in individual initiative was a statistical illusion. The planets are predictable because their individual atoms and molecules conform to certain statistical laws and any little individual initiatives or free actions in the individuals cancel out in the blurred vision we have of their behavior. Determinism took its idea of causal order from the behavior of individuals no one had ever seen as individuals and applied the idea, thus based on a mere guess, to individuals we have seen and know (if we know anything), namely ourselves and other vertebrate animals. Quite literally the known was interpreted by the unknown.

It was Leibniz who (partly) understood the fallacy and therefore (partly) reversed the traditional procedure and insisted on interpreting the unknown by the known. I say that he partly understood and reversed the traditional procedure. Let me explain. The tradition had (by implication) interpreted the unknown micro-individuals by analogy with the apparent individuals—really groupings of individuals—composing inorganic nature, rocks, planets, suns. From this came the idea of wholly lifeless and mindless individuals. Leibniz, knowing about Leeuwenhoek's microorganisms, interpreted the seemingly mindless objects as collectives of extremely simple or primitive but not mindless individuals. Like the ancient atomists he assumed that to be is to be active; hence the inactive rocks or grains of sand can only be assemblages of active singulars, monads. Since we do not observe them one by one, and their lack of *visible* activity is deducible from their extreme smallness, and since the only active individuals we know are living organisms, animals (and, here he hesitated, also plants) the only source for our idea of individual activity is our experience of ourselves and other organisms. Leaning on Leeuwenhoek's discoveries, he leaped to an anticipation of the cell theory: visible organisms are collectives of invisibly tiny organisms. Moreover, since, in spite of Descartes, the other animals exhibit all possible signs of having at least sensations or feelings, whether or not thoughts, we have no evidence for the assumption that there can be individual activity apart from feeling or sensing, however remote in quality and complexity from human sensing. The idea of insentient single individuals was thus at last revealed as being without valid basis in experience. So far Leibniz was thinking as Peirce, Bergson, and Whitehead (partly helped by Leibniz) later did, the difference being that it took greater genius to think thus in Leibniz's time than two centuries later.

Leibniz attributed sentience to plants for the same reason that Aristotle assigned a vegetable soul to them: that plants grow and, in that sense at least, seem active, self-changing things. What both writers lacked was knowledge of the nervous system and its function of enabling a colony of cells to act as one whole, which is the behavioristic indication of feeling as one. Plant cells multiply, and this is the growth of the plant. Only in animals can a group of cells give convincing evidence of forming a single acting, feeling agent or individual. I hold that the cell and nerve cell theories have yet to be adequately assimilated by speculative philosophy, although Whitehead gives many indications of how this is to be done. "A tree is a democracy" is one picturesque example. There is no dominant monad or individual (Whiteheadian "personally-ordered society") in trees, but we know in ourselves such a dominant individual. And we know our nervous systems and some of their ways of functioning.

We come now to the incompleteness of Leibniz's insight. The principle of sufficient reason, in the strong form then natural (which implies strict determinism), made it not surprising that Leibniz did not interpret animal behavior, including that of human animals, as free or active in the sense of self-movement, self-determination of present awareness by that very awareness. Otherwise expressed, becoming was not, for Leibniz, creative, but merely unwound the divine decision to make our world. Thus an absolute gulf was put, not between the human and the subhuman, but between any and all creatures and the Creator. Only the latter has any genuine power to decide. To claim to cross this posited gulf with thought is irrational.

Not only did Leibniz reduce his idea of activity to a meaningless equivalence with portions of the content of the timeless decision of deity, he also reduced the idea of animals as experiencing other animals to the absurdity of the preestablished harmony. Whereas to perceive is to be influenced by what is perceived, Leibniz denies interaction between monads. (This involved his absolutizing of the idea of genetic identity. One's childish self is the very self that is also one's adult self; its "law of succession" of states is in it at all times. So of course there seemed no need for interaction. Thus Leibniz had too much unity within each monad and too much disunity of monads with one another. In this respect also he was a sharpened, extreme example of an old Western tradition.)

Comparing Leibniz to Epicurus is interesting. Both attributed active individual micro-constituents to inanimate nature; however, the materialist left the supposed lifelessness and mindlessness intact, yet did attribute freedom to the constituents, whereas Leibniz attributed to them life and mind but not freedom. By now, every combination has been tried. It is our privilege to choose.

Leibniz himself by implication gave a reason for choosing a combination that no one until Peirce (unless Boutroux in France) seems to have thought of. In metaphysics, Leibniz said, it is what philosphers deny that gets them into trouble, not what they assert. (I have elsewhere given an argument for this.) Very well; Epicurus denied sentience to much of reality, while Leibniz admitted freedom, genuine causative initiative, *only* in divine form, not as universal category. Combining the positive universals, sentience or feeling and creative initiative, decision-making power, as categories (or in the medieval sense transcendentals), we have two basic features of neoclassical metaphysics. One more step and we come closer still. With Buddhism, Whitehead, and a few Western predecessors, let us admit that actuality contrasts with potentiality or possibility as the discrete with the continuous, here breaking with nearly everybody else in West or East, including Aristotle, Leibniz, Peirce and Bergson, who have largely denied actual discreteness at least in temporal form, to becoming; we then have much of the basis for Whitehead's concept of actual entity.

A great advantage of substituting primitive forms of experiencing or mind for mindless matter is that experience, as we know it in ourselves, furnishes clues for the solution of basic philosophical problems. Why does the past influence the present? Consult your own experience—and not your experience of billiard balls, which is what Hume consulted in this matter. Your senses do not tell you what the individual agents in such phenomena are. You however are an individual agent. Consider how, in yourself and others like you, the past obviously influences the present. In memory the past obviously does influence the present. Memory just is a way of being influenced. To say that you remember how you felt or thought a moment ago and yet are wholly uninfluenced by this past feeling (or thought) is to talk nonsense. (Hume never considered memory as a case of the influence of the past on the present. He missed the point as if by magic.) Consider also perception. The sound you hear was made a second or more before you heard it, and the events you see happening have already happened when you see them. Perception and memory are both ways of being influenced by the past. If you distrust memory and perception, what is left for you to trust? To dismiss these obvious cases of influence from consideration seems wonderfully irrational. To experience *is* to be influenced by the past. This is the clue. There is no other. Materialism has no clue. It simply takes the influence of the past for granted.

The other aspect of causal order is something in addition to the influence of the past; it is the *orderliness*, at least statistical or approximate, of the past. That we can relate, in memory or perception, to the past is possible only because the past is reasonably ordered. A coherent experience of a totally incoherent jumble of items is self-evidently impossible. In aesthetic terms there could be no value in such an experience, no motivation to have it. I take it as axiomatic that all experience is motivated by some value or other.

We are back to the problem of adaptation. Experience is in principle adaptive, and it presupposes order. Again we come to the need for a supreme form of freedom to decide upon the basic cosmic directives for all lesser forms. Otherwise, the door is wide open for a hopeless amount of maladaptation. Any conceivable world is an order, any conceivable world is a God-directed world. This, for some of us, is the bottom line.

Looking again at *Hartshorne and Neoclassical Metaphysics* I find not simply reconfirmation of my recollection of its excellence but intensification of my admiration for its author. Not only was Peters a careful scholar who gives a remarkably accurate account of my philosophy; he also was—and, by objective immortality, is—an extremely good writer. His neat, pleasantly readable sentences could be taken as models of how to present ideas attractively. I wish I could remember more vividly than I now can having adequately expressed to him the gratitude I feel for his having taken the pains to do such a beautiful job with that book. Such a gift from a fellow philosopher is not to be taken for granted.

Although when Peters wrote his book my *Creative Synthesis and Philosophic Method* was not yet published, he knew much of what went into it. The main outlines of my metaphysical system are about as he saw them. In the sixteen or seventeen years since, I have not been able to make any substantial changes in my conclusions; if there have been improvements they are chiefly in the method of argument for the conclusions and in the manner of relating them to the history of thought. I miss somewhat in Peters' account the way Karl Popper, who for me has been the most stimulating writer since Whitehead, has influenced my analyses, especially by his stress on elimination of erroneous theories as the way to approach truth. According to Popper, the possible theories are infinite in number, which makes it seem that no finite number of eliminations would accomplish much. In metaphysics, whether or not in physics (Popper admits we need both: "We are all metaphysicians"), one can, I argue, reduce the possibilities to a finite number, from which, by a similarly finite number of axioms or institutions, one can eliminate all but one answer to a metaphysical question. True, as Peters holds, the axioms can be questioned. A thinking animal has no absolute evidence, in spite of Descartes and Husserl. We do the best we can. With Popper I hold that full use of the method of discussion with others, (openness to criticism, avoidance of evasive or offensive tactics that tend to prevent effective communication) is the best definition of rationality in thinking. A compliment that came to me second hand from Popper that I cherish was: "He is a theologian—but, he argues." Peters presents me as a metaphysician rather than as a theologian. True, my metaphysics is theistic, but so have been most metaphysical philosophies. Many forms of theism have been bad metaphysics; but then their religious merits are also open to question. Indeed, perhaps the only great metaphysical tradition that can at all reasonably be called nontheistic is Buddhism, and even in that case there is some room for doubt. The Advaita form of Vedantism can, with some justification, be considered nontheistic; but it is hardly a live option for most Westeners. I am a metaphysician who takes religion *and* science seriously and has tried to make some contributions to both. Fundamentalist religions, arrogant toward one another as well as toward the efforts of philosophers and scientists—these and scientisms are the enemies, so far as I am concerned. Both seem remarkably visible in the present world.

Eugene Peters was remarkably free from either form of arrogant onesidedness. With his modesty, humor, and quiet charm, he was a very pleasant man to know.

From Pre-Panpsychism to Pansubjectivity

Lewis S. Ford

Whitehead's mature philosophy definitely ascribes subjectivity to all actualities. Actual entities are prehending subjects (e.g. PR 23/35). Since *Science and the Modern World*, his first essay into metaphysics proper, already appears to be panpsychist, there has been little inclination to determine when and how Whitehead came to adopt this position. These problems have seemed incapable of solution.

My study of *The Emergence of Whitehead's Metaphysics* suggests a way of addressing these questions. I find that Whitehead frequently altered his philosophical position during the composition of his books (at least in SMW and PR), without, however, thoroughly erasing traces of his earlier positions. Thus, by careful analysis we can isolate the various layers of composition. Each layer is basically consistent within itself, although there are tensions and anomalies between layers. By ordering these different layers it becomes possible by genetic interpretation to discern a progressive series of changes and to propose reasons for the shifts. Genetic interpretation seeks to determine the meaning of each layer by itself, methodologically restricting itself to the smallest hermeneutical unit, taking into account only the theories which Whitehead had held up to and including that compositional layer, but none of his later ones.

Compositional analysis and genetic interpretation are not the same. Genetic interpretation is dependent upon compositional analysis, but the compositional analysis may only suggest and cannot determine the genetic analysis. Differing interpretations are possible on the basis of the same compositional analysis. This essay illustrates the point. Although it makes few revisions, if any, of the earlier genetic analysis (in E W M) of the literature prior to *Process and Reality*, its genetic interpretation reverses the order between pansubjectivity and panpsychism.*

Yet what difference does it make how Whitehead developed his ideas? If his thought were wholly of one piece, such that each new idea slips into place with no modification of earlier ones, then it would make little difference. If, however, Whitehead *did* shift his position significantly, then the order is vital to the determination of the meaning of the texts. It is also a very important clue as to Whitehead's reasons, which are left largely implicit. Critics have often felt the need for further argument in Whitehead's writings; too much is simply claimed to be so without supporting warrant. I suspect this is primarily the result of his decision to present his views in the conventional form of an extended treatise and wanting the book to have this outward appearance, at least. Yet once his initial metaphysical position was formulated in the Lowell Lectures of 1925 which constitute the core of *Science and the Modern World* (EWM 22-45), Whitehead tended to develop his position largely in opposition to what he had already written. Thus, his reasons are often criticisms of himself and, even more importantly, of texts that he still wished to retain within the total composition. Were he to specify his reasons, he would alert his readers to inadequacies in texts still retained. Given the dialectical and self-critical bent of his mind, Whitehead would have been much better served with a format such as a philosophical journal. Not only would we then know from his own hand the order of his development, but he could have felt much freer to tell us why his newly won positions were superior to earlier ones. As it is, we can often reconstruct the reasons once the compositional order has been determined, although the particular case in hand shows how precarious this can sometimes be.

If we neglect to observe how the order of composition can suggest reasons for Whitehead's positions, then the absence of explicit reasons

---

*As we shall see in the next section, a compositional analysis concerning the revised subjectivist principle situating it relative to other texts turns out to be extremely important.

For our purposes the two most important compositional layers are (C) what I call "the Giffords draft," the 9 1/2 chapters Whitehead wrote during the summer of 1927 (EWM 179f), and (D) the first, and most revolutionary, level of revision. Before and during the Giffords draft Whitehead appears to hold implicitly that concrescence is a being caught up in the flux of appropriating and reintegrating an initial datum already containing whatever externally influences it (EWM 189-98). Whitehead revised this by identifying the feelings of the Giffords draft with the (positive) prehensions of *Science and the Modern World*, thus enabling the concrescence to reach out beyond itself to the many past data, unifying everything in a single act. This meant that the incomplete concrescence had no unified being, but was a sheer act of the coming into being of being with the satisfaction. This revised view of the subjectivity of concrescence appears to have led to the revised subjectivist principle.

in text may lead us to ascribe alien ones to him (e.g. WP 118f). So both finding the right reasons and distinguishing them from other reasons can be fostered by genetic interpretation. Not only do the reasons give a sounder philosophical basis for Whitehead's claims, but they may also aid in rendering those claims more precise, more distinctively his own.

Thus I take it to be important that the first *explicit* espousal of 'panpsychism' (using 'mind' in the sense in which Whitehead understood it) occurs in the 1926 essay on "Time." In *Religion in the Making*, Whitehead had distinguished between mental and physical occasions on the one hand and ground and consequent on the other, suggesting that physical occasions alone could have their own novel consequents (EWM 130-33). Later, however, a growing awareness of the inextricable connection between novelty and mentality seems to have led him to reinterpret the ground/consequent distinction in terms of physical and mental occasions. It then follows that "in place of Descartes' doctrine of the two species of substances, bodies and minds, we must hold that each occasion is dipolar, and that one pole is the physical occasion and the other pole is the mental occasion" (IS 240 = 303). From then on it was clear that every occasion has a mental pole (EWM 153f), although just what Whitehead's previous doctrine was is quite problematic.

In my study I rather incautiously postulated a basic 'pansubjectivity' to *Science and the Modern World* (EWM 22-50, 89f). While Whitehead did not then ascribe mentality to all events, conceiving mind in terms of 'ego-objects' which characterized only some of them (EWM 40-42), other senses of 'subjectivity' might be thought to apply. As the title of this essay indicates, however, I now think that Whitehead's original position can be more accurately described as "pre-panpsychist." I no longer think that *Science and the Modern World* is either pansubjectivist or panpsychist. 'Pansubjectivity' presupposes a refinement in our understanding of forms of panpsychism, and so would seem overly sophisticated for a position that has not yet attained to panpsychism. Secondly, I find that only the designation 'pansubjectivity' can do justice to the revolution in Whitehead's conceptuality brought about by the revised subjectivist principle that "apart from the experiences of subjects there is nothing, nothing, nothing, bare nothingness" (PR 167/254).

While I now reverse the order in which Whitehead moves from 'pansubjectivity' to 'panpsychism,' the shift is not as drastic as might seem, since it is based on a different interpretation of 'pansubjectivity,' which now renders it inappropriate as a description of Whitehead's original position. In the first section, then, I seek to illustrate this new meaning of 'pansubjectivity' by contrasting it with the better-known panpsychism, and here I take as my illustration the 'psychicalism' of Charles Hartshorne.*

In this *Festschrift* we aim to honor Eugene H. Peters, and what better way would there be than to make use of his study of *Hartshorne and Neoclassical Metaphysics*? This tightly organized book presents Hartshorne's methodological key, that there are no purely negative realities, and illustrates this with respect to three basic polarities: materialism vs. psychicalism, determinism vs. freedom, and atheism vs. (neoclassical) theism. We shall make use of three arguments Peters formulates from Hartshorne's writings on psychicalism, the view that reality is primarily mental rather than material.

I.

Psychicalism is not the silly doctrine that all macroscopic objects possess mentality, let alone consciousness. A stone neither thinks nor feels. Yet its elementary particles may betray by their spontaneity some faint trace of mental activity. Only the final actualities which constitute such aggregates, which exhibit some kind of inner activity within themselves, have some degree of interiority or mentality. There are no final actualities which are mere matter, devoid of any subjectivity.

1. One argument for psychicalism Peters presents is derived from Leibniz, "who reasoned that if all visible things are made up of parts too small to be discerned individually, then we have no visual acquaintance with any instance of individuality . . ." (HNM 32f). If so, our only hope for any experience of individuation would have to be through introspection. Thus "introspective experience furnishes not only our sole means of intuiting individuality but the principle of individuality itself" (HNM 33). "So (1) if a physical object such as a rock is not itself an individual but merely a mosaic of imperceptible individuals, and (2) if the only individuals we know are unities of experience—can the ultimate, simple individuals be other than animate and sentient?" (HNM 33).

This argument adopted by Hartshorne could not be used by Whitehead without serious modification. Whitehead distinguishes between

---

*Section 2 argues for my reading of SMW against those who would interpret it as already panpsychist, while section 3 explores the emergence of this full-blooded 'pansubjectivity' in PR.

subjectivity as present immediacy contrasted with the objectivity of past fact (EWP 323f) and mentality as the introduction of novelty, as contrasted with blind repetition (EWP 327f). The argument from Leibniz turns on the role of interiority, a role Whitehead assigns to subjectivity. It ignores the temporal status of such present immediacy, which is essential to Whitehead's account of subjectivity. Furthermore, all considerations of novelty are quite absent.

Temporality is essential to Whitehead's approach not merely because his actualities are events or occasions (as opposed to enduring substances, such as Leibniz' monads), but because of his contrast between becoming and being. For any (concrete) occasion or being $_w$ to be, it must first become $_w$ in the distinctively Whiteheadian sense, i.e., it must first come into being. Its subjective act of becoming $_w$, its concrescence, must complete itself before it can acquire any being $_w$ of its own. If subjectivity as the interiority of experience is exhausted in becoming, it can only be the present immediacy as contrasted with past being $_w$. As past being, therefore, the actuality is devoid of subjectivity, which is exclusively assigned to present becoming $_w$.

Whitehead could accept the elements of interiority, experience, and individuation Leibniz' argument uses, but not their conceptualization in terms of being. Subjectivity for him is not a characteristic of being $_w$. Insofar as there is a relevant characteristic of being $_w$, Whitehead assigns this to (as objectified) mentality, in terms of the already accomplished introduction of novelty, which as we have seen plays no role here. The properties of interiority and experience, since Leibniz and Hartshorne assign to them mentality, are thus considered to be aspects of being $_w$.

Hartshorne understands being and becoming somewhat differently. Generally speaking, by 'becoming' Hartshorne means a dynamic or temporal type of being $_w$ in contrast to static endurance, which is being proper. This is rather different from becoming $_w$ as the coming into being or the creation of a being (understanding creation as immanent and pluralistically self-reflexive, rather than as derived from one transcendent, divine source). Thus Whitehead's notion of being $_w$ includes Hartshorne's notions of both being and becoming, while becoming $_w$ addresses the dimension of concrescence whereby occasions, and therefore both endurance and change, come into being.[1]

Using Whitehead's distinctions, then, we may say that the functional difference between mentality and subjectivity concerns what is assigned to being $_w$ and what to becoming $_w$. Since for Hartshorne these properties can be maximally assigned to being, mentality is the controlling concept, while for Whitehead it has only minimal meaning.

2. A second argument Peters presents uses Hartshorne's distinctive axiom of positivity. After showing that neither extendedness and predictability nor any other positive trait can be taken as evidence for mere dead matter, he argues: "then no individual entity can be known to be lifeless. Thus, materialism is false in some cases—for there *are* living, experiencing beings—and cannot be known to be true *as a fundamental interpretation* in any case. Or putting it another way, psychicalism is true in some cases and could not be known to be false *as a fundamental interpretation* in any case. Using the methodological key, we must draw the conclusion that materialism, since it involves sheer negation, is necessarily false and psychicalism therefore a metaphysical truth" (HNM 37).

That which must be described negatively, as lacking e.g. mind, is the more abstract. As Hartshorne puts it, "'Mind' and 'matter' are not two ultimately different sorts of entity but, rather, two ways of describing a reality that has many levels of organization. The 'mind' way I take to be more final and inclusive, so that my position is the opposite of materialism" (LP 217).

The negative is the more abstract as long as we remain on the level of the concreteness of being, but matters can become complicated when subjectivity is involved, particularly when, as in the case of Whitehead, it is identified with becoming $_w$. When defined in terms of the being $_w$ to be attained, becoming $_w$ appears as a lack, as that which does not yet have being. Since it is not a being, a thing, subjectivity is nothing. While Whitehead has not exploited this line of dialectic, Sartre and other (e.g. contemporary Buddhists) have. Subjectivity can be conceived as negativity over against being's positivity. This need not mean, at least not in Whitehead's case, that subjectivity is thus to be regarded as something abstract, as if becoming were dependent for its existence upon being. The exact opposite is the case.

Hartshorne specified 'mind' and 'matter' as "two ways of describing a reality," which gives no hint that either (or both) *essentially* pertains to becoming rather than being (as would be the case with Whitehead's subjectivity). The question is rather: whether mind or matter offers the most appropriate inclusive description of reality. For Whitehead, if we prescend from the subjectivity of becoming, and consider only the attributes of being, we find that a sort of 'neutral monism' reigns. It is true that, generally speaking, every (objectified) actuality has accomplished some degree of physical response. No concrescence has been devoid of physical prehension. The inclusive category is neither the physical nor the mental but the prehensive, understood in terms of being, has no application to Whitehead's approach.

3. The third argument is based upon degrees of awareness. Hartshorne writes: "Relatively and for many purposes we may say that the dog is mindless; still more that a protozoon, and even more emphatically that a molecule is mindless, unconscious, purposeless. But that such creatures are absolutely without the least degree of that which reaches a high degree in human awareness and purpose—this the panpsychist will not admit. . . . The limit of any decrease in vividness is not matter but non-existence. The absolute opposite of infinite awareness is simply complete unawareness" (BH 169f).

In another context Hartshorne adds: "There is no lower limit to the psychological problem. Amoebae react to stimuli, and this is what we mean by perception, as seen from the standpoint of the external observer. But molecules react too, and so do all the primary individuals in nature" (WP 118f). All primary individuals, i.e. those capable of acting on their own as one, possess some degree of awareness, because ultimately any severance of psychological interiority would be arbitrary. Again, this is an argument pertaining to beings. Its Whiteheadian counterpart would be that all beings are the product of present concrescences, which in their present immediacy enjoy subjectivity. Such subjectivity does not admit of different degrees.

Peters applies Hartshorne's principle of degrees of awareness to the problem of evolution: "The evolution of life and mind is unintelligible if in the final analysis nature is nothing more than tiny, lifeless BBs. For on these terms evolution would mean that the later products of the process were wholly different in nature from their sources, the qualitative having arisen from the quantitative. Causes need not entail their effects, but they must make them possible. One may, of course, have recourse to sheer emergence—or to miracle. But in either case, explanation is sacrificed. We gain explanatory power by conceiving the lower levels of nature, all the way down, to have affinity with the higher" (HNM 40f).

This argument may be compared with Whitehead's: "a thoroughgoing evolutionary philosophy is inconsistent with materialism. The aboriginal stuff, or material, from which a materialistic philosophy starts is incapable of evolution. This material is in itself the ultimate substance. Evolution, on the materialistic theory, is reduced to the role of being another word for the description of the changes of the external relations between portions of matter. There is nothing to evolve, because one set of external relations is as good as any other set of external relations. There can merely be change, purposeless and unprogressive. But the whole point of the modern doctrine is the evolution of the complex organisms from antecedent states of less complex organisms. The doctrine thus cries aloud for conception of organism as fundamental for nature" (SMW 107).

Both of these arguments essentially operate on the plane of being$_w$. (As we shall see in the next section, Whitehead had not yet developed a concern for the level of becoming$_w$.) Both use evolutionary considerations to attack materialism. Though they are superficially similar, the important point to note is that Whitehead's makes no use of degrees of awareness, while this is essential to Peters': "We gain explanatory power by conceiving the lower levels of nature, all the way down, to have affinity with the higher" (HNM 41). If there were no continuity in the degrees of awareness, Peters allows that there could be no emergence. This is just what does take place in Whitehead's theory, for we may conceive of concrescence as emergence generalized. To be sure, major jumps in emergence may be rare, if there are any at all, but there may be gradual emergences linking the insentient with the highly conscious over long periods of evolution. Whitehead makes little use of the evolutionary cosmologists, particularly in *Process and Reality*, perhaps because he is proposing a metaphysics which is invariant for all evolutionary epochs, but he may have used the central insight of C. Lloyd Margan's 'emergence' in his theory of concrescence, even if somewhat inadvertently.[2] The important feature of Whitehead's argument concerns the conditions under which evolution is possible. Peters points to a feature—psychicalism—which does not evolve. Evolutionary changes merely intensify that which is already present, even if only in very implicit and inchoate form. Whitehead argues that if materialism is correct, no evolution is possible, and lays down some preliminary conditions for its possibility. These conditions are refined in the course of his philosophical development. In terms of the final theory we may argue that subjectivity is essential for any emergence whatever, because only in the presence of subjectivity can there be any appropriate response to novel possibility. Ultimately novelty must have a source out of this world in God. Evolutionary emergence requires subjects (in becoming) which can respond to initial subjective aims.

Clearly, these two arguments have considerable affinities, yet their structure is quite different. Whitehead's pansubjectivity is based on becoming$_w$ as the coming into being (or self-creation) of actualities (occasions). It has its differences, even if rather subtle, from Hartshorne's psychicalism. These differences did not arise all of a sudden; at one point, Whitehead's position did not differ significantly from Hartshorne's. To see the ramifications of Whitehead's final view, we should examine how he got there.

II.

To see how Whitehead's views on pansubjectivity matured, we need to examine some important texts from *Process and Reality*, and this we shall undertake in the next section. First, however, we should consider why this term 'pansubjectivity' is inappropriate with respect to the earlier *Science and the Modern World*.

More precisely, our comments need to be directed at the Lowell Lectures of 1925, not the later additions inserted before publication (EWM 1 21). Only the added material (chapters 10 and 11 on "Abstraction" and "God" and some eighteen paragraphs of chapters 6–8) propose the epochal theory of time whereby occasions cannot be divided into smaller actualities, whereas the Lowell Lectures of 1925 speak only of events, conceived as indefinitely subdivisible into smaller events. The later additions, with respect to the questions at hand, have already been sufficiently discussed (EWM 89-91, 131f). Basically, Whitehead discusses almost exclusively 'natural events,' mentioning the more inclusive 'complete occasion' in the last four paragraphs of this account. "A complete occasion includes that which in cognitive experience takes the form of memory, anticipation, imagination, and thought" (SMW 170). No decision is made as to whether all natural events must be complete occasions, or whether only complete occasions are actual. The same strategy, under somewhat different terminology, is also adopted in *Religion in the Making* (1926), which mostly talks of 'physical occasions' and 'mental occasions,' while noting that "the most complete concrete fact is dipolar, physical and mental" (RM 114). But no decision is made as to whether only complete occasions are concretely real, or whether purely physical occasions might also be real.

The initial draft of *The Emergence of Whitehead's Metaphysics* found very little evidence for panpsychism (broadly construed) in the Lowell Lectures of 1925. David Ray Griffin, one of the readers for the press, challenged me on this. In response to these very helpful arguments, I used the strategem of restricting panpsychism only to mentality (EWM 90) because the texts on this point are much more definitive. Whitehead ascribes 'mentality' (as he understands 'mentality') to all occasions first in the 1926 "Time" essay. I then, rather unfortunately, used the term 'pansubjectivity' as a comprehensive term for all those traits in the early books which were thought to pertain to the issue.

Griffin's published critique is carefully spelled out in the first part of his critical study of my book appearing in *Process Studies*. It persuades me that some revision of its views on panpsychism is called for.

Renewed investigation, however, results in our differing even more sharply. Griffin holds Whitehead to be panpsychist (more precisely, 'panexperientialist') already in *Science and the Modern World*, while I now believe he was neither a psychist nor a pansubjectivist then.

The position I meant to hold in the book is well summarized by Griffin.* As he is able to show, however, my revision was only partially carried out. More importantly, my choice of 'pansubjectivity,' drawn from a different context altogether (EWP 322-331), was singularly inappropriate. It was meant to specify interiority, intrinsic pattern, and a very nonsubjectivist interpretation of prehension (EWM 42). If so taken strictly denotatively, it is consistent with the claim that "While it makes some sense to ascribe interiority to every event whatsoever, to claim every event has subjectivity is highly implausible" (EWM 42). Taken in *any* connotative sense, however, it is radically inconsistent; how can there be pansubjectivity if any actuality lacks subjectivity? Therefore I move we eliminate the term 'pansubjectivity' from our analysis of the early works (SMW and RM), and find another term for this interiority, intrinsic pattern, and prehension.

The distinction between panpsychism and pansubjectivity, while implicit in the later theory of *Process and Reality* (EWP 322-31), is too subtle for his earlier theory. To my knowledge no philosopher other than Whitehead has found it necessary to distinguish the two. Usually mentality and subjectivity are held to entail each other. Hartshorne's arguments illustrate how claims about subjectivity are specified as arguments about mentality. If so, we should not expect to affirm pansubjectivity 2 while denying panpsychism.

(The paucity of our terms here leads me to use subscripts: pansubjectivity 1 means the placeholder for the doctrines affirmed, i.e. interiority, intrinsic pattern, and prehension; pansubjectivity 2 means the ascription of subjectivity as ordinarily understood to all actualities; pansubjectivity 3 means Whitehead's particular understanding of subjectivity as present immediacy as applied to all actualities.)

For Whitehead's first metaphysical theory, we must examine the Lowell Lectures of February 1925. These lectures comprise nine

---

Ibid., bottom paragraph, pp. 195f. I can agree to this specification with two exceptions: (1) I find it most unwise to assimilate 'prehension' to 'perception,' since the early notion of 'prehension,' a way of understanding internal relatedness, had no necessary connection with subjectivity whatsoever (EWM 23-25). (2) While it may be possible to read my remarks as saying that Whitehead tentatively introduces panpsychism in SMW "Abstraction," as Griffin suggests at the end of this paragraph, I find it more plausible to hold that Whitehead was deliberately holding the question open.

chapters of *Science and the Modern World*. Apart from three additions, they present a philosophical position different from that of the later chapters. The theory of the Lowell Lecture is based upon the event, which can be of any size whatsoever, and is infinitely divisible into smaller events (EWM 22-50), while the later theory is based upon actual occasions, which are very small yet incapable of further division without loss of actuality (EWM 510125).

If any event is any region of space-time, then pansubjectivity 2 would require that it always remain subjective. That is surely contrary to the later Whitehead's theory of the perishing of subjective immediacy, but it is contrary to the Lowell Lectures, where "the primary fact" is taken to be "an impartial world transcending the 'here-now' which marks the ego-object [Whitehead's term here for 'subject'], and transcending the 'now' which is the spatial world of simultaneous realisation. It is a world also including the actuality of the past, and the limited potentiality of the future, together with . . . the realm of eternal objects . . ." (SMW 151). The subject, or ego-object, is only here-now, not ingredient in past, future, or contemporary events. Yet pansubjectivity would demand that all these other events be in some sense subjective.

It is particularly difficult to see how there could be many future events enjoying subjectivity. I have argued elsewhere that there could be one event embracing the whole of the future that might possess subjectivity, provided it did not concresce into any determinate state,[3] but it is difficult to conceive how any plurality of such future concrescences could be possible.

Events of any size could be wholly arbitrary, such as last night's dinner or the Crimean War. If these events cannot meaningfully be said to enjoy subjectivity, then there is no pansubjectivity of all events.

Pansubjectivity would also require any all-inclusive event, embracing the whole world process from everlasting to everlasting, to be subjective, and probably that to the greatest extent. Not only does Whitehead not present such a view of God, but the Lowell Lectures are quietly naturalistic (EWM 101-107). No view of God is present. If the event of the whole is not subjective, then there is no pansubjectivity of events.

The 'discovery' of temporal atomism gave Whitehead a natural class of events, the occasions, that could plausibly be subjective, particularly as atomization could be restricted to the present alone. Yet we do not find Whitehead immediacy embracing pansubjectivity or panpsychism. Neither is a direct outcome of temporal atomicity, the way his revised theism is (EWM 109-16). He persists in describing subjectivity in terms of ego-object (EWM 45ff), while panpsychism is very gingerly and tentatively contemplated in terms of a mental supplement to actual occasions (EWM 89f, 131).

Yet if all this is true, why is it that *Science and the Modern World* seems so panpsychist? First, these features, particularly the elements of interiority and prehension will naturally appear to be subjective to the reader schooled in the thought of *Process and Reality*. The etymology and association of 'prehension' with 'apprehension' and 'comprehension' suggests it. Besides, neither characteristic is appropriate to that which is purely objective.

We need to appreciate that Whitehead is active on two fronts: fighting against pansubjectivity while at the same time trying to put mind back into nature. Many hold this to be impossible for there are only three alternatives: Materialism, Dualism, or Idealism (panpsychism being pluralistic idealism). To bring mind back into nature without becoming completely panpsychist seems to many an impossible eclecticism combining elements of dualism (which Whitehead surely rejects) and idealism.

Interiority and prehension, I submit, should be regarded not as subjective themselves but as the preconditions for subjectivity. Subjectivity cannot emerge from blank objectivity, but it can emerge—or at least the early Whitehead hoped it could—from these preconditions. This is quite analogous to Whitehead's later theory of consciousness, which also has its preconditions (EWM 224-27). Consciousness is the subjective form of an intellectual feeling, which in turn is the synthesis of more primitive feelings. The primitive feelings are the necessary preconditions for conscious feelings, yet they are not themselves conscious. In fact, they cannot individually be conscious, if consciousness presupposes their synthesis. By the same token, the preconditions of subjectivity cannot be subjective.

Yet every event can plausibly possess the preconditions that interiority and prehension signify. In this way there is an underlying unity which prevents any dualistic disruption. All events possess interiority and prehension, so while some events can remain purely objective, others may build on this common heritage by specializing in subjectivity. Let us now examine these two preconditions:

(a) Interiority is clearly ascribed to events. " 'Value' is the word I use for the intrinsic reality of any event" (SMW 93). This intrinsic reality is characterized by an intrinsic pattern, that "pattern of aspects of other events which it grasps into its own unity" (SMW 103). This is sufficient for some to ascribe subjectivity and even mentality to all events, on the grounds that interiority necessarily entails subjectivity.

The converse is clearly true, but does interiority entail subjectivity for the Whitehead of 1925? Consider the percipient event: "This event is not the mind, that is to say, not the percipient. It is that in nature from which the mind perceives" (CN 107). (He speaks of 'mind' and not 'subjectivity,' but we may take the mind/nature dichotomy for these purposes to be the same as with the subject/object dichotomy.) A conscious perceiver inhabiting that percipient event would perceive the world, but how about the percipient event itself? It is a standpoint geometrically related to all other standpoints in the universe. These other standpoints are its outside, while the way it unifies them constitutes its inside. Interiority, conceived without subjectivity, is precisely the percipient event. (While there can be perceiving from a percipient event, if it should be inhabited by some subject, the percipient event per se does not perceive.)

Interiority per se may be a more abstract concept than that which we have ascribed to percipient events. For while even eternal objects have some sort of interiority, they certainly lack all subjectivity. (The interiority of an eternal object would be its individual essence, as opposed to its relational essence (EWM 80-82). Each is a distinctive entity, yet internally related to all other eternal objects.)

The reason we are not tempted to ascribe subjectivity to eternal objects or to any complex concatenations of them is that they lack the preconditions for subjectivity. Percipient events have them, even though not yet subjective themselves. This three-layered approach, pure objects, preconditions of subjectivity, and subjects, when the middle layer alone is assigned to all actualities, enables Whitehead to avoid dualism.

(b) Prehension is used for the way in which "every volume mirrors in itself every other volume" in space-time (SMW 65). The notion is derived from his 1906 memoir "On Mathematical Concepts of the Material World," a work which Whitehead regarded as one of his best. Its fifth concept defined a point in terms of 'projective points,' the bundle of lines from every other point converging together to form this point. Analogously, an event is constituted out of the convergence of the prehensions from all other events (EWM 23-25).

No subjectivity need be involved in prehension, as originally understood, unless we think of it as a perception which, even if unconscious, remains still subjective. Here the texts are inconclusive, because Whitehead is only concerned to rid prehensions of being necessarily conscious, and says nothing about whether or not they are necessarily subjective.

There is possibly a clue in his use of Bacon on 'perception': "Also in the previous lecture I construed *perception* (as used by Bacon) as meaning *taking account of* the essential character of the thing perceived, and I construed *sense* as meaning *cognition* [i.e. consciousness]" (SMW 69). Whitehead approves of Bacon's use of 'perception' beyond the limits of consciousness. Does this also mean the limits of subjectivity? Bacon certainly thought so, applying it to all bodies, including the way the weatherglass perceives the weather or the way the magnet perceives iron (SMW 41f).

Prehension is often explained in terms of perception, but this simply means that conscious perception is an instance of prehension, the one most immediately accessible to us. It does not mean that all prehension shares the characteristics more complex instances have. Clearly consciousness has been excluded, but in contexts concerning prehension and events generally it is not at all clear whether subjectivity is also excluded.

We may infer this, however, from how he conceives of 'the ego-object' and its role. Paradoxical as it sounds, the ego-object is the subject. In the Lowell Lectures, 'subject' is not the contrast to 'object.' 'Event' is. All actuality is constituted out of events which differ in terms of the objects they exemplify. Thus those features ascribed to all actualities are ascribed to events, whereas those characteristics which apply only to some events rather than others, like subjectivity, are designated as objects (EWM 40-42). Whitehead has another reason for not using 'subject': if 'subject' is taken in terms of the Aristotelian 'subject-predicate' schema, we are eventually brought to the solipsism of the individual subject with its private experiences (SMW 151).

Thus, while it is possible to interpret some of the texts concerning the preconditions of subjectivity as entailing pansubjectivity, none of them need be so read, and they must be qualified in terms of the implicit problematic that pansubjectivity would pose for Whitehead's theory of events, and by his own understanding of subjectivity in terms of ego-objects.

Not only are interiority and prehension preconditions of experience, but they can be ascribed to all events whatsoever, without introducing the difficulties pansubjectivity does. At the same time these preconditions cannot apply to any entity whatsoever, such as an eternal object. No eternal object can prehend another.

III.

How subjectivity as a distinctive property comes to be introduced is most problematic. On the one hand, it would seem that whatever enjoys mentality thereby also enjoys subjectivity, for subjectivity may be defined (though not explicitly by Whitehead) as 'the capacity to be affected by (novel) possibilities.' On the other hand, Whitehead had not yet worked out a satisfactory theory of subjectivity, for he still maintained the traditional assumption that the subject, like the object, was a being. This was inappropriate for his philosophy, which called for the identification of subjectivity with becoming, objectivity with being.

In the *Original Treatise on Perception*, probably composed during the spring of 1927 (EWM 181f), Whitehead distinguishes between two moments of being in concrescence, the original objective datum from which it flows, and the final subjective outcome. This 'datum' is a revision of the earlier 'physical occasion' as it presents itself to the mental occasion which supersedes it (= the concrescence). The 'physical occasion' in turn is derived from the prehensive unity of the earlier (SMW) actual occasion. The original datum may also be derived from the 'ground' which is "formed by all the facts of the world" (RM 145) is the "one actual fact" from which the creative process (= the consequent) starts (RM 109). Thus we learn that "Perception . . . is the appropriation of the datum by the subject, so as to transform the datum into a unity of subjective feeling" (PR 180/273B). [4]

The innocuous 'subject' mentioned in the passage just quoted proved to be quite troublesome, for if it is a being, it does not clearly exist during concrescence, unless we fuse being and becoming by treating becoming as some sort of being. Whitehead found it difficult to gain clarity on the issue, so quietly dropped it in some subsequent formulations, such as these from the Giffords draft: "The philosophy of organism [in contrast to Kant's philosophy] presupposes a datum which is met with feelings, and progressively attains the unity of a subject" (PR 155/234C). As a being the subject first exists as a unity at the end of the process. While commonly called the 'subject,' this outcome should be more properly termed the 'superject': The 'satisfaction' is "the final characterization of the unity of feeling of the one actual entity, the 'superject' which is familiarly termed the 'subject'" (PR 166/251fC).

For this reason "the satisfaction' is the 'superject' and not the 'substance' or the 'subject'" (PR 84/129C). It does not underlie the process, but only emerges at the end. Thus "the operations of an organism are directed towards the organism as a 'superject,' [for only this will have being] and are not directed from the organism as a 'subject'" (PR 151/228C).*

---

*As yet Whitehead has no 'subjective aim' directing the concrescence (G). Its ancestor in this context is the ideal: "The ideal, itself felt, defines what 'self' shall arise from the datum; and the ideal is also an element in the self which thus arises" (PR 150/228C).

From the perspective of Whitehead's final theory, the theory of the Giffords draft seems strange. It conceives concrescence as starting from a single unified datum rather than from a vast multiplicity of physical prehension. This is partly an accident of the way the original theory was put together. Whitehead apparently regarded his analysis of "transition" (not yet so named) as constituting the original datum in terms of prehensive unification (so SMW) as an unproblematic account of perceived nature. Nature was more or less taken care of, but the problem arose as to how to place mind within nature. Thus he concentrated his attention on "concrescence" in order to account for what he had earlier ascribed to the mental occasion. But problems in the interrelation of "transition" and "concrescence" led him to recast the theory of the Giffords draft in terms of the theory most familiar to us, which has one single act of unification.[5]

A particular feature of the Giffords draft theory we have observed is the assimilation of the subject to the superjective outcome of the concrescence. Only the superject has the being i.e. the unity to serve as the subjective being counterbalancing the objective being of the original datum. This theory of two beings, the datum and the superject, framing the concrescence suggests that the occasion is a process of two successive acts of unification. The unity of the original datum needs to be explained, and this is most naturally accounted for by a transition from past occasions effected by the prehensive unification previously proposed (in SMW). In that case, however, there would be two acts of becoming, first of the datum by means of transition, then of the subject through concrescence. This is contrary to the atomicity of becoming, according to which the act of an occasion "is not extensive, in the sense that it is not divisible into earlier and later acts of becoming" (PR 69/107C).

By identifying the subjective feelings of the Giffords theory, which had been restricted to the interiority of the concrescence, with prehensions, as originally conceived (in SMW), which connected the various actual occasions with one another, Whitehead broke through to the conception of a single unification starting from a multiplicity of past data and concluding with the final superject.[6] But this simply exacerbated the problem: who or what feels the feeling *during* the concrescence, if the subject first fully exists only at the end? On the earlier theory, while the original datum cannot serve as a subjective substratum for the concrescence, it can be an objective being underlying the process until the superject appears. Now, however, even that basis has been removed. Until satisfaction is reached, the occasion has no unity as a whole, which is to say, it has no being.

We are already somewhat prepared for the claim that subjectivity, thought in some sense real, has no being. Objective unity is clearly identified with being; the problem remains only whether there is also subjective being. The notion of 'objective immortality' is already examined in the 1926 essay on "Time" (ES 243f = EWM 305f). This is correlated with perishing in the Giffords draft, although Whitehead does not yet explicitly identify what perishes with the subjectivity of the occasion: "the 'perpetual perishing' (cf. Locke, II. XIV, 1) of individual absoluteness is thus foredoomed. But the 'perishing' of absoluteness is the attainment of 'objective immortality'" (PR 60/94C). In another formulation, the process perishes in the attainment of the superjective being: "In the organic philosophy, an actual entity has 'perished' when it is complete. The pragmatic use of the actual entity, constituting its static life, lies in the future. The creature perishes *and* is immortal" (PR 81f/126C). Something perishes in concrescence, and it is not some objective being. Could it be the subject?*

The doctrine of perishing effectively restricted subjectivity to present immediacy, since only that which is objective could survive the moment. This suggested the identification of objectivity with attained unity, which is past relative to supervening occasions, allowing subjectivity to be unity in attainment in the present moment.**

While not a being, the subject was all the more real in the revised theory, for now *all* unification is effected by means of the concrescing subject. There is no longer any autonomous efficient causation effecting the original datum as in the Giffords draft. Prehension, by being identified with concrescent feeling, is now understood to have a subjective pole. Subjectivity grounds prehensive activity by bestowing continued being on the objective data prehended. Thus sensa are given being through perceptual experiencing. Without it they would not exist, at least not for the experience.

---

*In the final revisions, Whitehead comes to recognize this: "actual entities 'perpetually perish' subjectively, but are immortal objectively. Actuality in perishing acquires objectivity, while it loses subjective immediacy" (PR 29/44).

**As long as Whitehead sought to understand the subject as a being, 'subject' was used interchangeably with 'superject.' Once the subject was no longer considered as being but as becoming, while superject remained as the being attained, he adopted the hyphenated form 'subject-superject' to emphasize the essential continuity of the two sides, despite the ontological diversity, for what was once subject is now superject (EWM 208n15).

All this underscores the importance Whitehead gave to the present: "The present contains all that there is. It is holy ground; for it is the past, and it is the future."[7]

Thus everything depended upon subjectivity, but subjectivity which was less and less conceived in terms of being. Yet while an incomplete concrescence has no unity or being as a whole, this does not mean that it is simply nothing. For becoming ₙ contains all as beings prehended, and thus has at least some being in this distributed sense. More importantly, they are not a sheer disconnected multiplicity, for they are all 'together' in the concrescence. While not simply a ???, they do not yet form a unity, for the outcome of the concrescence has not been reached. This 'togetherness' represents an intermediate state between multiplicity and unity appropriate only to subjectivity: "There is a togetherness of the component elements in individual experience. This 'togetherness' has that special peculiar meaning of 'togetherness in experience.' It is a togetherness of its own kind, explicable by reference to nothing else . . . the consideration of experiential togetherness.' The denial of any alternative meaning is the 'subjectivist' doctrine. This reformed version of the subjectivist doctrine is the doctrine of the philosophy of organism" (PR 189f/288D).

'Togetherness' is not just objective unity, nor is it the multiplicity that many ones might have for themselves. But a multiplicity is not an aggregate or a collection which has some, even if very thin, unity. It is a useful conceptual device, an abstraction from experience, for in itself a multiplicity has no unity at all and must therefore be regarded as an improper entity (PR 29f/44f). The 'togetherness' of the multiplicity depends upon the concrescent experience entertaining it. While 'unity' may be objective, 'togetherness' is incurably subjective as the process whereby the initial multiplicity becomes the one superjective unity.

These many reflections concerning the primacy of the present moment, the primacy of subjectivity, and the role of 'togetherness' come together in the inversion of the traditional relationship between being and becoming. Becoming is traditionally understood as the dynamic species of being. Becoming is flux, which is either itself being or dependent upon some underlying being. But if subjectivity cannot be understood as being, yet underlies all objective beings, then it must be understood as the becoming which underlies beings. This is an ontological inversion of the tradition, issuing into a new understanding of becoming. Becoming is creation, for all new being is emergent as the superjective product of concrescence.

Whitehead had already recognized that the ontological principle entailed that "in separation from actual entities there is nothing, merely nonentity—'The rest is silence' " (PR 43/68C0). But the formulation of the ontological principle operative during the composition of the Giffords draft was restricted to past actual occasions: "That every condition to which the process of becoming conforms in any particular instance has its *reason* in the character of some actual entity whose objectification is one of the components entering into the particular instance in question" (EWM 323f). Now, however, Whitehead realized that subjectivity is the reason for the 'togetherness' of past actualities in concrescence, and even for their continued existence. According to the reformed subjectivist principle, "apart from the experiences of subjects there is nothing, nothing, nothing, bare nothingness" (PR 167/254D).

Previous to the adoption of this principle, a being such as the original datum of concrescence could exist apart from the subject first emergent in the satisfaction, and even be implicitly thought of as the underlying substratum. Now, however, no such beings could exist, nor could there be any actual entities that were not in their origination subjective. This entails a pansubjectivity of concrescing actualities. But now this pansubjectivity is fully justified, for subjectivity has been understood in terms of the immediacy of present becoming (which all occasions must at some time or other undergo), and this becoming is seen to form the ontological basis for all (objective) beings. This is certainly a different basis than that provided by most panpsychist theories, and sets Whitehead's theory apart.

The reformed subjectivist principle is Whitehead's distinctive teaching on this subject, won as a reflection upon the transformation of his theory of concrescence. Its importance cannot be measured by the two or three passages that explicitly mention it, for it was very quickly assimilated to (a revised understanding of) the ontological principle (PR 166/252fD).

Whitehead has gone a far way towards distinguishing between mentality and subjectivity. In particular, the theory of physical prehension shows how subjectivity even underlies efficient causation as the present appropriation of the past. This suggests that there could be purely physical activity dependent upon subjectivity, apart from any mentality. This is not, however, the way it is phrased by Whitehead, who stresses that there is mentality "all the way down": "in its lowest form, mental experience is canalized into slavish conformity. It is merely the appetition towards, or from, whatever in fact already is. The slavish thirst in a desert is mere urge from intolerable dryness. His lowest form of slavish conformity pervades all nature. It is rather a capacity for mentality, than mentality itself. But it *is* mentality. In this lowly form it evades no difficulties: it strikes out no new ways: it produces no disturbance of the repetitive character of physical fact. It can stretch out no arms to save nature from ultimate decay. It is degraded to being merely one of the actors in the efficient causation" (FR 33-34).

The issue here is partly semantic, and turns on the claim that "it is rather a capacity for mentality, than mentality itself." If we understand by mentality the effective actualization of novelty, no matter or what degree, then slavish conformity has no mentality. If mentality simply means the capacity for mentality, then subjectivity is the better candidate. Subjectivity is first and foremost the capacity to be affected by (novel) possibility, although it is also the capacity to be affected by past actuality. It underlies both the physical and the mental. What Whitehead is driving at in this passage, I believe, can best be formulated by saying that while some actualities may be purely physical, all must necessarily be subjective.

If so, we may say that in moving from panpsychism to pansubjectivity, panpsychism is finally discovered to be unnecessary.

Key to References

HNW	Peters' Hartshorne and Neoclassical Metaphysics
WP	Whitehead's Philosophy
BH	Beyond Humanism
LP	The Logic of Perfection
SMW	cited according to the Free Press Paperback 1967
RM	cited according to the Meridian Edition
EWM	The Emergence of Whitehead's Metaphysics (1925–1929), Albany: State University of New York Press, 1984
EWP	Explorations in Whitehead's Philosophy, e.d. Lewis S. Ford and George L. Kline NY: Fordham UP, 1983.
FR	The Function of Reason, Beacon Press, 1929.

Notes

1. This issue is explored in some detail, with the necessary qualifications, in my essay on "Hartshorne's Interpretation of Whitehead," forthcoming in the volume on Hartshorne in The Library of Living Philosophers, ed. Lewis E. Hahn (Open Court).

2. George R. Lucas, Jr. has indicated Whitehead's somewhat surprising neglect of the evolutionary cosmologists in "Evolutionist Theories and Whitehead's Philosophy," *Process Studies* 14/4 (Winter, 1985) 287–300.

3. "The Divine Activity of the Future," *Process Studies* 11/3 (Fall 1981), 169–79.

4. 'B' at the end of this citation indicates that it is assigned to the second Level in the order of the composition of PR (see EMW).
Process Studies 15/3 (Fall 1986), 184–207, particularly part I.

5. The outlines of this shift are sketched in EWM 198-217, but the crucial transitional texts, particularly III.1.2, are analyzed in my essay on "The Concept of 'Process': From 'Transition' to 'Concrescence,'" pp. 73–101 in *Whitehead und der Prozessbegriff/Whitehead and the Idea of Process*, ed. Harold Holz and Ernest Wolf-Gaxo (Freiburg/Munich: Verlag Karl Alber, 1984), especially pp. 85–95.

6. The second section of "The Theory of Feelings" (III.1.2: PR 220f/337fD) appears to be the decisive transitional text.

7. *The Aims of Education* (New York: Macmillan, 1929). Quoted by George Allan, *The Importances of the Past* (Albany: State University of New York Press, 1986), p. 13. While AE was first published in 1929, the essays it contains were composed much earlier, most before 1917, the latest by 1922.

Essays in Process Thought and Christian Faith

- John B. Cobb, Jr.
- Schubert M. Ogden
- David Ray Griffin

The Adequacy of Process Metaphysics for Christian Theology

John B. Cobb, Jr.

My own view of Christian theology has been so informed by a processive mode of thought that the issue raised in the title does not arise acutely for me. I will explain briefly why this is so and then turn to the alternative, more common, view of theology and spend most of the paper responding to the issue to which that view gives rise.

I understand Christian theology as the whole range of thinking which is intentionally Christian. In the great tradition, when Augustine, Thomas, Luther, and Calvin discuss issues of political theory, they are, in my view, still functioning as theologians. Similarly, when I try to understand what is wrong with the development programs promoted in the third world by idealistic representatives of the first and second worlds, I understand myself still to be functioning as a theologian. Also, when I engage in metaphysics, I have not put on another hat.

To be a Christian, for me, is to gain my identity in conscious and committed participation in a community whose acknowledged and prized historical roots are in Israel and in primitive Christianity. This community interprets this history through which it came into being and in relationship to which it maintains its unity in light of Jesus who is, for this community, the center of this and of all history.

For this community, the Bible is the indispensable authority. It is only through the Bible that the community knows who it is. It exists as

An earlier and shorter paper by this title was presented to a meeting of Christian philosophers at Westmont College in March 1982. Much of the expansion has been in response to a critique by Jim Mannoia.

the community of those who remember the events recorded in the Bible as *their* history. Its central acts as a community consist of encountering again and again portions of the story, hearing them explained in their relevance to the present, and re-presenting the death and resurrection of Jesus in thanksgiving.

At every point in the history of this community, many beliefs about the past, the present, and the future are of utmost importance. The clear and accurate statement of these beliefs is essential to the health of the community. The most central of these beliefs have to do with what God has done and is doing in the world, and especially in Jesus, among believers and in the hoped-for future.

The need for doctrinal norms poses a problem for the community with respect to its tolerance of those who share its history but reject the official formulations of their time. The problem is an inescapable part of the life of the community, which must make some judgment as to the limits of toleration, yet must also recognize the great harm that has been done repeatedly in the past when such limits were badly drawn.

For the most part, the limits with respect to beliefs are to be drawn in terms of consequences for the community. For example, there are debates about just what the authority of the Bible means. Some suppose that it implies divine authorship in a quasi-literal sense. Others see it as a collection of human writings. Generally, they can live together as long as both understand themselves and the community as living from these writings. On the other hand, the belief that we should give no more attention or authority to these writings than to any other ancient documents, or that we should now identify ourselves primarily from more recent events and ideas, places one outside the community of Christian faith.

The beliefs of one century or epoch of the community's life are continuous with those of earlier periods, but never identical with them. They change by virtue both of inner developments within the community and of encounter with relevant ideas developed outside the community. The Reformers primarily express the former mode of development, whereas the assimilation of Greek philosophy by the Church Fathers and of scientific modes of thought in recent centuries primarily express the latter mode. Both are desirable and healthy.

When Christians experience an opposition between what they judge to be the best thinking of their time, based on the most convincing evidence, and what they find their heritage leading them to think, the community suffers. The sacrifice of the intellect is not a healthy expression of Christian humility. It forces compromise and it leads to lukewarmness or idolatry. When these are the only apparent alternatives, theologians are called upon to lead the community to new modes of thought which break out of this impasse.

We have, in fact, been living in such an impasse for some time. There have been deep tensions between our biblical heritage and the worldview of Descartes, Newton, and Kant. A variety of brilliant strategies were developed to deal with this tension, but a price has been paid for all of them.

Today we are fortunate that the worldviews of Descartes, Newton, and Kant no longer present themselves to us as reflective of the best current thinking. What is replacing them is not yet altogether clear, but it does appear far more congenial to our heritage. It is time for Christians to move from the defensive to positions of leadership in the reshaping of worldview. Whitehead's philosophy is of great help to us here.

When one sees Christianity itself, in this way, as an historical movement, continuously fashioning its beliefs in light of its historical experience, Whitehead's formulation of a post-Newtonian worldview offers itself as a positive and fruitful aid to theology. It cannot be, of course, the last word. If "the adequacy of process Metaphysics" in my title meant that this metaphysics by itself constituted the sole need of Christian theologians, the question would be absurd. Christian theologians need historical, scientific, and practical knowledge as much as philosophical help. They also need deep rootedness in the community and its history and rich participation in contemporary Christian experience and praxis. But if the adequacy of process metaphysics means only that among the ways of dealing with issues of worldview today, process thought has much to commend it to Christian theologians, then I strongly affirm such adequacy.

As I indicated at the outset, I am aware that those who question the adequacy of process metaphysics often do so from a different understanding of theology. In this more widespread view, being a Christian involves subscribing to some core of beliefs established for all time. The theological task is articulating, clarifying, and justifying these beliefs. The question of the adequacy of process metaphysics is the question of its compatibility with this core. Even though I regard the quest for a timeless essence of Christianity or a normative core of Christian beliefs as misguided, I recognize its historical and present importance. I shall devote the remainder of this paper to attempting to address the question posed by the title in terms of this other, dominant approach.

Whether process metaphysics is compatible with the core of Christian beliefs depends, of course, upon how that core is formulated. If the core is formulated as including the idea that God is Being Itself and that Being Itself cannot be affected in any way by what takes place, then process metaphysics is incompatible with the core, for Process theology polemicizes against this view of God. Or if the core is defined in terms of "the six fundamentals" or the imminent rapture, then the uncongeniality of spirit between process metaphysics and the core is so great that any technical possibility of bridging the gulf becomes irrelevant. But when the core is more plausibly considered, the question of the adequacy of process metaphysics is a serious one to be treated in far more detail than will be possible here. I suggest four plausible definitions of the core. I will call them Lutheran, ecumenical, conservative Calvinist, and moral. In the remainder of this essay, I will consider the adequacy of process metaphysics in relation to these definitions of theology.

I.

In the sphere of the influence of Martin Luther, the core is sometimes considered to be the doctrine of justification by faith alone. In itself, this doctrine seems relatively neutral with respect to alternative metaphysics. It can be interpreted in terms of religious psychology, and although this cannot grasp the whole of Luther's meaning, it is an important part.

There can be no doubt that we human beings have a great need to justify ourselves. We are aware that we do foolish and sinful things and cause harm to others. We want to explain ourselves or to compensate in some way. We do not like to feel that we are in the wrong. In order to avoid such a feeling, we try to deceive both ourselves and others with respect to what actually happened and with respect to our reasons for acting as we did. At a still deeper level, much of our life's work can be understood as a way of trying to justify our existence.

Luther was peculiarly sensitive to the distortions and corruptions of his motivations, even in his effort to repent of them and compensate for them. His efforts to justify himself only deepened his awareness that fundamentally, he was in the wrong. In this context it came to him as redemptive revelation that he had no need to justify himself, that God already viewed him as just, not on the basis of any merit on his part, but because of Christ. To benefit from this objective fact of justification by God, Luther concluded, one needs only to believe it or trust in it. In Tillich's language, one needs only to accept one's acceptance. Then one is free from the need to justify oneself and can be genuinely open to others and their needs.

On the subject of just how Christ is the basis of God's acceptance of believers, Lutherans vary. Process metaphysics is open to some, but certainly not all, of the theories of atonement that have tried to explain this. Luther's own views were in the context of a worldview in which few today share. But this worldview has rarely been understood to be at the core of faith for Lutherans.

Far more important is the question of whether process metaphysics can help the theologian affirm the reality of justification by God. Does it make metaphysical sense to say that God justifies or accepts us? Here the answer is an unequivocal affirmative. For Whitehead, the doctrine of God's justification or acceptance of us as we are is metaphysically grounded.

It is true that for Whitehead, as for Tillich, the issue is more the threat of meaninglessness than of guilt. But his doctrine of the Consequent Nature of God, in which our lives are everlastingly affirmed and continued, is equally valid for both concerns. God's love and acceptance are not dependent on our works or our worth. They depend only on God's own grace. For us to believe that we are thus affirmed and saved in God is to be free from anxiety and able to respond to the needs and possibilities of the world with confidence. We can be freed from the self-preoccupation that blocks our openness to others and to God.

Although the most common summary of this Lutheran core is the one I have used, "justification by faith alone," the fullest statement is "justification by grace through faith alone." It is not enough for Luther that we emphasize that faith and not works is the key. We must also avoid the danger of thinking of faith itself as a work, that is, as a human achievement. Once we think of faith as a human accomplishment, we are thrown back into the quagmire of uncertainty. Have we produced true faith, or do we deceive ourselves? Are we really trusting God, or are we substituting some other feeling for real trust? Are we taking pride in our faith as something for which God rewards us with justification?

It is doubtful that there is any way in which correct doctrine can prevent all doubts from arising. But Luther rightly saw that the faith through which we are justified must itself be acknowledged as a gift of God rather than a human achievement independent of God. Otherwise, it does indeed become another work through which we try to justify ourselves or to win God's favor.

Can process metaphysics help us to understand how faith is itself a gift of God? Yes, but it cannot agree fully with some of Luther's formulations on this point. In order to safeguard the gift character of faith, Luther at times writes as if there is no responsible human participation in faith at all. He argues against any notion of human freedom. Indeed, his opposition to human freedom goes further than any other major Christian thinker.

But Luther's own writings imply, all the same, that we do have some responsibility as to how we respond to God. We are not automata. Even faith appears within the context of real human feelings and attitudes as part of ourselves for which we are responsible. In short, Luther gives with one hand what he takes away with the other. What is needed is a doctrine of the relation of grace and faith that makes clear the primacy of grace as giver without rendering human beings into passive objects on which God works quite arbitrarily.

In this connection, Whitehead's metaphysics is remarkably helpful. In Whitehead's analysis of each actual occasion of experience, the initiation lies with God. God determines its locus and its aim. The locus decides what world it will inherit as its past. The aim gives it direction and freedom in its response to that past. Neither the direction, nor the freedom are inherent elements in an autonomous creature. Nor are they contributions of the past world. They are the founding gift out of which the creature comes into being.

This locates creaturely freedom and responsibility quite differently from most metaphysical systems that allow for them at all. Generally, they are seen as properties of creatures, more often of human creatures alone. They may be regarded as gifts of God, but they are permanent possessions, inherent attributes, of creatures over against God's present working. For Whitehead, this is not so. There are no enduring creatures with inherent properties and possessions. The enduring creatures come into being as successions of ephemeral creatures. And each of these ephemeral creatures is called into being individually by God. Further, it is only because of the way God calls them into being that they can transcend the mere repetition of the past and have some responsibility for the way they constitute themselves. Freedom is not a general gift bestowed on Adam and inherited in broken form from him. Freedom is an immediate expression of the working of grace in our lives moment by moment.

The gift is not a blank freedom. It is the enablement to become what the occasion ideally should be in the concrete situation, but by the same token, it is the enablement to refuse that possibility and to become something less and different. The occasion may be called to trust the enabler. No doubt that is an element in the call of all human occasions. But how trusting the occasion will be depends on many things, including its understanding of the giver. The church's message of God's love and acceptance provides a context in which the call to trust God takes on new force. We can still resist, but we can also recognize the truth of what we are told. That recognition is God's gift, but it is a gift received in freedom and enlarging our freedom.

II.

The core may be understood as the ecumenical creeds. This is the core which is most often pointed to in discussions between the Eastern and the Western churches, since it expresses the shared judgments of the Christian community before the great rift. Here, too, if these creeds are taken in their strictest interpretation, involving the philosophical categories which the Fathers used and the worldview of the period, there would be obvious problems. But this is not usually insisted upon by those who identify these creeds as the core. They are ready to differentiate the theological meaning of the creeds from these inevitable accompaniments of every theological formulation.

If this is done, then Whitehead's conceptuality can be helpful. Whitehead explains, in a way that has previously been rare, that the belief that God is incarnate in the world is a metaphysically accurate one. The central point of Nicea is that what is incarnate in Jesus is truly God and not, as Arius taught, a creature—however exalted that creature might be. Whitehead can help us make clearer both what is at stake in this affirmation and also its truth. The central point of Chalcedon is that God is truly constitutive of Jesus, but in such a way that Jesus is fully human. Again, Whitehead can help us to understand what Donald Baillie also pointed out, that the more grace is operative as God's effective presence in a human creature, the more human that creature is. No sacrifice of the intellect is required to accept the doctrine that the perfect case of God's constitutive presence, far from reducing the humanity of the one thus constituted, perfects it.

Although process thought strongly affirms this incarnational way of thinking, it is not committed to any particular doctrine of how Jesus resembles and differs from other human beings. Jews and Buddhists can accept much of the conceptuality without raising these questions at all. The issue here is whether process metaphysics is adequate for Christian theology. To be adequate it must be open to the expression of Christian claims about what happened in Jesus. These include the claim that God was present in him without any lessening of his true humanity, but the claims are not exhausted by that.

For some Christians, the emphasis is that Jesus is the model of a perfect realization of God's presence while in others of us this presence is fragmentary and obscured. For some Christians, the difference is that

Jesus was called by God to a particular work different from that to which others are called. For some, it is held that God was present in Jesus in such a way that there was no human "self" or "I," but rather that God's own presence constituted that self.

All of these views and others can be formulated in process categories. No one view is dictated by those categories. For reasons that have more to do with my reading of Bible and tradition than my use of process metaphysics, I prefer to emphasize a different speculation. I agree with the last of the proposals in the preceding paragraph that Jesus' existence was structurally distinctive, but I do not agree that there was no human "self," or "I," in Jesus. This conflicts with my reading of the gospels. In them, with the partial exception of the Gospel of John, Jesus appears to speak as a truly human self. Further, much of the struggle in the early church was to preserve this insistence on the true humanity of Jesus while affirming that Jesus as a person is co-constituted by God. The later interpretation of Chalcedon as implying that the humanity of Jesus was "impersonal" appears to me both a misreading of the creed and a misrepresentation of scripture. I believe it has done great harm. Hence, I have tried in *Christ in a Pluralistic Age* to show how the one person or self can be conceived as co-constituted by the human past and the divine presence.

III.

In conservative Calvinist circles, the core of Christian belief is often defined in relation to the Bible as such. A particular view of biblical authority is sometimes taken as the crucial test. Earlier, I gave some indication of the limits of views of biblical authority that I find acceptable within the church. Here, the question is whether the sort of views held by conservatives in the Calvinist tradition can be compatible with process metaphysics.

One such view is that the scriptures are divinely inspired through human agents whose human minds are not set aside in the process. Hence the different language and literary style of the writings is recognized, and the same idea may be expressed through different authors at different times in different ways. But the ideas are given in divine inspiration and God protected the writings from errors.

That such a position would not be congenial to Whitehead and to most of those he has influenced, goes without saying. Yet this is not primarily because what is claimed is excluded from the sphere of metaphysical possibilities. It is more because it is theologically distasteful. The Bible itself seems not to make any claims of inerrancy for itself, and these are associated in church history with efforts to escape the relativity of all creaturely life. An inerrant Bible is juxtaposed to an inerrant Pope. Many of us think we would be better off to give up all efforts to absolutize anything creaturely and to acknowledge the fallibility of all our beliefs and thoughts.

Nevertheless, in terms of abstract possibility, something close to what is claimed cannot be excluded. The qualifications arise because of the close association of the doctrine of inerrancy with notions of divine power that *are* metaphysically excluded in process thought. Indeed, it is differences in the understanding of divine power that lead to tensions not only with respect to biblical authority, but also with respect to the appropriation and interpretation of other doctrines arising out of the authority of scripture between process theologians and conservative Calvinists.

In Section I, I suggested that a contribution process conceptuality can make to Christian thought is to show that the operation of God's grace creates and increases human freedom. For process thought, God's power cannot be separated from this operation of God's grace. God does not act on us in some other way than through this enlivening, inspiring, liberating, and empowering grace. This grace works quite diversely in differing instances, so that we may sometimes speak primarily of empowering or inspiring instead of enlivening and liberating. Hence, there is no difficulty in affirming that the biblical writers were inspired by God quite literally. Nevertheless, as this theory recognizes, they were also influenced by their own past and by their cultural settings. Thus far, there is agreement. The difficulty arises at the point at which it is asserted that God protected the inspired writers from error. This sounds like a quite distinct type of power on God's part, one that overrules or displaces human freedom. It is this kind of power that is alien to Whitehead's metaphysics. Whitehead's metaphysics does not exclude the idea that God, having inspired and empowered, would then also inhibit the exercise of that human power.

There is, thus, an important tension between certain conservative Calvinist theories of divine inspiration and process metaphysics. On the whole, the adoption of process categories encourages openness to historical-critical study of scripture. To some conservatives, this is anathema. On the other hand, Whitehead's metaphysics paves the way for certain criticisms of the work of biblical critics that lead to greater congeniality with conservatives than might be initially recognized. For example, higher criticism has often seemed to absolutize a worldview that predetermines the impossibility of miracles. From a process point of view, this is a mistake. If there are good historical reasons for denying the reliability of a particular account, then it should be denied. But this should not be done on grounds of *a priori* suspicion, simply because the event does not fit the dominant worldview. In this respect, much of Pannenberg's argument about historiography is convincing.

Conservative Calvinists are not interested in the question of biblical authority only for its own sake. It is the core, because from it they can move to many other doctrines. The belief in miracles is one. I have indicated that the possibility of miracles is a point of commonality between process thought and conservative Calvinists. But again, some approach miracles with a view of power that differs from that of process metaphysics.

In their view, God may be causally involved in some way in all events, but in this universal activity, God is acting according to the principles of natural law. On the other hand, God sometimes acts contrary to these laws so as to demonstrate lordship over them or to achieve some goal that cannot be attained through natural law.

Process thought rejects this distinction. There is no nature bound by a system of imposed law. There is some measure of spontaneity or self-determination in all natural events made possible by God's presence in them. For process thought, laws have a descriptive character that can be expressed statistically. They evolve as nature evolves. Given these assumptions, events cannot be understood to violate laws. Some of them may be unpredictable and extremely surprising, but that is a different matter. Their remarkable character may be due to the way God is working in them, but still God's working there is continuous with God's working everywhere. Even the most extraordinary occurrences can be analyzed in terms of their continuity with other events and their partial dependence upon them, as well as their discontinuity. An event truly disconnected from its past or its environment is strictly inconceivable.

Now we may ask whether there exists in the Bible a clearcut distinction between God's acts in and through natural law on the one side and in the abrogation of natural law on the other, so that an open-ended and non-reductive theistic naturalism is fundamentally alien. I would argue that this is not the case. Extraordinary occurrences are certainly reported. Usually they reflect unusual spiritual greatness on the part of the human beings who effect them, but at times they are attributed to darker powers. There is no conception of a self-enclosed nature governed by immutable imposed laws which these extraordinary occurrences suspend or violate. Indeed I am convinced that the process view is more congenial to the Bible than the dualistic one which has been so influential in post-Cartesian hermeneutics.

Critics of process thought sometimes point to the doctrine of creation out of nothing as a cornerstone of biblical understanding of the power of God. When it is taken in a very straightforward and unqualified sense, it implies a beginning of time, and the act which initiated time must, indeed, be radically different from acts which shape the process. Further, it must be granted that the notion of a beginning of time is extremely difficult to conceive from a process perspective. Indeed, it is strictly inconceivable from any human perspective whatsoever. If this is part of the core of Christian theology, then there is an important limitation on the adequacy of process metaphysics for its purposes.

It is important to notice, however, that this doctrine is never clearly formulated in the Bible. It is not the doctrine expressed in the creation story in Genesis. It is very doubtful that it was in the mind of any biblical author. If it is to be declared a part of the core of Christian theology by a biblicist, this must be on the basis of complex argumentation. This argumentation usually is to show that alternative doctrines violate the intention of the biblical authors, whereas this one does not. For example, if we posit an eternal matter alongside God, then creation as such cannot be declared good, for the matter may be a principle of evil, or aspects of the world may belong to another power over against God. Ancient heresies enable us to see where such doctrines lead.

Process theology, however, claims to have another view which, equally with creation out of nothing, excludes the offensive teachings. It teaches that no event has ever come into being except as God has brought it into being. Nothing ever has or ever will exist apart from God. But, this does not require the doctrine of a first event. Although the idea of the everlastingness of the world is as difficult as that of a beginning, it should not be rejected on supposed biblical grounds. Before the Big Bang, something was probably going on.

More important than the question of origins is that of destiny. Critics of process theology often argue that part of the core of Christian theology is the affirmation that at some point in the future, God will act in a way that is discontinuous with all God's acts hitherto and with all that the creatures do. This will be a unilateral act of God which brings into being something discontinuous with the existing world. Sometimes this is taken to be the end of time.

Here again, we encounter a doctrine that could hardly be rendered in process terms. But before it is supposed on biblical grounds that this type of eschatology is part of the core of Christian theology, the Bible should be reexamined. When this is done, it appears that at least the last point, the idea that God's act brings an end to time, does not fit with biblical language or imagery. Believers look forward to a new age, but not to a cessation of events. The new age will be one in which God's will is done on earth as in heaven. That will indeed be a remarkable change, but it does not entail metaphysical discontinuity.

There is no doubt that the author of the new age is to be God and not human beings. But it is by no means clear that this entails such radical discontinuity as is sometimes asserted. Scholars have great difficulty in their analysis of Jesus' teaching in discriminating the senses in which the kingdom is purely future and those in which it is already in the midst of the disciples. No doubt utterly unique events are anticipated, and they are awaited as acts of God, but this does not entail that they are disconnected from human acts. To turn such disconnection into a part of the core of Christian theology says more about the advocate of such a position than about the Bible.

How fully, after nineteen centuries and more, a process theologian can share in the sense of imminent expectation that characterized the early church is an important question. But that is a question for all Christians. Process thought as such does not conflict with the expectation that God will do great and surprising things. It conflicts only with certain ways of conceiving the mode of divine action in those events.

Some critics of process theology are committed to the view that whatever occurs in the world must be what God decides will occur. This, too, expresses a view of divine power which process theology rejects. But, we should not deny that there are some biblical passages which point in that direction, as when human sins are attributed to God's hardening a human heart. We can only reply that the reason the author notes that God intended those particular sins may well be that in the general Biblical view it is human beings, and not God, who are responsible for human sins. The Bible generally assumes that human beings may and do act in ways quite contrary to the divine will and intention. No one human response seems usually to be necessitated by divine commands and calls. Human beings genuinely struggle to decide whether or not to obey; their pervasive disobedience is not willed by God. God is Lord of History more in the sense that God perseveres with new initiatives toward God's ultimate purposes, than that God determines exactly what the response to the initiatives will be. I am not willing to concede that the view that everything that happens is exactly as God wills it to happen is the normal and normative biblical view. On the contrary, for the Bible in general, an account of what happens requires that both God's acts and human agency be treated. This is systematized better in process terms than by those who draw logical deductions from supernaturalist views of divine power.

The critics of the adequacy of process metaphysics for Christian theology on the topics treated show that the understanding of divine power in process thought differs from that in much of the tradition. But since we are dealing here with those who appeal strongly to the Bible, this is not the real issue. The claim of process theologians is that the process understanding of divine power is genuinely helpful in understanding the Bible.

In concluding this discussion of power, let us consider the doctrine of divine omnipotence. Process metaphysics is sometimes rejected for Christian use on the grounds that it cannot affirm God's omnipotence. But is omnipotence a biblical doctrine? I believe it is not.

It is true that the word "Almighty" appears in the English Bible extensively in Genesis, Job, and Revelation and occasionally elsewhere. But generally, it translates the Hebrew "El Shaddai," in the Old Testament and the Greek "Pantocrator," in the New. One cannot base a philosophical notion of omnipotence on that. Certainly in the Book of Job, there is heavy emphasis on God's power verging at times on omnipotence, but in the context of that book, it is difficult to say whether this view is affirmed or rejected. Elsewhere, several times, the image is used of God as the potter molding the clay; this certainly suggests great power over the world, but hardly omnipotence. The clay is both a condition of the potter's work and a limitation upon it.

A conservative Calvinist New Testament scholar, a believer in divine omnipotence with whom I discussed this recently, asserted that the clearest teaching of divine omnipotence comes from the lips of Jesus. In the Garden of Gethsemane, for example, Jesus expresses the knowledge that God can do all things. This ability to do all things she took to imply omnipotence. In context, however, the thing God is asked to do is to release Jesus from the need to go to his death. It is doubtful that creation out of nothing or reversal of the expansion of the universe were the kinds of things Jesus had in mind! It should also be noted that Paul claimed he could do all things through Christ, but few would suppose he is claiming metaphysical omnipotence.

I by no means intend to assert that every biblical affirmation of divine power fits comfortably into a process framework. Many do not. But I do believe that the theological tradition has seriously misrepresented biblical thinking about God by stressing a unilateral determination of events by God that is rarely asserted in scripture.

IV.

For many believers the core of Christianity circles around the idea of righteousness. This is central both for some who emphasize private life and some who seek above all that justice be done in the public sphere. The near absence from process philosophy, and from most process theology as well, of the moral language of righteousness, justice, judgment, and will, renders the adequacy of process metaphysics profoundly questionable for these believers. They see that process philosophers make aesthetic categories more basic than moral ones, and they regard this as rendering process thought quite alien to Christian faith.

In part, this criticism is based on misunderstanding. Whitehead is certainly not supporting aestheticism. He is not suggesting that primary importance lies in the creation of art objects, valuable though these are. He is more interested in beauty of character or spirit than of paintings and sunsets. The locus of value for him is in human experience as such, and the aim at some perfection of human experience is closer to that of the ethicists than the difference of language initially suggests.

Nevertheless, the critique cannot be dismissed as based simply on misunderstanding. If we consider Immanuel Kant as representative of a philosophy which locates Christianity in the moral sphere, the contrast with process philosophy is apparent.

For Kant, the only thing that is purely good is a good will. A good will is defined in terms of the intention to obey the moral law. Whitehead, on the contrary, does not rate moral law so highly. It is useful because it provides us, in congealed form, with the cumulative wisdom of the community. But one cannot deduce from it infallibly what is now to be done. The one thing that is purely good is perfect conformation to God's present aim. That may or may not coincide with following the divine law, but Whitehead believes it will always involve the realization of some optimum of beauty in the present experience compatible with contributing to the beauty of future occasions. In short, Whitehead denies that God is a cosmic moralist, and here he parts company with Kant. The question now is whether he also parts company with the Bible.

There is no doubt that moral law plays a large role in the Bible. There is also no doubt that some Christians have interpreted the Bible primarily in these terms. Especially in the eighteenth century, there were those who believed that what is valuable and valid in the Bible is a body of moral teaching, combined with the assurance that the divine source of that teaching also rewards and punishes human actions in accordance with it.

But few Christians subscribe to such legalism without qualification. Most affirm that there is also forgiveness. Some hold that forgiveness is an everlasting characteristic of the way God deals with us. Others hold that it is dependent on the atoning death of Jesus. In either case, God's justice is qualified by God's mercy. Our salvation depends on the latter rather than on the former.

At this point, therefore, it is Kant, rather than Whitehead, who deviates from the tradition. But in this formulation, it still remains the moral law whose violation places us in the need of forgiveness. Here, it is Whitehead who differs. For him, there is no moral law with such sacred authority that it is always wrong to break it. There are times when God calls us precisely to transcend the law. Whitehead is closer to Kierkegaard than to Kant.

But are not Whitehead and Kierkegaard here closer to the Bible than is the tradition which has emphasized the moral law? Does not Jesus also break the law in the service of human need? Does not Paul teach that in faith we are free from bondage to the law? Has not the church's effort to establish an absolute law of God been an expression of faithlessness rather than faith?

Paul does not, of course, dismiss the law as worthless. On the contrary, it serves as a teacher. Similarly, Whitehead affirms the need for moral law as a general guide to conduct in most circumstances. But for Paul, when we live in Christ, when we are indwelt by the Spirit, we no longer need the external teacher. We are led to fulfill the law precisely in our freedom from the law. Similarly in Whitehead, God indwells each moment of our lives and directs us toward that new possibility which is truly appropriate. This is not a rejection of morality, but a fulfillment of its deepest intention by transcending it.

There remains a contrast of language. Justice or righteousness is a central characteristic of God in both the Old and the New Testaments. These terms hardly appear in process metaphysics and are rare in process theology. Does this mean that process metaphysics draws its users away from biblical modes of thought? If so, must we not deny its adequacy for theology?

Clearly, Whitehead felt distaste for the word "justice." In his social theory, he speaks of freedom and equality, but not of justice. Presumably, justice was connected in his mind with rewards and punishments duly apportioned according to merit. Life gives no evidence of that kind of justice, and Whitehead did not affirm it of God. The whole notion of merit with which it is bound up is alien to him.

Does this separate him from the New Testament? It seems to me that the notion of justice he opposed is opposed there too. Jesus noted that the sun shines on the unjust as well as on the just, that the killing of eighteen by the fall of the tower of Siloam did not imply that they were any more sinful than others. The parable of the laborers in the vineyard clearly warns against expecting from God the correlation of reward with merit. Jesus notes that it is sinners and not the righteous who respond to his message. To turn his own teachings into a new law by which we would be judged works so badly that it has only rarely been tried. All of this suggests that the idea of justice alien to Whitehead was alien to Jesus as well. Would it be going too far to say that Jesus redefines divine justice in terms of divine love and that it is faithful to him to take God's universal love for sinful human beings as central and normative? If not, then process preference for the language of love over the language of justice does not count against the adequacy of process metaphysics.

Sometimes the concern about the inadequacy of process metaphysics to express biblical modes of thought about justice centers on the question of punishment. There has been a strong element in the tradition that has viewed the assurance that the wicked will be punished is important, both for the satisfaction of the saved and to make sinners aware of the urgency of repentance. It is quite true that this element is absent in process metaphysics and would be difficult to incorporate. It is also clear that interest in the punishment of sinners has expression in the Bible, especially in the apolcalyptic writings, but elsewhere as well.

Of course, process thinkers are far from alone in their silence about hell. The idea of God's inflicting punishment on the wicked simply as punishment rather than as purgation or discipline, has been difficult to reconcile with the revelation of God in Jesus. Yet it can be argued that it is only because of a soft humanism and liberalism that this biblical note has been so widely silenced. In that case a metaphysics that enforces this silence is inadequate. On the other hand, the greatest and most biblical of twentieth-century theologians, Karl Barth, meditating on the meaning of Jesus Christ, came to the conclusion that in him God saved all human beings. Barth cannot be accused of soft humanism or liberalism.

Whitehead does speak of judgment, although it is the judgment of love. We are judged as our lives are taken up moment by moment into God's life. Both our good and our evil take on thereby everlasting significance. God gives our contribution what meaning it can receive in the total context, but that does not equalize the good and evil or do away with their differences.

Whitehead's thought is open to the possibility of life after death, and process theology can pursue the theme of judgment there without violating the metaphysics. That does not mean that it can think of God imposing on sinners a punishment that is not the inherent consequence of their sin. That would be alien to the nature of God as process metaphysics depicts it, and many feel it would be alien also to the nature of God as that is revealed in Jesus. It is, however, possible to provide images that suggest punishment of another sort.

One that I like is suggested in the prologue of John. When light comes into the world some turn to the light and others turn away. Those whose deeds are evil are made miserable by this light. This is no punishment inflicted upon them extraneous to their sin. It is a heightening of a reality of self-hate that is already there. Suppose then, that after death all that enables human beings to hide from the Light is removed. What then? Is that reward or punishment? Surely it involves both. Those who long to see God face to face have their deepest hunger satisfied. Those who have lived the lie, who have endured life by self-deception, are forced to face the reality. For them, the truth is hell.

I do not propose this as a prediction of what life after death will be like in any straightforward sense. Neither the Bible, nor process metaphysics, carries me very far in imagining such a mode of existence. But the image does suggest the kind of judgment that makes sense in process and, I think, in Christian terms.

For some who object to the downgrading of moral categories in process theology, the primary issue is social justice. Whitehead began as a mathematician and developed his thought through physics to metaphysics and theology. Throughout his life he had broad humanistic interests, and in later years he worked out his conceptuality in its relation to history as well. His concern for freedom and equality is a small part of his total work. Those seeking extensive help from philosophers in this area will do well to turn to such traditions as the Frankfort School.

The situation is similar among process theologians. Many of those Christians who have been attracted to Whitehead's thought have emphasized its fruitfulness in relation to the scientific worldview rather than the quest for justice. Most of them looked to Reinhold Niebuhr rather than to Whitehead for guidance on social issues. Hence the impression could well be given that process categories are inherently inadequate for these needs of Christian theology.

Recently, however, a considerable literature has appeared relating process categories to concerns for world history and destiny. This literature goes far toward overcoming the plausibility of the critique. I will leave it to speak for itself.

My paper is an argument *for* the adequacy of process metaphysics to Christian theology. I have stressed that such an argument depends on prior agreement as to what Christian theology is. It is obvious that process metaphysics is incompatible with many traditional and contemporary Christian theologies. The argument is that this is because of the particular commitments of those theologies, rather than because of anything essentially Christian. Most of what process theology rejects on the subject of power in these other theologies is being rejected in various ways by many other Christian theologians as well. Dietrich Bonhoeffer and H. Richard Neibuhr will serve as good examples along with most of the liberation theologians. Most of what process thought rejects in the moralism often associated with "justice" has been long since criticized by Martin Luther. I hope that process metaphysics can contribute to the clearer and fuller articulation of the positive insights of such theologians as these.

Concerning Belief In God

Schubert M. Ogden

In our society and culture, the traditional and still predominant form of religious belief is theistic—specifically, the theistic religious belief of Judaism and Christianity as well as of classical Hellenism. Theistic religious belief is constituted explicitly as such by the foundational belief in the reality of God. Consequently, for any of us who has been socialized and accultured into our society and culture, whether into its traditional forms or into one or the other of their more or less radical revisions, the most important question concerning religious belief is almost certain to be the question concerning belief in God. Because all the other religious beliefs and practices in our social and cultural context presuppose an answer to this question, one must be concerned with it, above all, if one is to seriously engage in religious inquiry of the sort that I propose to pursue in this essay.

I stress that my concern is with belief in God from the standpoint of religious inquiry, because this is certainly not the only standpoint from which one may find oneself concerned with such belief. Belief in God is also a proper object not only of the inquiries constitutive respectively of philosophy and metaphysics but also of the inquiries necessarily pursued by such human sciences as psychology, sociology, and anthropology as well as by history. Even so, my concern here is not as a philosopher or a metaphysician, much less as a human scientist or a historian, but as a theologian and a student of religion—both of whom engage, in somewhat different ways, in what may be properly distinguished as religious inquiry. Of course, I have no intention of separating the present inquiry as religious from any of the other inquiries from whose standpoint belief in God is also in some way a proper object of study. As a matter of fact, I shall presently be explaining why religious inquiry concerning belief in God necessarily implies both philosophical

This was a lecture given at the Center for Process Studies in Claremont on March 9, 1986.

and metaphysical inquiries concerning the same belief. But, contrary to Hume's famous dictum that any things that can be distinguished can be separated, it is possible—and in some cases necessary—to distinguish things without separating them. And so we may, and even must, distinguish the present inquiry as properly religious, without thereby separating it from any of the other inquiries that in their own way are also properly concerned with belief in God.

Before explaining further what I understand by religious inquiry and what can be said about belief in God from its standpoint, I want to comment briefly on why such belief typically becomes a question for us. To grow up in our society and culture, I have said, is in one form or another to internalize its traditional religious beliefs, including, above all, the belief in God constitutive of the radically monotheistic religions of Judaism and Christianity. In the case of those of us who have been raised in church or synagogue, this internalization is most likely to have taken the form of the positive acceptance of a more or less traditional belief in God, while in the case of others of us, this internalization may very well have taken the form of a negative rejection of traditional belief in God because of a positive acceptance of some more of less radically ultimate belief. But in either case, continuation in the process of maturing involves being confronted with questions about the truth of our religious beliefs. Although none of us could live humanly at all without being socialized and acculturated, and thus internalizing in some form or other the beliefs of some human group, none of us can become a truly mature human being without critically appropriating our inheritance of beliefs once the question of their truth is raised in our minds. To try to repress this question once it has arisen is to live dishonestly or insincerely, whatever our particular beliefs.

The question of truth is bound to arise, however, as soon as we recognize, as we must, that all our religious beliefs are controversial, and that this is so in several different respects or at several different levels: as between different traditions or movements within religions (e.g., Reform, Conservative, and Orthodox in the case of Judaism, or Protestant, Catholic, and Orthodox in the case of Christianity); as between different religious (e.g., Judaism, Christianity, and Islam); as between theistic religions and nontheistic religions (e.g., the three theistic religions just mentioned and, say, Theravada Buddhism or Zen); and, finally, as between religious and nonreligious ultimate beliefs (e.g., any of the religious beliefs previously referred to and the ultimate beliefs, say, of Marxism, or scientism or some other form of modern secular humanism). As a matter of fact, a different but no less important kind of controversy is evident today in all of the major religious traditions. I refer to the often embittered controversies between traditionalist interpretations of the traditions and their more or less revisionary reformulations—such as, for example, the controversy in the contemporary Christian community between those who still interpret the Christian life as simply a matter of moral responsibility within the given social and cultural order and those who see the tasks of Christian love as including the specifically political task of transforming the structures of society and culture.

Whatever the kind or level of controversy, there is nothing to be done by any of us who wishes to become a mature person in his or her religious beliefs once the question about their truth has arisen than to try to find reasonable answers to this question. This requires us to engage in religious inquiry, by joining with any and all others who are similarly moved in a cooperative search for truth in which the only constraint, just as in any other serious inquiry, is the constraint of the better argument. Such inquiry is likely to occupy us to some extent all our days, even if, as we may hope, it will not take too long to find sufficient reason either to reaffirm our inherited beliefs or else to affirm some alternative beliefs, so that we may identify ourselves religiously in the same way in which we grow up otherwise by identifying ourselves morally, politically, aesthetically, and so on.

If we now ask about the question of the truth of belief in God, analysis discloses that it is essentially two questions—distinct and yet closely related: (1) What, properly, is to be understood by the term "God"? (or How is God properly conceived?); and (2) Is there sufficient reason to believe that, when the term "God" is properly understood, something is real to which it applies? (or Does God properly conceived also exist?) Obviously, it is the second of these questions that we are most likely to have in mind when we speak of the question of belief in God. But it is hardly less obvious that any answer to the second question depends on some answer to the first. As a matter of fact, not only does the question whether God exists depend for its answer upon how God is conceived, but the same is true of any answer to the crucial procedural question of the modes of reasoning or kinds of argument that are and are not appropriate to answering the question of God's reality. There are the very best of reasons, then, why we should take some pains in pursuing the first of our two questions concerning belief in God.

I trust it will seem reasonable, in the light of my opening comments about the traditional and still predominant form of religious belief in our society and culture, if I appeal to the foundational belief of traditional Jewish and Christian theisms in responding to our first question as to how the term "God" is properly understood, or how God is properly conceived. There can be no serious question that the term "God" is primarily a religious term, since it is first employed by religion, and its religious use always remains its primary use, however it may also come to be used in philosophy or metaphysics. Consequently, it is always to religion that we must finally appeal if we wish to understand the proper use of the term; and for reasons that should now be clear this means in our context that it is to the foundational beliefs of Judaism and Christianity that we must look for an answer to our first question.

The difficulty, of course, is that this belief has been formulated over the centuries in both of these religious traditions in widely different ways and, therefore, cannot be simply identified with any of its formulations but can be retrieved only by critically interpreting all of them. Without minimizing this difficulty, I believe one can argue— although I shall not develop the argument here—that Jewish and Christian theisms are constituted by essentially the same use of the term "God" and that this use suggests that the concept of God as it figures in both of these religions involves a certain characteristic duality or tension.

On the one hand, God is conceived in both religions to be a distinct individual who enters into genuine interactions with others—both acting on them and, in turn, being acted on by them. On the other hand, God is conceived in both religions to be strictly universal, in the sense that anything that is so much as even possible has its primal source and its final end in God. Thus if God is an individual, God is the *universal* individual, the one individual with strictly universal functions, whose action on others is an action on *all* others and on whom, in turn, *all* others somehow act or make a difference. Similarly, if God is universal, God is the only *individual* universal, the one universal that functions individually, by not only acting on all other things but also interacting with them, and thus also being acted on by them.

If it be objected that this concept of God that I find expressed in Jewish and Christian theisms is really an ideal type, I should readily agree that it has rarely if ever been expressed in such a way as to bring both of its essential aspects to clear and coherent expression. In the more religious and often mythological formulations of theistic belief, the individual aspect—or the aspect of God as an individual—so predominates as to call into question the universal aspect—or the aspect of God as universal. On the other hand, there is something like the reverse difficulty in the more philosophical or metaphysical formulations of Jewish and Christian theisms, where the emphasis upon God as universal obscures or contradicts the aspect of God as an individual. In other words, there are two main ways of going wrong in thinking and speaking about the God conceived by these radically monotheistic religions, and both of these ways are illustrated many times over by the history of Judaism and Christianity. I could also express this by saying that the history of these two religions exhibits the possibility of two main types of theoretical idolatry: a *concrete* type, according to which God is thought and spoken of as an individual without taking sufficient account of God's universality, and an *abstract* type, according to which God is thought and spoken of as universal without doing justice to God's individuality.

But if God is properly conceived only as the universal individual, or the individual universal, more or less adequately attested in Jewish and Christian religious belief and practice, certain consequences follow that are of the utmost importance for the question concerning belief in God. On the one hand, it follows that an answer to this question is by no means entirely dependent on the fate of classical Jewish and Christian theisms at the hands of modern and postmodern criticism. There seems little doubt that the more metaphysical among the classical formulations of theistic belief tend to be determined by what I have called the abstract type of theoretical idolatry. By this I mean that they so think and speak of God as universal as either to deny or to obscure the genuine individuality of God. Thus, for instance, while God is said to act on all things, and, therefore, to be externally related to them, and so to be in the strict and proper sense "absolute," God is also said to be in no sense "relative," because internally related to nothing, and so in no way acted on by other things as any genuinely interacting individual perforce has to be. But, then, any predicate expressing or implying God's individuality, and hence God's interaction with others, such as the familiar personal predicates of loving others, knowing others, judging others, caring for others, and so on, must either be denied of God altogether or else be asserted of God more or less unclearly or incoherently.

The truth, I suspect, is that the classical formulations or theistic belief are neither clear nor coherent, since they continue to assert the personal predicates that are certainly characteristic of primary religious belief and practice in a theistic religious context. But as serious a criticism as it may be to say this, it is, after all, a criticism of the classical formulations of theistic belief, not of this belief itself. Provided one so expresses the concept of God as to take account of both of its aspects—and this is exactly what is attempted by all revisionary, especially all neoclassical, formulations of the concept such as those of process theologies—there is every reason to suppose that belief in God remains an open question, however devastating modern and postmodern criticism of classical theism has proved to be.

On the other hand, it also follows from the concept of God whose propriety I am urging that an answer to the question of belief in God cannot be settled by any merely empirical or factual mode of argument, such as has again and again been insisted on by modern and postmodern critics of classical theistic belief. Ever since Hume, it has been widely supposed that statements about anything real or existent, and hence about any individual, can be true only empirically or factually, and this only contingently, rather than necessarily. But if God is properly conceived only as the strictly universal individual, this modern supposition is exposed as involving, in effect, the concrete type of idolatry, and thus of begging the question of belief in God instead of rationally answering it. Otherwise put, if Hume's rule about the necessary contingency of all assertions about individuals calls the reality of God into question, the existence of religious traditions such as Judaism and Christianity, for which God is nothing if not the universal individual, is at least sufficient to challenge the unrestricted application of Hume's rule. Because God is properly conceived only as the strictly universal individual, the question of theistic belief, in the sense of belief in the reality of God, lies beyond the scope of all merely empirical or factual modes of reasoning, and must be settled, if at all, by some very different kind or kinds of argument.

Nor are these the only procedural consequences that follow once appeal is made to the Jewish and Christian religious traditions for a proper concept of God as the universal individual or the individual universal. For if the question of belief in God is thus shown to be independent both of the abstract idolatry of classical theism and of the concrete idolatry of modern secularism, it is just as certain that it cannot be settled by some merely fideistic appeal to particular religious traditions but only by appropriate modes of inquiry and argument. By "fideistic" here, I mean the kind of position that proposes to answer all questions as to the ultimate justification of religious belief by appealing simply to the claims and warrants of some already given religious faith (the word "*fides*," from which "fideistic" and its cognates are derived, being the Latin word for faith in this sense.) Such a position has been taken again and again throughout Jewish and Christian history right up to the present time, when it is often represented in a peculiarly sophisticated form by certain analysts of religious language. But not the least objection to any such fideism is that it is implicitly contradicted by the concept of God constitutive of radically monotheistic belief. If God can be properly conceived only as the strictly universal individual, then God must also be conceived as ubiquitous or omnipresent, and hence as immanent in anything whatever insofar as it is so much as even possible. But, then, God must also be conceived as somehow omnipresent in any and all possible beliefs or experiences, so that everyone must in some way, or at some level, believe in God or experience God, and no one could in every way, or at every level, disbelieve in God, or fail to experience God. In other words, belief in God by the very meaning of "God" and by the very nature of such belief must be somehow warranted not only by the particular faith and experience of those who explicitly believe in God in terms of some inherited religious tradition such as Judaism or Christianity, but also by any and all human experience and belief simply as such. Thus, contrary to the claim of fideistic accounts of belief in God, including those of certain forms of contemporary analytic philosophy, if anyone is indeed justified in believing in God, then no one could really be justified in not believing in God—or, alternatively, if anyone is indeed justified in not believing in God, then no one could be really justified in believing in God.

To recognize this, however, is to realize the importance of asking about the kind or kinds of inquiry whereby the question of belief in God can, in fact, be properly answered. And so we are led to develop further what has already been said about distinctively religious inquiry as a necessary step toward any answer to the second of our two questions concerning belief in God—the question, namely, of whether the term "God" as properly understood has any application to reality, or whether God properly conceived also exists. If we are to answer this question, or, at least, understand how one properly goes about answering it, we must understand the kind or kinds of inquiry by which alone it is appropriately answered; and as we have seen, this means that we must primarily understand the kind of inquiry distinctive of religion, even if there may be other kinds of inquiry that are also appropriate to answering it.

To pursue the question as to the nature of religious inquiry, then, I would observe, first of all, that the constitutive question of such inquiry is the primary explicit form of what I call "the existential question," or, alternatively, "the question of faith." I speak of it as "the existential question" because it has to do with the ultimate meaning of one's very existence as a human being and, therefore, is and must be asked and answered at least implicitly by anyone who exists humanly at all. Alternatively, I call it "the question of faith" insofar as I reflect on the "basic supposition" underlying it. Like any other question, it can be asked at all only because or insofar as one supposes certain things to be the case. But in asking *this* question, what one necessarily supposes to be the case is what is perforce supposed by our basic faith simply as human beings in the ultimate meaning of our lives—namely, that reality is ultimately such as to authorize some understanding of ourselves as alone appropriate to it and as, therefore, our authentic self-understanding.

So far as I can see, at least this much in the way of faith is basic to our very existence as human beings, because it is implicitly presupposed as the necessary condition of the possibility of all that we think or say or do. Even suicide, to the extent that it is the intentional act of taking one's own life, necessarily presupposes faith in this basic sense of the word. But if this is correct, such underlying faith in the ultimate meaning of life is the basic supposition of the existential question, and it is this to which I intend to call attention by speaking of the question as also "the question of faith."

This same question, however, may also be called "the religious question," assuming as I do, that what is properly meant by "religion" is the primary form of human culture in which the existential question, or the question of faith, is explicitly asked and answered. If this question is and must be asked at least implicitly insofar as we exist humanly at all, because the basic faith underlying it is a necessary condition of whatever we think or say or do, some answer to the question is necessarily implied by all forms of culture, secular as well as religious. The distinctive thing about religion, however, is that it not only *implies* an answer to the question, but also *explicates* such an answer—just this being its unique function as a primary form of culture alongside of the other, secular cultural forms.

But if this explains why religious inquiry is possible, what makes such inquiry necessary? That it is necessary seems evident enough from the existence throughout human culture and history of particular religions and—as we noted earlier—from the various kinds and levels of controversy instituted by their existence. Yet if we ask for the reasons of the various religions, basic faith in the ultimate meaning of life, while certainly a necessary condition, is not sufficient. Religion comes to exist not simply in order to explicate our basic faith, but only because our faith in some way becomes problematic. Even though we have no alternative, finally, but to exist and to act in the faith that life somehow finally makes sense, how exactly we are to understand our faith is so far from being unproblematic as to be continually called into question. Why? Because our life is perforce lived under conditions that threaten to undermine any naive assurance we may have as to its ultimate meaning. Thus, for instance, there are the inescapable facts that each of us must suffer and die, that we inevitably involve ourselves in guilt, and that all our undertakings are continually exposed to the workings of chance. Or, again, there is the loneliness that overtakes us in even the most intimate of human relationships and, still worse, the gnawing of doubt and the threat of final meaninglessness when we recognize, as we must, that our ultimate beliefs are just the ones of whose truth we must always be the least certain at the level of explicit belief. And these conditions are only exacerbated in the case of those who must suffer the injustices and oppressions of the existing social and cultural order. Indeed, the deeper misery of the oppressed is the constant sense that they are excluded from participating in a meaningful human life of the sort that they are nonetheless compelled to believe in as soon and as long as they exist humanly at all.

Of course, none of these conditions would pose the kind of problem it poses for us but for our prior assurance that our lives somehow finally make sense and are worth living. This is why the question of faith, to which all religious concepts and symbols in one way or another offer an answer, is never the question *whether* life is ultimately meaningful—any more than the question answered by a properly scientific assertion is *whether* the world has some kind of order. Rather, the question of faith, and, in its explicit form, the religious question, also, is always only *how* the meaning that we are sure life finally has can be so conceived and symbolized that we can continue to be assured of it—just as the question of science is always *how* we are to understand the order that we are certain the world must have, so that we can sufficiently predict and control the future as not only to survive in the world but also prosper in it. Even so, all the negativities of our existence, insofar as we experience and reflect on them, challenge our basic faith, driving us beyond any simple understanding of it. In this way, the conditions of human life as we unavoidably lead it again and again create the profound need for *re*-assurance, for an understanding of ourselves and the world in relation to ultimate reality that will enable us to make sense of the basic faith we inevitably have.

It is to just this need to make sense somehow of our basic faith in the ultimate meaning of life that religion generally, and hence each religion in particular, is the response. All of the various religions are so many attempts under the pressure of this need to solve the problem of understanding our basic faith, given the negativities of existence as we all, in fact, undergo it. How different religions, in particular, manage to do this, or with what radicality of insight, is, naturally, historically variable, depending on which of the conditions of human life are taken to focus the problem and on the depth at which these conditions are grappled with and understood. Even so, the whole point of any religion is so to conceive and symbolize the great inescapabilities of life as to solve the problem of our existence as such: the problem of our having to believe somehow in the ultimate meaning of life under conditions that make such faith seem all but impossible.

The upshot of the preceding analysis, then, is this: the structure of religious inquiry is constituted by a single question that is neither merely metaphysical nor merely moral but distinct from both of these other kinds of inquiry, even while having aspects that respectively relate it to each of them. Accordingly, it can be described as the question about the meaning of ultimate reality for us, which asks at one and the same time about both ultimate reality and ourselves: both the ultimate reality that authorizes some understanding of our existence as authentic and the authentic self-understanding that is authorized by what is ultimately real. As such, the religious question has, on the one hand, a *metaphysical* aspect in which it is distinct from all properly metaphysical questions, even while being closely related to them. It is distinct from metaphysical questions insofar as it asks about the meaning of ultimate reality for us, while they ask about the structure of ultimate reality in itself. But it is also closely related to metaphysical questions insofar as any answer to it necessarily implies certain answers to them. This is so because it is only insofar as ultimate reality in itself has one structure rather than another that it can have the meaning for us it is asserted to have in taking it to authorize one self-understanding rather than another as the authentic understanding of our existence. On the other hand, the religious question has a *moral* aspect in which it is both distinct from and closely related to all properly moral, including specifically political, questions. It is distinct from moral questions insofar as it asked about the authentic understanding of our existence authorized by ultimate reality, while they ask about how one is to act and what one is to do in relation to the interests affected by one's action. But the religious question is also closely related to such moral questions insofar as any answer to it has certain necessary implications for any answer to them. This is the case because it is only insofar as acting in one way rather than another is how one ought to act in relation to relevant interests that ultimate reality can have the meaning for us it is asserted to have in taking it to authorize one self-understanding rather than another as authentic.

Of course, as thus analyzed, the religious question might be said to be two questions rather than one, insofar as in asking it one asks about both ultimate reality *and* authentic self-understanding. But as true as this certainly is, there is an overlap between the two questions that speaking of them simply as two fails adequately to take into account. In asking about the meaning of ultimate reality for us, one asks about ultimate reality only insofar as it authorizes authentic self-understanding, even as one asks about authentic self-understanding only insofar as it is authorized by ultimate reality. Recognizing this, I prefer to speak of the question constituting distinctively religious inquiry neither simply as two questions nor simply as one question, but, rather, as one question with two essential aspects, metaphysical and moral, each of which necessarily implies the other.

If this is the logical structure of religious inquiry, and if the standpoint from which it perforce must deal with belief in God is the meaning of ultimate reality for us, how our second question concerning belief in God is to be answered should be clear enough. There is indeed sufficient reason to conclude that the term "God," properly understood, actually applies to what is real, or that God so conceived also exists, insofar as belief in God can be shown to be the most appropriate way of answering the religious question, and thus solving the problem of our existence as such. In other words, the distinctively religious question of the truth of belief in God, given the understanding of "God" previously clarified, is the question whether the ultimate reality authorizing the authentic understanding of our existence is best conceived as God in this sense of the word, and hence as the one universal individual, or individual universal.

To establish that this is, in fact, the case is the objective of all arguments for God's reality of existence, insofar as such arguments are understood as belonging to properly religious inquiry. Thus, however many may be the ways of developing it, there is really only one such religious argument—to the effect, namely, that we exist humanly at all only because of our at least implicit belief in God and that, as a consequence, this belief must also be affirmed explicitly if the reflective inventory of our beliefs is to be both complete and consistent. As for whether I myself take this religious argument for God's reality to be sound, my answer is affirmative on two conditions: provided God is conceived neoclassically as genuinely individual no less than universal, and provided one repudiates the secularistic insistence that God as individual can exist only contingently, by maintaining, to the contrary, that God is genuinely universal as well as individual, and hence exists necessarily. In short, in my view the truth of belief in God from the standpoint of religious inquiry depends upon so understanding the term "God," or so conceiving the God to whom it applies, that both the abstract and the concrete types of theoretical idolatry are overcome.

On the other hand, insofar as both of these misconceptions *are* overcome, belief in God seems to me to have a strong claim to be religiously true; for the two aspects of God as properly conceived, as individual and as universal, correspond exactly to the two demands implicitly placed on any truly profound answer to the distinctively religious question of the meaning of ultimate reality for us—the individuality of God constituting a ground of life's meaning such as only a genuine individual can possibly provide, and the universality of God constituting this ground as in principle unsurpassable, because God is the primal source and the final end not only of our own existence but of everything else, possible as well as actual.

In sum: belief in God thus understood explicates an understanding of our basic faith as well as of all the negativities of our existence that enables us to reaffirm the faith we inevitably have even while coming to terms with the inescapabilities of life that confound any less profound understanding of our existence.

I have two concluding comments. The first is that, while a religious argument for belief in God such as I have just outlined is the primary way of going beyond any mere fideism by rationally arguing for theistic belief, it is not, in the nature of the case, the only way of giving reasons for such belief. I explained why this is so when I argued that the religious question, although distinct from both properly moral and properly metaphysical questions, nevertheless has two aspects that closely relate it to both of these other types of questions—namely, in such a way that any answer to it necessarily implies certain answers also to them. Because this is so, there not only can, but also must, be both metaphysical and moral arguments for belief in God if such belief is, in reality, religiously true.

To be exact, there are and must be as many metaphysical arguments for God as there are transcendental concepts of completely unrestricted or strictly universal application—like the concept of God itself, provided God is properly conceived as the universal individual or the individual universal. Because any such transcendental concept is and must be implied by any concept, including perforce any other transcendental concept, if theistic belief is true, one can begin with any transcendental concept whatever—including the concept of God—and validly infer therefrom God's existence. As for moral arguments for belief in God, there is, so far as I can see, really only one such argument, however many may be the ways of developing and formulating it. It is an argument to the effect that, if anything is morally binding on us at all with respect either to what we are to do or to how we are to act, then God must exist or be real as the only intelligible ground of our obligation and of the other conditions that must be present in the very nature of things if fulfilling our obligation is to be possible or finally to make any sense.

But if there are to this extent both moral and metaphysical ways of rationally arguing for belief in God, one may say that belief in God is also the proper object of philosophical as well as of metaphysical and moral inquiry. For while philosophy, in the broad classical sense of the love of wisdom—of any and all wisdom, whether secular or religious—is more than metaphysics and morals taken simply as such, it essentially includes both of them and thus comprises within its own distinctive kind of inquiry the inquiries respectively distinctive of them. Thus, if, as we saw earlier, modern secularism notwithstanding, belief in God cannot be appropriately a matter of scientific inquiry or of any other merely empirical or factual mode of reasoning, it *is* the proper object not only of religious inquiry but also, in their respectively different ways, of metaphysical and moral, and hence of philosophical, modes of inquiry and argument.

My second and final comment is by way of emphasizing the necessary limits not only of all arguments for belief in God, religious and otherwise, but also of belief in God itself. It lies in the nature of any deductive argument, including religious, that one can always rightly refuse to accept its conclusion by successfully questioning either its formal validity or the material truth of one or more of its premises. For this reason, the most that any such argument can ever achieve is so to connect various assertions that one more fully grasps their meaning by understanding the price one has to pay for asserting or denying any one of them—in the way, namely, of denying or asserting the other assertions with which this one assertion is necessarily interconnected. Thus the function of any well-constructed argument for belief in God, whether religious or philosophical, moral or metaphysical, is to connect assertions of such belief with certain other beliefs or assertions so far less controversial that the absurdity of denying one or the other of them will seem too great a price to pay for denying the truth of theistic belief. In this sense, all arguments for belief in God have the logical structure of *reductio ad absurdum* arguments. They seek to show, in one way or another, that the only alternatives to such belief are either so much less clear or else so much less coherent that it is thereby established as the most reasonable way of terminating the inquiry giving rise to the arguments. Naturally, the same can be said for any clear-headed argument *against* belief in God. It, too, will seek to show that affirming the falsity of such belief is more reasonable than the contrary, because it involves a far lower price in the way of more or less hopeless unclarity or no less hopeless incoherence than is involved in opting for any other alternative.

But whatever the outcome of arguments for and against belief in God, such belief itself also has its limits in that *belief* in God is one thing, *faith* in God, something else. Certainly, from the standpoint shared by Judaism and Christianity, faith in God is primarily a matter of trusting in God and being loyal to God, as distinct from asserting— even sincerely asserting—God's reality. Faith in God, in a word, is existential, while belief in God as such is merely theoretical. This is why liberation theologians can say quite rightly, however one-sidedly, that, according to scripture, to know God is to do justice. Of course, to know God through faith necessarily implies the truth of theistic belief, and if such belief were finally to prove false or unsupportable, faith would be exposed as an inauthentic response to the way things ultimately are. But this connection between faith and belief cannot be reversed; for one may very well believe in God, and do so ever so honestly or sincerely, even while neither authentically trusting in God as the sole ultimate ground of one's life nor authentically serving God as the sole ultimate cause one is called to serve by seeking justice.

This is no doubt a disturbing reflection to those of us who are seriously concerned with belief in God, and hence are only too likely to succumb to the existential idolatry of making the truth of our beliefs an essential part of our basic faith in the ultimate meaning of life. But I submit that it can also be a profoundly liberating reflection. In becoming aware that the meaning of our life, finally, is not dependent on the truth or falsity even of our religious beliefs, but only on our continuing to trust and to be faithful, whatever we may be led to believe, we may be sufficiently free from ourselves and for others really to examine our beliefs—to ask, perhaps for the first time, just what they really mean and whether we have sufficient reason to continue to hold them.

Creation *Ex Nihilo*, The Divine *Modus Operandi*, and The *Imitatio Dei*

David Ray Griffin

In the 1970s many Christian theologians began rethinking the doctrine of creation in response to the ecological crisis. This was motivated by the widespread perception that the anthropocentrism of the received doctrine had contributed significantly to the modern dualism of humanity and nature and to an exploitative attitude toward "nature." The movement to which I belong, process theology, has contributed to this effort. This process of rethinking the doctrine of creation in the light of the ecological crisis needs to continue.

However, in this essay, I look at the Christian doctrine of creation from the viewpoint of the other major threat to the viability of our planet—nuclear holocaust.

In the first part I examine the traditional idea of God's *modus operandi*, which both supported and was supported by the traditional idea of *creatio ex nihilo*. I suggest that this view, besides being responsible for several well-known problems that have led to a widespread decline in the perception of our world as divine creation, has also contributed to the nuclear crisis. The key notion here is that our basic religious desire is to imitate the divine reality. In the second part I suggest that an alternative view of God's mode of agency, which supports and is supported by an alternative understanding of creation "out of nothing," is more authentically Christian and avoids the disastrous implications, both theoretical and practical, of the traditional view.

I. The Traditional View of God's *Modus Operandi*

A. Coercive Omnipotence and *Creatio Ex Nihilo*

In speaking of the "traditional" doctrine of God, I am referring to the Western Christian tradition, with Augustine, Thomas, Luther, Calvin, Descartes, Newton, Edwards, and Barth as major representatives. This tradition, in thinking of God's mode of operating in or on the world, has thought in terms of coercive omnipotence. This idea of the divine *modus operandi* in relation to the world and the traditional idea that the world was created *ex nihilo* imply each other.

I must first explain some distinctions and define some terms. The first distinction is between immanent and transitive power. Immanent power is the power of an individual to exert causation *within* itself, i.e., the power of self-determination. Transitive power is the causal power exerted by one thing upon another.

Transitive power is of two basic kinds, coercive and persuasive. Here I am using these terms in a strict, ontological sense. Transitive power is *coercive* when it *achieves its result without any cooperation from the thing upon which it is exerted*. When one billiard ball hits another, the second one does not make any self-determining response to the power exerted upon it. The result, which is the locomotion of the second ball, is achieved without any free response on its part. It is not a bilateral product, due to cooperation. Coercion in the ontological sense is exerted when the result is *unilaterally produced by the agent's transitive power*.

Transitive power is persuasive when it does not unilaterally bring about the effect. The result produced is a change *within* the being upon which the transitive power is exerted, and this being, with its immanent power, makes a self-determining response to the transitive power, thereby determining what the precise effect will be. So, the final effect is a bilateral product, due to the cooperation of at least two agents.

Thus defined, persuasion in the ontological sense applies to a continuum of forms of agency, some of which are, in ordinary parlance, called coercion. For example, when one man is robbed by another at gun-point, we would normally not say that the victim handed over his money freely, but that he was coerced. However, in the strict sense, this is a case of persuasion, since the victim had a choice—as implied in the classic line, "Your money *or* your life." We recognize this by ironically referring to a hand-gun as a "persuader." The victim had to make a self-determining response, to decide whether to hand over the money or risk the probable consequence of being shot. The resulting action, the handing over of the money, was produced by the joint agency of the robber's threat and the victim's grudging consent.

This very coercive persuasion contrasts with pure persuasion, at the other end of the continuum, in which a presented possibility evokes a response from an individual by its inherent attractiveness. The individual is persuaded that the actualization of this possibility would be its own reward. In the less pure forms of persuasion, on the other hand, one is motivated to do something not for its own sake, but because of some outcome extrinsic to the activity itself. In the *very* coercive forms of persuasion, this extrinsic outcome is a threatened use of coercion in the ontological sense. The robber threatens to pull the trigger, which will fire a bullet which will unilaterally bring about destructive effects in the victim's body. This is the connection between the two meanings of coercion: Coercive persuasion, often called "psychological coercion," depends upon the threat, implicit or explicit, to exert coercion in the ontological sense.

This brief analysis oversimplifies a very complex issue. But this complexity involves the intertwining of elements of coercive and pure persuasion on the continuum of forms of persuasion. For the purposes of this essay, the important distinction is between persuasion and coercion in the ontological sense, which is an absolute distinction. A result either involves some self-determining response to the transitive causation or it does not. If it does, then the agent exerting the transitive causation does not unilaterally bring about the effect, and is accordingly not totally responsible for it.

Traditional theism said that God had coercive power to exert in relation to the world. God could unilaterally bring about effects in the world. In fact, in calling God "omnipotent," it meant that God has this kind of power to the greatest conceivable extent. God was credited with coercive omnipotence. Nothing could resist God's transitive power. No cooperation by creatures was needed for God to produce effects in the world.

One noteworthy feature of this view was that God's power completely to control the action of creatures applied not only to inanimate things, such as rocks, but also to living beings, including the inner motions of the human soul. For example, although Augustine said that God uses persuasion on human beings rather than coercion, this distinction turns out to be, ontologically, a distinction without a difference. He says that even those wills

"which follow the world are so entirely at the disposal of God, that He turns them whithersoever He wills, and whensoever He wills."[1]

Further:

> "The Almighty sets in motion even in the innermost hearts of men the movement of their will, so that He does through their agency whatsoever He wishes to perform through them."[2]

Traditional theists thereby took that mode of transitive power which in our experience can only be exerted upon *inanimate things*, or the *bodies* of animate things, and said that God exerts it upon *all* things, including the *souls* of animated things. That is, in the causal interactions among creatures, the only things that can be coerced in the strict sense are ones with no immanent power of self-determination. An aggregate of molecules such as a rock has no such power, *qua* rock (although the individual molecules making it up may). Nor does the body of a human being; that is, *qua* body, it is just as susceptible to the unilateral effects of a knife as is a corpse. The human being as soul, *qua* soul, i.e., as an experiencing individual, does have immanent power to determine its own state. Hence it cannot be totally determined by other creatures. But according to traditional theism, souls as well as rocks were subject to total determination by their creator.

This idea of coercive omnipotence over all creatures led to, and was in turn supported by, the doctrine of *creatio ex nihilo*. The *nihil* was taken to be *absolute* nothingness. If the Bible gives any support for this doctrine, it is minimal and ambiguous. Much more support is given to the notion that the present world was created out of a "formless void" (Gen. 1:1) or some other prior state. But in large part due to the conviction that God exercises absolute control over every aspect of the creatures' existence, the idea of creation out of absolute nothingness was accepted. This doctrine ruled out the possibility that our world was formed out of a pre-existent realm which had some power of its own and hence some kind of "necessity" to which God's creative activity had to conform. Since every aspect of the world's reality was created by God out of absolute nothingness, every aspect is totally subject to the divine will.

The ontological implication of this doctrine of creation was that the creatures have no *inherent* power at all. All power inherently belongs to God alone. Any power apparently belonging to the creatures—whether the immanent power of self-determination, which at the human level we call freedom, or the transitive power to exert causation upon other things, such as the destructive power of nuclear weapons—is totally under God's control.

There is an important distinction at this point between the theologian's doctrine and the more popular idea. The theologians held that God in fact causes all things that happen. Not a leaf stirs on a tree, nor a passion in a human heart, but that God caused it. Popular belief has more generally held that God grants transitive power to all creatures, and immanent power to some of them (human beings at least), normally letting the world develop according to the exercise of these creaturely powers. However, since all power inherently belongs to God alone, God always retains the power to intervene in the world to bring about certain effects unilaterally. But whether omnipotence was thought of as omnicausality, or as a power usually held in reserve, traditional theism attributed coercive omnipotence to God and supported this attribution with the doctrine of creation out of absolute nothingness.

B. Problems Arising from the Traditional View

The idea of the divine *modus operandi* implied by this traditional doctrine of creation has been a disaster for Christian theology and, through it, for the world. Most of the problems arising from the doctrine of coercive omnipotence are well known, and will only be listed here. (1) It led to an insoluble problem of evil. (2) It led to the expectation of "miracles," in the sense of events caused unilaterally by God and hence having no natural causes. (3) It led to the expectation of infallibly inspired scriptures. (4) It led to resistance to the evidence that all complex forms, including life and the human soul, have evolved out of less complex forms over a long period of time, with no "gaps" pointing to the need to posit unilateral divine effects. (5) It led Newton and others in the seventeenth century to the idea of a purely material, insentient nature, which led in turn in the following centuries to the belief that there was no way to think of God as influencing nature. (6) This view of nature also contributed to a sense of alienation from nature and an exploitative attitude towards it. (7) The traditional doctrine of omnipotence has led many to suppose that God's existence must be denied if human freedom and responsibility are to be affirmed, and if the political *status quo* is not to be regarded as divinely sanctioned. (8) This doctrine of omnipotence has led many to a complacency in the face of the possibility that we will destroy our planet's viability through gradual pollution or nuclear war, since they believe that such an event cannot occur unless it be God's will. These are all problems that have led to a decline in the idea of the world as God's creation, and which a reconstructed doctrine of creation should address. But there is one other way in which the traditional doctrines of creation and divine omnipotence have had ill effects. Since this problem has not been much discussed, I will develop it at some length.

C. The Divine *Modus Operandi* and the *Imitatio Dei*

There has been much controversy as to whether there is anything that all religions have in common, and whether human beings are inherently religious. My suggestion is that human beings all do have a common religious motivation: the desire to be in harmony with the ultimate power of the universe, which is felt to be the Holy Power. This motivation is the formal element common to all these movements that we call religions and quasi-religions. It is also present in many other group and individual phenomena that are often labeled "religious" in a somewhat derogatory sense because they seem irrational. Religious behavior *is* irrational if by "rational" we mean behavior that is calculated to achieve some worldly good. Religious activity, insofar as it is distinctively religious, is motivated by the feeling that *being in harmony with the Holy Power is good in itself*, not by prudential, utilitarian calculations about how to achieve some extrinsic good. If the desire to be in harmony with the Holy Power is common to all religious activity, what most fundamentally differentiates the various religions are their different visions of the nature of the Holy Power. The Taoist, the Marxist, the Nazi, the Moslem, and the Quaker all want to be in harmony with the deity; what distinguished them is the effective visions of deity with which they seek to align their lives. When Matthew's Jesus says, "Be ye perfect as your heavenly father is perfect," he was in one sense saying nothing original, but was only enunciating the universal religious desire. What was distinctive was his substantive idea of what the Perfect Power is like. According to Jesus in Matthew 5:43–48 and in Luke 6:32–36, being in harmony with the Perfect One rightly understood entails loving and being merciful toward those who do not love us.

There are different ways to be "in harmony with" the Holy Power. This is especially the case if, as in the biblical religions, the Holy Power is understood to be a personal, purposive deity. One could be in harmony with such a deity in at least three ways: (1) obeying God's commands, (2) helping to bring about God's goal for the world, and (3) imitating God's own mode of agency, insofar as possible.

Christian morality has usually been understood in terms of the first two possibilities, and the fundamental tension between Christian ethicists in recent times has been between those who put primary emphasis upon express commands and those who stress alignment with the divine goal, the kingdom of God. The theme of imitation has also played an important role in the form of the *imitatio Christi*. But this imitation has usually been interpreted in terms of one or both of the first two themes; little explicit attention has been given to the motif in the sense of the imitation of God's own mode of agency. In fact, those features of Jesus that were models for us to imitate were understood to be expressions more of his human nature than of the presence of God in him.

However, I am suggesting that, of these three possibilities, the one that is the most effective, in terms of shaping actual human feelings, attitudes, and behavior, is the third, the desire to imitate the *modus operandi* of the ultimate power of the universe. Insofar as it is in conflict with either of the other two ways of being in harmony with deity, it will win out.

An example of such a conflict is found in a common reading of Romans 12:14–21. Paul says: "Bless those who persecute you; bless and do not curse them. . . . Repay no one evil for evil. . . . Beloved, never avenge yourselves." Up to this point, Paul sounds very much like Jesus as quoted in Matthew and Luke. But, whereas for Jesus the reason for acting in this unworldly manner was to imitate God, Paul offers a quite different reason: "Beloved, never avenge yourselves, but leave it to the wrath of God; for it is written, 'Vengeance is mine, I will repay, says the Lord.' " Now, we know how ineffective it is when parents say to their children: "Don't do as I do, do as I say!" The desire to imitate the parents' behavior usually wins out, even when the express commands are backed up with threats of punishment. And yet Paul seems to portray God as saying just this. This passage can be taken as paradigmatic of the double message that Christians have been given in much traditional teaching. On the one hand, they are told to be gentle, loving and forgiving. On the other hand, they are told that threats and the vengeful, violent destruction of evil-doers are the divine ways of getting things done.

Although Jesus' life and message could be interpreted as a rejection of this previous understanding of God, Paul's citation of the statement about God's vengeance has generally been read as an endorsement of that understanding,* and hence of passages such as Psalm 94, which begins:

O Lord, thou God of vengeance,
thou God of vengeance, shine forth!

---

*As several biblical scholars have pointed out, divine "wrath" in Paul's thought, and in that of most of the Bible, does not refer to a divine emotion that results in punishment. Rather, it refers to retribution that comes to people naturally when they violate the God-rooted structures and principles of reality. See Anthony Tyrrell Hanson, *The Wrath of the Lamb*, (London, SPCK, 1957), esp. 69–75. Hence the popular reading of the passage at hand probably misrepresents Paul's meaning. But it is this popular reading that has been historically effective.

Rise up, O judge of the earth;
render to the proud their deserts!

The Psalm ends with these sentiments:

The Lord will bring back on them their iniquity,
and wipe them out for their wickedness;
the Lord our God will wipe them out.

I suggest the claimed ineffectiveness of Christian ethical teaching upon the behavior of Christians is significantly explained by the conflict between explicit Christian teaching about the way of life appropriate for human beings and the implicit teaching provided by the dominant Christian images and doctrines about the Divine Way of achieving ends. Explicit Christian teaching commands us to be loving, forgiving, patient, peaceful, gentle, not jealous, not insistent upon our own way, and to overcome evil with good. But dominant Christian teaching has portrayed God as quite short on patience, as employing forgiveness only as a temporary policy to be followed by vengeance, and as being at least as filled with wrath as with love. The final triumph of the good over evil is achieved not by patiently winning the evil-doers to good, but by destroying and banishing them: "the Lord our God will wipe them out." The reign of peace is ushered in not by peaceful means but by an unprecedented use of violence—the war to end all wars. The "gentleness" mentioned in 1 Corinthians 13 as the way love acts has hardly been a dominant feature of God's own *modus operandi* in Christian doctrine and imagery.

So, when we look at the sorry history of Christian peoples—the Crusades, the brutal colonization, the genocide, the ecological despoliation, the ruthless bombing of hundreds of thousands of civilians with conventional and atomic bombs, and the attempt by the still largely Christian United States to dominate the world by military means, including the threat of nuclear attack—we do not have to conclude that Christian teaching has been ineffective. It is rather that the desire to imitate God's own imagined *modus operandi* has been more powerful than the desire to obey the express commands believed to come from God.

Alfred North Whitehead, whose philosophical notion of the God-world relation is used by process theologians in our reformulation of the doctrine of creation, himself made this connection between the traditional idea of deity, who creates *ex nihilo*, and rules by imposition, and the violence of this deity's devotees. He says:

> "the doctrine of [a] . . . transcendent creator, at whose fiat the world came into being, and whose imposed will it obeys, is the fallacy which has infused tragedy into the histories of Christianity and of Mahometanism."*

Process and Reality (Corrected Edition, Free Press, 1978), 342. Whitehead's oft-quoted rejections of the idea of God as creator of the world should be understood as the rejection only of the doctrine of creation out of absolute nothingness. That this is his concern is shown in a number of statements throughout his various books. In *Science and the Modern World* (Mentor, 1948, 258) his criticism is aimed at conceiving God "as the foundation of the metaphysical situation with its ultimate activity" (258). In *Religion in the Making*, (World, 1960), he rejects the idea of God as "the one ultimate metaphysical fact . . . who decreed and ordered the derivative existence which we call the actual world." This same concern is shown even where he refers to God as creator. In *Process and Reality* he says that, since God provides each finite actual occasion with an initial aim, from which its self-creativity begins, "God can be termed the creator of each temporal actual entity." His next statement shows why he usually shies away from the term: "But the phrase is apt to be misleading by its suggestion that the ultimate creativity of the universe is to be ascribed to God's volition" (225). This ambivalence about the term "creator" shows up in a later statement: "He does not create the world, he saves it: or, more accurately, he is the poet of the world, with tender patience leading it by his vision of truth, beauty, and goodness" (346). His "more accurate" statement indicates that God creates the world in the sense of persuading it with this vision. (In his personal copy, Whitehead crossed out the word "leading" and wrote both "persuading" and "swaying" in the margin.) Besides speaking of God as creator, in a sense, of each finite event, Whitehead also speaks of God as creator, albeit not *ex nihilo*, of our present world. Without committing himself to the details, Whitehead explictly endorses Plato's *Timaeus*, according to which "the origin of the present cosmic epoch is traced back to an aboriginal disorder, chaotic according to our ideals." He contrasts this with the theory endorsed by Newton of "a wholly transcendent God creating out of nothing an accidental universe." Whitehead endorses the idea that "the creation of the world is the incoming of a type of order establishing a cosmic epoch. It is not the beginning of matter of fact, but the incoming of a certain type of social order" (95, 96).

In *Adventures of Ideas* (Macmillan, 1933), Whitehead continues to protest against the idea of God as "the one supreme reality, omnipotently disposing a wholly derivative world" (213). But the sense in which he thought of God as creator not only of each actual entity but of the world as a whole is further shown in the chapter on "Laws of Nature." Here he rejects the doctrine that the laws are externally imposed by a wholly transcendent deity in favor of the idea of laws as immanent, flowing from the internal characters of things. However, if there were nothing but a multiplicity of finite things, there would be "absolutely no reason why the universe should not be steadily relapsing into lawless chaos." Accordingly, the universe must also have "a stable actuality whose mutual implication with the remainder of things secures an inevitable trend toward order. The Platonic 'persuasion' is required" (142–47). In other words, it is through the omnipresence of the divine individual, with its unchanging vision, that creation out of chaos occurs.

Elsewhere, in reflecting upon the idea of God portrayed in Psalms such as the one quoted above, he says:

"This worship of glory arising from power is dangerous. ... I suppose that even the world itself could not contain the bones of those slaughtered because of men intoxicated by its attraction."[3]

This "intoxication" is the key. The feeling of being in step with the Sacred Reality is, at its highest pitch, a kind of intoxication. Whether being God-intoxicated is a good thing or not depends upon the image of God that has captivated one's religious passion. The traditional Christian view of God has been a mixed blessing, and its negative aspect is now threatening to lead us to destruction. The human tendencies to control others for one's own ends, to divide human beings into "us" and "them," to identify this division as that between good and evil, and to use force to destroy evil—these tendencies are reinforced by deeply implanted teaching telling people that this behavior puts them in harmony with the divine goal of the universe and the divine way of achieving it.

The greatest irrationality of our day is the endless build-up of larger and larger nuclear arsenals. It is irrational because it far exceeds anything a "rational" doctrine of deterrence would require. It is irrational because the values that could be destroyed by these arsenals are absurdly disproportionate to any values that could be defended by them. It is irrational because the use of even a small portion of the Warsaw Pact or NATO arsenal would destroy the users as well as their enemies. But when we realize that this build-up of nuclear arsenals is *religious* behavior, it becomes understandable. True religion is *not* rational, in the sense of prudential. Being in harmony with the divine power of the universe is good in itself. The arms race is, as its critics charge, mad; but it is a *divine* madness. When defenders of these arsenals treat with contempt those who suggest that even unilateral disarmanent, with all its risks, would be less risky than the present situation, this is the same contempt that true believers have always shown for those who put prudential considerations above the thrill that comes from being in harmony with the Holy Power of the universe. The fact that, in risking martyrdom, these nuclear-age saints are willing to include the rest of the planet's life in their sacrifice, may make their devotion less admirable. But it does not make it less religious.

It should be added that the continued effectiveness of this religious dynamic does not depend upon continuing literal belief in an apocalyptic second coming of Christ in power (although this belief is still strong, at least in the United States, and these literalists have been becoming increasingly active and influential politically). Where this literal belief has disappeared but has not been replaced by a fundamentally different religious vision, the sensibility remains that the use of unilateral power is the way to get things done. Thus far, the decline in adherence to traditional theism has been replaced by a "scientific" worldview which portrays the world as controlled by Omnipotent Matter.* The resulting religious ideologies can foster policies that are even more brutal than those of Christian Crusaders, since blind matter does not encourage the respect and compassion for individuals which have been fostered by devotion to the Christian God, and which have served to mitigate and often even to over-balance the desire to imitate this deity's *modus operandi*. And these materialistic ideologies, whether embodied in capitalistic or communistic systems and rhetoric, encourage the conviction that spiritual impulses are irrelevant in human relations, especially between nation states, so that "realistic" policies must be based upon material power, namely economic and military power, alone.

Each religion produces its saints—people with extraordinary intensity and devotion who take the implications of that religion's worldview with ultimate seriousness and, when the vision itself makes this appropriate, infect the masses with their enthusiasm. As long as our dominant worldviews, whether called "religious" or "secular," portray unilateral, coercive power as the ultimate power of the universe, our saints will be people who are intoxicated by the power of brute force. Religious zeal will join with prudence to lead us to repent, to turn away from our current trajectory of death and destruction, only if a fundamentally different sense of what is going on in this mysterious universe in which we find ourselves develops and spreads.

---

*In "A Free Man's Worship," Bertrand Russell reveals the strategy adopted by many ethical philosophers in response to the belief that the world, including human life, is the product of "omnipotent matter." He called upon people to worship Goodness rather than Force, recognizing that this meant to worship ideals of our own creation rather than fact—for "the world of fact, after all, is not good." The dilemma is: "Shall our God exist and be evil, or shall he be recognized as the creation of our own conscience?" (*The Basic Writings of Bertrand Russell 1903–1959*, ed. Robert E. Egner and Lester E. Dennon [Simon and Schuster, 1961], 66–72). He, along with many others who called for the autonomy of ethics from metaphysics (and theology), did so in order to reject the ethic of "Social Darwinism," according to which being in harmony with nature meant a ruthless, competitive, exploitative ethic. As noble as this effort was, it was futile, if our ineradicable religious motivation is to live in harmony with the ultimate power of the universe. A new ethic will not be created by attempting to divorce morality from our understanding of reality, but only by coming to a new understanding of the ultimate power of reality.

II. An Alternative Christian View of God's *Modus Operandi*

Should the acceptance of Jesus of Nazareth as the decisive revelation of God lead us to an alternative view of the *modus operandi* of the Holy Power of the universe? Whitehead thought so, and meant his own philosophical theology to be a way of developing this alternative. After the passage in *Religion in the Making* criticizing the worship of glory arising from power, Whitehead says:

> The life of Christ is not an exhibition of overruling power. Its glory is for those who can discern it, and not for the world. Its power lies in its absence of force.[4]

And after the passage in *Process and Reality* connecting the idea of a transcendent deity who creates by fiat and rules by imposition with the tragic histories of Christianity and Islam, he says that "Galilean origin of Christianity" contains "another suggestion" about God, but that Western theologians missed it:

> In the official formulations of the religion it has assumed the trivial form of the mere attribution to the Jews that they cherished a misconception about their Messiah. But the deeper idolatry, of the fashioning of God in the image of the Egyptian, Persian, and Roman Imperial rulers, was retained. The Church gave unto God the attributes which belonged exclusively to Caesar.[5]

What is the "suggestion" contained in the Galilean origin?

> It does not emphasize the ruling Caesar. . . . It dwells upon the tender elements in the world, which slowly and in quietness operate by love.[6]

Finally, in his most explicit essay in Christian theology, which he called "The New Reformation," Whitehead said:

> The essence of Christianity is the appeal to the life of Christ as a revelation of the nature of God and of his agency in the world.[7]

What should Christian theologians conclude about God's mode of agency from this appeal?

106

That the divine element in the world is to be conceived as a persuasive agency and not as a coercive agency. . . . The alternative doctrine, prevalent then and now, sees either in the many gods or in the one God, the final coercive forces wielding the thunder . . ., the supreme agency of compulsion. . . ."[8]

That Whitehead meant his own cosmology to be a way of formulating an "alternative suggestion" about the divine mode of agency contained in the life of Christ is clear. But, before we could advocate taking his cosmology as the framework for a fundamentally new form of Christian faith, we need to deal with several questions. First, is Whitehead's claim about "the life of Christ" justified, i.e., that insofar as it is taken as a revelation of God's agency, it is less suggestive of overruling power than of persuasive love? Second, were there reasons in earlier times for assuming divine coercive omnipotence that no longer obtain? Especially, given the notion that the world is the creation of a loving Holy Power, is our current knowledge of the world less suggestive of a creator who works coercively? Third, can the Christian doctrine of creation be reformulated so as plausibly to portray the world as the creation of a Holy Power who works only evocatively or persuasively, never coercively, and also to avoid or solve the various problems that have undermined the sense of the world as divine creation in recent centuries?

A. Jesus as Decisive Revelation of the Divine *Modus Operandi*

Our first question is: If the life of Jesus is taken as a revelation of the mode of agency of the creator of the universe, what does it suggest?

If the God we worship is held to have the kind of power which the world generally thinks of as power, i.e., the power to control, to coerce, to dominate, to destroy, one would expect that the decisive incarnation and revelation of our God would have been in someone with political power, or economic power, or military power, or all three, such as a Caesar. And yet we take as the central revelation of the Holy Power of the universe a man with none of these forms of worldly power. Of course, we can attempt to overcome this great incongruity by speaking of "kenosis." But is this not perhaps simply a way of calling Jesus "Lord" without letting this confession challenge the kind of power in which we put our ultimate trust?

Furthermore, there is much in the New Testament portrait of Jesus that directly rejects the reliance upon force as the way to deal with evil, such as Jesus' admonition to turn the other cheek (Matt. 5:39), his statement that those who live by the sword will perish by it (Matt. 26:52), and his admonition to Peter to put away his sword (Luke 33:49–50). It may be significant that in Luke 4, in which Jesus is reading from Isaiah 61, Luke has Jesus close the book just before getting to the phrase referring to "the day of vengeance of our God." It surely is significant that the tradition about Jesus' temptations, as reported by both Matthew and Luke, includes the authority and glory of ruling over worldly kingdoms—precisely the kind of authority and glory the Caesars enjoyed. And note that such rule could be had only by worshiping demonic power. Also relevant to the distinction between the power of the world and the power Jesus was understood to represent is the statement attributed to Jesus in John 18:36—his servants would fight on his behalf if his kingship were of "this world."

Fully consistent with this portrait of the life and message of Jesus is the tradition about his death. For example, 1 Peter 2:23 portrays it as exemplifying Jesus' admonition about turning the other cheek: "When he was reviled, he did not revile in return; when he suffered, he did not threaten." And, beyond the details, is it not supremely incongruous that a religion that has as its chief symbol a man dying on a cross, as the non-resisting victim of the chief political and ecclesiastical powers of the time and place, would develop a theology according to which this man was the chief incarnation and revelation of a God with the power to overrule all worldly powers—and in fact of a God who is the sole power of the universe, and who therefore caused the worldly powers to crucify Jesus? Again, rationalizations were invented to reconcile the historical facts with the theological dogma. But we are asking, not whether confessing Jesus as the chief revelation of God can somehow be made *compatible* with the substance of traditional theism. We are asking what notion of divine power is *suggested* by taking Jesus to be the decisive revelation of the ultimate creative power of the universe—if we are open to the possibility that the chief significance of Jesus might lie precisely in posing a radical challenge to the idea of divine power presupposed by Rome and Jerusalem alike.

One other signficant fact is that the central image the early Christians were led to use to understand God's relation to Jesus was "incarnation." But, instead of taking the incarnation of God in Jesus as the Supreme Revelation of how God works always and everywhere, Christian theologians, at least in the West, took it to be the Great Exception. One result of this non-incarnational theology was the Boyle-Newton picture of nature as composed of utterly solid, insentient bits of matter in which no divine presence could be imagined, so that the laws of nature had to be understood as externally imposed. But if Jesus is our best clue to God's general *modus operandi*, and if *incarnation* is our best image for thinking of God's active presence in Jesus, a quite different way of understanding God's activity in the world is implied.

Now, accepting the idea of incarnation does not automatically mean giving up the idea of total divine control, as the various christological attempts to reconcile Jesus' full humanity with an all-controlling incarnate Logos demonstrate. But the very unsatisfactory nature of these attempts shows that the idea of total divine control and that of divine presence in a fully human and hence self-determining individual can only be joined artificially. Again, the revelatory idea suggested by the early portrait of Jesus was not allowed to revolutionize the idea of God's *modus operandi*. Instead, the idea that the culminating revelatory act of the biblical God was an act of becoming incarnate was forced into the straightjacket of the preconceived idea of divine omnipotence.

Of course, there were aspects of the portrait of Jesus that *were* taken to be direct exemplifications of overruling omnipotence. These were the so-called miracles and the resurrection. Traditional christology took these to be manifestations of the divinity, or divine nature, of Jesus, while the other features of his life, especially his sufferings, were said to be manifestations of his humanity, or human nature. Conservative theology still interprets the miracles as evidence of divine power. Most liberal theologians have accepted the general consensus of modern Western culture that such events simply do not happen. However, there is a third view which seems more consonant with the facts. During the past 100 years, psychical researchers or parapsychologists have, in a disciplined, scientific manner, studied precisely those kinds of phenomena that were traditionally called miracles. They are now called telepathy, clairvoyance, psychokinesis, psychosomatic healing, psychic healing, etc. On the basis of laboratory studies, investigations of spontaneous phenomena, and historical studies of virtually all literate societies, the most reasonable conclusion seems to be (a) that such phenomena do occur and (b) that, although they are extraordinary, they are not supernatural. That is, they are the product of the powers of certain finite beings, usually human beings. Even if some phenomena are produced by discarnate beings, such beings are still finite, and their powers natural, i.e., creaturely. Like all the powers of the contingent beings making up our world, these powers can be regarded as having developed under the influence of the creative power of God.

In regard to the question of the distinctive form of divine power suggested by taking Jesus as God's decisive revelation, I have thus far talked about the distinction between persuasive and coercive power. But as important as this shift is, it only points to one side of the radical suggestion contained in the New Testament account of Jesus as the Christ. The other side is pointed to by Paul in the first chapter of Corinthians, where he speaks of the word of the cross as the power of God. He also refers to Christ crucified as the "wisdom of God," which contrasts with the "wisdom of the world." Should we not see these contrasting ideas of wisdom as related to contrasting ideas of power? What is more basic to the wisdom of "the world" than the idea that the only kind of power that counts, the only kind to which we can safely entrust our security, is coercive power—the power to control, to threaten, and to destroy? What higher foolishness could there be from the viewpoint of worldly wisdom than to say that human relations could be based instead upon forgiving, reconciling love, which is willing not only to turn the other cheek, but to absorb the abuses of others even to the point of death, if need be, rather than to return evil for evil?

The power involved would hence have two aspects, with both a receptive and an out-going side. On the receptive side, it would be the strength to receive abuse without reacting with the desire to retaliate. This strength would require genuine love for the other. If one wants the best for the other, one would not *want* to inflict evil upon him or her in return. This idea leads to the outgoing aspect of this "unworldly" form of power. Instead of returning evil for evil, one returns good. Instead of responding to coercive power with coercive power, one relies upon persuasion, seeking to elicit good from the other.

Of course, if such a way of being is thought of as a "strategy" to be evaluated in terms of its short-term results, it often fails. The cross stands as a clear symbol of this fact. But to dismiss it as foolish on this basis—would this not be to accept the wisdom of the world as the highest wisdom? From the viewpoint of this wisdom, now called "realism," the power of the cross is not power at all; it is weakness. But Paul suggests that "the foolishness of God is wiser than men, and the weakness of God is stronger than men" (1 Cor. 1:25). Now that the wisdom of the world has brought us to the brink of self-destruction, might we not be ready to challenge the conventional wisdom on this most basic of all questions: What is truly powerful? What kind of power creates and saves?

B. Other Reasons for Revising Our View of God's Mode of Operation

Our second question is: Were there reasons for the early Christian fathers to ascribe coercive omnipotence (as defined here) to the God of Jesus Christ that no longer obtain today? The change from a doctrine of

110

coercive agency to one of persuasive agency would not be a minor change in Christian thought; it could well be the most radical change ever made. And the early Christian fathers were sincere and intelligent Christians, doing their best to formulate the implications of the belief that the ultimate saving truth of the Holy One of the universe had been made manifest in Jesus of Nazareth. Such a radical change in their formulation of Christian faith should not be made lightly.

The pragmatic reasons given above for such a change are not insignificant. But pragmatic considerations alone cannot be decisive in matters of truth. And the issue of the best interpretation of the revelatory significance of Jesus is complex, a matter of judgment which is inevitably influenced by a host of considerations. It is hence important to ask whether there were presuppositions that would have made the notion of coercive divine agency natural, even virtually inevitable, in the formative period of Christian thought, but that have now been replaced by beliefs that do not suggest coercive divine agency. I shall mention seven important presuppositions that have changed.

1. Surely the most important is the change from sudden creation to evolution. When it was believed that the world in its present form was created suddenly, it was natural to assume that the creator had the power to bring about effects unilaterally. It would be hard to imagine a creator persuading a chaotic realm of finite things with inherent power into the present form of the world in six days! Creation out of nothing, in the sense of absolute nothingness, was a reasonable supposition. But now we think in evolutionary terms, and of a time-span 100 million times longer than six days. Not only is it plausible to think of the cosmic creative power as exercising power by persuasively evoking new forms in entities having their own power, it is implausible to think in the old terms. Why would a creator who could bring things about unilaterally take so long to get to things thought to have significant intrinsic value? Furthermore, the main point of the evolutionary perspective, besides the amount of time involved, is that all complex forms show evidence of having been fashioned out of earlier forms; in many cases the present structures are very imperfectly adapted to their present functions (such as the Panda's "thumb").[9] Everything points to creation out of something earlier, nothing to creation out of absolute nothingness.

2. In earlier centuries, it was reasonable to take extraordinary events, especially psychokinetic events, as "miracles," in the sense of events unilaterally determined by God. But today, whether one denies that such events occur, or more reasonably, interprets them as products of the parapsychological powers of certain creatures, this major empiri-

cal basis for believing in unilaterally caused "acts of God" is gone.

3. In earlier centuries, belief in infallibly inspired scriptures provided another support for the presupposition that at least some events are unilaterally determined by God. But the modern study of the Bible makes this belief no longer a reasonable one.

4. In earlier centuries, matter was thought to be passive, in the sense of devoid of self-moving power. Hence it could be assumed that the material part of the creation was unilaterally controlled by the creator. And, since most of the world appears, to the unaided senses, to be passive matter, it was easy to take this total divine control as paradigmatic for the creator-creature relation in general, in spite of the problem thereby created for belief in freedom. But now we know that apparently passive things are composed of enormously energetic, constantly moving individuals. The formula $E = mc^2$ even says that energy and mass are convertible. Matter can be understood as frozen energy, since matter can be transformed into energy, and vice versa. Also, the view that we cannot speak separately of space and time, but only of space-time, implies that there is no nature in a non-durational "instant." The basic realities making up the world must be events, which take (or make) time to be what they are. This idea suggests that the energetic activity which all material things embody is not primarily locomotion, i.e., movement through space, but an internal process of self-constitution. This suggestion is further supported by the "mind-body problem," which is the impossibility of understanding how a temporal, nonspatial, self-creative, experiencing mind could interact with non-durational, spatial, passive, insentient matter. The idea of the actual world as made up exhaustively of spatio-temporal events with an internal process of experiential becoming overcomes this problem. Finally, this assumption fits with the evolutionary perspective, which suggests that every level of the world is composed of things with some self-moving, self-organizing capacity. Accordingly, there is today no "passive matter" whose motion and order beg to be explained by an omnipotent controller.

5. The formative centuries of Christian theology occurred in a milieu in which the complete immutability and impassibility of that which was fully divine was widely presupposed. This assumption, combined with the biblical presupposition that God knew the world, strengthened that aspect of the biblical witness which implied that God's providential influence upon the world was total control. The world could have no power of its own with which to do something unexpected, for such power could change the content of God's knowl-

edge and give God cause to make a new decision. However, today we are increasingly realizing that the ideal of impassibility is profoundly unchristian, and that the biblical notion that God "changeth not" only implies that God's basic character, God's "steadfastness," does not change. This idea allows for genuine interaction between God and the world, and hence for the world to have inherent power *vis-a-vis* God.

6. In earlier centuries, the intrinsic difficulty caused by the problem of evil could be dismissed rather easily. The proofs for the Christian God were generally assumed to be strong; most Christians had little exposure to opposing ideas; and, most importantly, the truth of Christian doctrine was assumed to be guaranteed not primarily by its intrinsic convincingness, but by *extrinsic* proofs, mainly the miracles, which in turn supported the belief in divinely guaranteed scriptures. But today, a Christian perspective on reality must make its case, in an increasingly pluralistic setting, on the basis of its *intrinsic convincingness*. There is no extrinsic proof: nothing can be asserted to be true simply because it is allegedly "biblical" or "Christian." In this context, theologians can neither ignore the problem of evil, nor rest content with self-contradictions under the guise of "mystery" or "paradox." This is especially the case as long as we take self-contradictions in opposing worldviews and ideologies as good reasons for rejecting *them*. With no extrinsic proofs for our own case, we cannot presume exemption from the criterion of intrinsic convincingness. This shift from extrinsic to intrinsic verification of the truth of Christianity means that the problem of evil, which had always stood as evidence against the traditional doctrine of omnipotence, presents an even stronger case today.

7. Correlative to the idea of a sudden creation in the relatively recent past was the idea of a sudden end of the world in the relatively near future. The expectation of a dramatic end of our world, with a transformation of existing things into a new heaven and earth, presupposed a cosmic agent with the power to transform things unilaterally. But now we expect our universe to continue for billions of years (regardless of what we do to our particular planet). And, with our evolutionary perspective, it is less meaningful to distinguish creation, providence, and eschatological salvation as different divine activities than to think in terms of *continuing creation*. That is, God's activity is always simultaneously creative, providential, and saving. God's bringing us to some ultimate wholeness will simply be one more achievement in God's ongoing creative activity. So if God's creative activity is best understandable as persuasion, so is God's saving activity. Our hope for ultimate saving transformation no longer requires belief in a coercive

Holy Power. There is time for loving, evocative persuasion to have its way with us.

Given the presuppositions generally held at the time, it is understandable that the early Christians retained the idea that God's power is coercive, even if they thereby missed the central revelatory significance of Jesus and also created an insoluble problem of evil. But in our day none of those reasons for thinking in terms of coercive omnipotence remain.

C. Creation Out of Relative Nothingness

The third question is: Can the Christian doctrine of creation be reformulated so as to portray the world as the creation of a Holy Power who operates only evocatively or persuasively in relation to the world, and also to avoid or solve the various problems that have undermined in recent centuries the belief that the world is a divine creation?

I believe that Whitehead's philosophy provides us with the best basis today for this reformulation. I will mention seven points which pertain to the issues raised earlier.

1. Although the doctrine of *creatio ex nihilo* need not be rejected, the "nihil" should be reinterpreted to mean relative (not absolute) nothingness. Here process theology agrees with Nicolas Berdyaev.*

Although *our* world, with its particular forms of order (e.g., electrons, protons, neutrons, etc.), is contingent, there has always been a realm of finite beings. The ultimate finite beings are momentary events, each having immanent and transitive power, i.e., the power partially to create themselves, and then the power to exert creative influence upon later events. That such a realm exists is as necessary as that God exists. That it has power is inherent to it, not due to divine

---

*Berdyaev distinguishes between two meanings of nothing or non-being: relative non-being, *MN OV*, and absolute non being, *OUK OV*. The former type of non-being includes freedom. He says: "freedom is not created by God: . . . it is part of the nothing out of which God created the world" (*The Destiny of Man* [Harper & Row, 1960], 25). Hence he speaks of the uncreated freedom as "meonic freedom." This idea corresponds to Whitehead's doctrine that "creativity" (along with "many" and "one") constitutes the "category of the ultimate." When Whitehead rejects creation *ex nihilo*, he is rejecting the idea that creativity itself was created. Although he used the notion that our world was created out of chaos, he could equally well have said that it was created out of creativity. Creativity cannot exist apart from a multiplicity of created things, so whether one speaks of the "nothing" out of which our world was created as a prior state of partially self-created creatures, or out of creativity itself, the main point is the same: the world was *not* created out of nothingness devoid of power.

volition. Whereas traditional theism said that creative power *as embodied in God* exists eternally, process theism suggests that creativity is eternally embodied in the Divine One *and* a non-divine many. This uncreated creativity is not divine: in itself it is not actual, it is devoid of character, and it is beyond good and evil. Nor is the plurality of finite embodiments of it divine. That *some* such realm of finitude exists is necessary; what kinds of beings in fact exist is contingent. God is the only individual who exists necessarily. Also, only God is omnipresent, and has perfect knowledge and love. From a Christian standpoint, it is these characteristics (not mere necessary existence) that constitute worthiness or worship, and that lead us to speak of divinity.

The plurality of momentary events can be organized in an indefinite number of ways. The most simple form of order is a purely temporal society of events, in which each event essentially repeats the form embodied in its predecessors. An electron provides an example. These simple enduring objects, or even perhaps more simple ones, e.g., "quarks," are the most simple enduring and hence identifiable *things* of our world. In a realm of events in which no such stable objects were present, there would be *no-thing*. This realm of chaos would hence be a realm of no-thingness—not absolute nothingness, but nothingness relative to the order necessary to have a cosmos. This is a way of understanding the "formless void" of Genesis 1:1. The "nothing" out of which our world has been created was hence an *active* nothingness, which could not be simply manipulated. It could only be coaxed.

2. Each event is, in Whitehead's terminology, an "occasion of experience." To say that an event has some immanent power implies that it has some internal reality. We can conceive of this internal reality only by analogy with our own internal reality, our own experience, which we know by identity. We can, therefore, think of each event as having some kind of feeling—not conscious feeling, and certainly not self-consciousness, but some kind of vague value-experience. The data for each experience comes from other experiences. Each experience arises by receiving feelings from previous experiences (which is *their* way of exerting transitive power upon the present). All causal interaction is finally understandable in terms of this transference of feelings.

Attributing feelings to even the most simple individuals making up our world explains in principle how our experiences can affect our bodies: our bodily parts are composed of webs of experiences which can feel our feelings and thereby respond to our wishes and moods. It also explains how God can influence the world. Every event in the world is an experience responding not only to the finite events in its past, but to that all-pervasive experience which is God. God influences a finite being by envisaging a novel possibility for it appetitively. When an enduring individual begins feeling this divine appetition conformally, a corresponding appetition is evoked in it for this possibility. This appetition for a possible way of in-forming experience is what Whitehead calls "mental" or "conceptual" feeling. (Mentality in this sense can occur far below the level of conscious experience.) When this novel form is no longer felt only mentally but also physically, i.e., as really characterizing the feelings of the individual, it becomes a full-fledged ingredient of the created order—for example, when one not only thinks it would be nice to respond non-violently to abuse, but actually does so. (God's role in this new creation is that of envisaging this possible way of being human with appetition, as an attractive ideal.) Whether this new ideal actually becomes incarnate in the world, as actually in-forming our responses, is then up to us. A new creation is always a result of cooperation, never of unilateral operation by God.

3. It is because all events inherently have the two-fold power to determine themselves and to influence their successors that the causal influence of God upon the events of the world must be persuasion; it could not be ontological coercion. God could not totally determine their internal reality, or the way they will affect other things.

God also cannot coerce enduring objects, such as electrons, atoms, and molecules, since each of these enduring things is a series of partially self-determining events. Nor can God coerce the larger things which are made out of these simpler enduring objects. These larger things are of two basic kinds. On the one hand, there are *compound individuals*, in which the order of the parts supports an integrating dominating experience which gives the society the power to respond and act as a unit. Since this central experience has the immanent power of self-determination, it cannot be coerced. We human beings and other animals with central nervous systems provide the main examples. Lower animals, living cells, molecules, and atoms are also compound individuals. On the other hand, there are *mere aggregates* of enduring objects, such as rocks, comets, clouds, oceans, pens, knives, guns, tanks, and bombs. They are mere aggregates in the sense that their order gives rise to no higher-order experience which would provide them the power to make a unified response to their environments. This kind of entity accordingly has no capacity as a unit to respond to God. Divine power exerted upon it is God's persuasive influence upon the experiential individuals making it up.

4. The central feature of the creation of our world through a long evolutionary process is the rise of more and more complex individuals with higher and higher forms of value experience. This feature, by hypothesis, reflects the divine purpose. This increased capacity for experiencing higher forms of value is accompanied, necessarily, by an increase in power—in both the immanent power of self-determination and the transitive power to affect others. This dual increase means an inevitable increase in the power to act contrary to the divine purpose and to make decisions that are destructive to oneself and to one's fellow creatures. Hence, the creation of a world with significant forms of value experience is necessarily a risky enterprise. Each increase in value means a correlative increase in danger. Each increase in the possibilities for good is necessarily an increase in the possibilities for evil.

The traditional doctrine of creation could not regard this positive correlation between value and power, which obtains as an empirical fact of our world, as a metaphysical principle, which would necessarily obtain in any possible world. The alternative metaphysical view led to an intractable problem of evil. Since the constituents of our world were said to be created out of *absolute* nothingness, theologians had to assume that all the principles descriptive of the interactions of the created things were purely contingent, due to divine volition alone. But if we accept the alternative hypothesis, that there has always been a realm of finite actualities interacting among themselves and with God, it follows that there are eternal principles applicable to these interactions. The universal correlation between value and power is an obvious candidate for this status as eternal, necessary principle. We cannot know absolutely that this is the case, but it seems more probable than the contrary hypothesis, that this correlation is purely arbitrary. It is by assuming this contrary hypothesis that traditional theodicists have had to deal with such questions as: Why did God not create "rational saints," i.e., beings who are like us in all respects, except that they would be guaranteed always to do the best thing? Process theology can say that this question is based upon a false assumption. God could not have created beings with our capacity for rational reflection and self-consciousness, and all the values these capacities allow us to enjoy, but with no power to act contrary to the divine will and to wreak havoc. God's creation of beings with the capacity for self-consciousness and rational reflection was necessarily a great risk. The risk could have been avoided only by foregoing such beings.

5. An individual acts directly only upon other individuals, and individuals by definition have some power to make a self-determining

response. Hence, the transitive power possessed by individuals is always the power of persuasion, in the ontological sense. However, an individual can have a "body," i.e., a complex society of subserviant individuals organized so as to be both a source of information and enjoyment and a means of expression. Although the individual in the strict sense is distinct from its body, it is intimately related to it, sympathetically feeling the feelings of its members and being responded to by these members in turn with a high degree of sympathy for its wishes. Because an individual's body, when healthy, responds so conformally to its wishes, the individual thereby has the means to exert coercive power indirectly upon other societies. For example, when my hand conforms to my persuasive wishes for it, I can use my hand to exert coercive power upon a stone, perhaps picking it up to hurl at an enemy.

Because we, as "compound individuals," have bodies, we have the power to exert coercive power, even though as individuals in the strict sense we have only persuasive power. Because our bodies are attuned, partly through billions of years of evolutionary development, to respond so conformally to our persuasive influence upon them, we indirectly have coercive power. The instruments developed by technology can be regarded as extensions of our bodies, greatly increasing our coercive power and the ethical questions this power poses.

If we have both kinds of power, it can be asked, why does not God? Because there is no divine body *between* God and us. Insofar as God has a body, it is the universe as such, which includes us. We are directly related to God, not indirectly through some divine body which mediates between God and us, and through which God could operate coercively upon the aggregates of the world, including the bodies of human beings and other compound individuals. Accordingly, as Whitehead says,

> "God's role is not the combat of productive force with productive force, of destructive force with destructive force; . . . he is the poet of the world, with tender patience leading it by his vision of truth, beauty, and goodness."[10]

From this perspective, traditional theism was guilty of an implicit self-contradiction. It insisted that God was "simple," which meant in the first instance that God was a non-composite individual. And yet, in ascribing to God coercive power *vis-a-vis* the creatures, it was attributing to God the kind of power only a composite being can have. It was thereby implying that God has "hands." This self-contradiction revenged itself in the problem of evil: if God has hands, then God has a *left* hand—this being the metaphor used for God's alleged destructive activity. By attributing hands to God, the distinction between the divine and the demonic, the creative and the destructive, was compromised.

6. The symbol of the devil can be taken to refer to the uncreated creativity of the finite realm insofar as it is used destructively by symbol-using creatures guided by hate or indifference. As embodied in God, the uncreated creativity is always used persuasively, is always based upon a sympathetic response to the welfare of the creatures, and thereby always seeks what is best for the creatures. This is a way of understanding the intuition behind the idea of the trinity: divine power is always characterized by receptive and creative love. Demonic power is the opposite of divine: it is based upon hate or indifference rather than on responsive love; it is aimed at the presumed good of the agent that does not include the good of others; and it is accordingly willing to use coercive power, which destroys the power of others to determine their own destinies.

This idea does justice to the two-fold, seemingly inconsistent, intuition behind the notion of the devil. On the one hand, the devil has been regarded as a creature, brought into existence through God's creative activity. On the other hand, the devil has been felt to be not merely a creature, but a power of cosmic proportions, in some sense comparable to God, hence a real adversary, not one arbitrarily created by God to make for an interesting game. This latter dimension is reflected in the idea that the created order embodies power that is uncreated and eternal. The former dimension—the creaturely, contingent character of the devil—is reflected in the idea that demonic power did not exist until God's creative activity has brought forth beings with the capacity for rational, symbolic thought. This symbolic power gives them the capacity to think of others *as others*, and hence to realize that there are many other centers of existence and value than themselves, all with needs and rights. But it also gives them the capacity to invent ideologies to justify special privileges for themselves, technologies to coerce and destroy those who would challenge these special privileges, and further ideological rationalizations to justify hatred or indifference toward these others. In this sense, demonic power is a product of God's creative activity. But, as stated before, it is a power the risk of which could not have been avoided if symbol-using creatures were to be brought about. And, once in existence, it is a power that cannot be withdrawn or overruled by God. It can only be overcome by persuasive conversion—ultimately by making the imitation of divine creativity seem more attractive than demonic destructiveness.

7. Although demonic destructiveness often wins out in the short run, as symbolized by the cross of Christ, we can live by faith that divine creativity, with its persuasive, evocative love, is ultimately stronger than the power of death and destruction. The resurrection of Christ symbolizes this power of love to bring about creative transformations, especially new creations that are not subject to the powers of death.

The first chapter of Romans refers to three exemplifications of divine power: the creation (vs. 20), the gospel (vs. 16), and the resurrection of Jesus Christ (vs. 4). Traditionally, the middle one, the preaching of the gospel, had been portrayed as God's use of persuasion, whereas creation and resurrection had been assumed to be manifestations of divine coercive omnipotence. I have been suggesting that in our time we can see creation as also an example of persuasive power. I now extend that suggestion to the resurrection.

By seeing the creation of the world in its present form as the gradual development, in which a continual increase in immanent and transitive power has occurred in some lines of development, and especially in that trajectory leading to and continuing with human beings, we can regard the power of the human soul to survive the death of its bodily environment as one more of the powers which the unceasing persuasive agency of God has evoked in the creation. When this power first emerged we do not know, though a good guess would be that it emerged simultaneously with the power to ask the question of survival.

Parapsychological studies are again relevant. In a variety of ways, they provide impressive evidence that the human soul not only can but does survive the demise of its physical body. The details and credibility of this evidence must be reserved for another time. Of course, relying upon this kind of evidence takes away from the absolute uniqueness of Jesus' "resurrection." But this is all to the good. For one thing, what it takes away in uniqueness, it gives back in credibility, which is surely more important. This does not mean that Jesus' resurrection is not special, but that is a topic which lies beyond the scope of this paper. The point to be made here is that it can be interpreted objectively, in the sense that the resurrection appearances to the first Christians were really based upon the continued activity of the individual who had been Jesus of Nazareth, without regarding it as a "miracle." And our own capacity to survive or be re-created beyond bodily death can be added to the other impressive achievements of the power of persuasive love.

It is often thought that belief in life after bodily death leads to a depreciation of the importance of preserving this planet. That has often been the case, and still is among some "nuclear Christians." But if divine creative power has taken many billions of years to bring about our planet, we must assume that this planet plays an extremely important role in the divine plan, whatever forms of life we may have beyond this earthly one. Although we cannot agree with those who claim that a nuclear holocaust would be the destruction of all meaning whatsoever, we can still say that it would be an evil far worse than anything nuclear arsenals are meant to avoid, even perhaps the greatest evil the universe has ever suffered. Far from leading to indifference to the fate of the earth, the kind of Christian faith envisioned here should increase not only our concern but also our courage to work for the disarming of our planet—an enormously risky endeavor, considering the degree to which religious conviction is united with the lust for power and riches in the nuclear powers and principalities of our age.

Conclusion

With the kind of approach suggested here, we can understand the creation of the world, the origin of Christianity, and the eschatological fulfillment of the world as creations which God brings about by the use of persuasive power alone. A Christian faith so understood will not encourage complacency about the threats to our planet's viability. But neither will it foster despair, since it shows that divine persuasive love is ultimately the strongest power in the world, and that nothing, not even nuclear holocaust, can separate us from it. And as Christians come to have their basic vision of reality formed by this version of Christian faith, their desire to be in harmony with the Holy Power of the universe will lead them to seek ways of living together in which the element of coercion is reduced to the greatest possible extent. They will be intoxicated not by the vision of using overwhelming force to bring about the final solution unilaterally, but by the dream of a society in which the present wisdom about what is foolish and realistic is turned upside down. Finally, this form of Christian faith will lead Christians to overcome their own continued reliance upon weapons of mass destruction for security, and to embolden them to engage in the most difficult, momentous, and dangerous task of all time: dismantling the nuclear megamachine, in which demonic power has reached its fullest embodiment ever. Of course, part and parcel of this task would be overcoming those patterns of injustice, exploitation, and privilege which military power is needed to protect.

This alternative vision of the world as creation and of the divine *modus operandi* is a vision that Christians can commend to others on its own merits. No special pleading or supernatural validation is needed.

This vision of reality, although inspired by the belief that a particular tradition has been especially revelatory, bases its case upon its intrinsic convincingness, not upon extrinsic proof or a special experience inducing a willingness to tolerate self-contradiction. If Christianity comes to reformulate its faith in these terms, we can hope that our Jewish and Islamic sisters and brothers might do likewise. And we can also hope to win ground back from these ideologies that, in reaction to the omnipotence of spirit, proclaimed the omnipotence of matter. In this way a reformulated Christianity could contribute to the greatest ecumenical task of our day.

Notes

1. Grace and Free Will, XLI, tr P. Holmes in *Basic Writings of St. Augustine*, ed. Whitney J. Oates (Random House, 1948).

2. Ibid., XLII.

3. Alfred North Whitehead, *Religion in the Making* (New York, Macmillan, 1926) p. 56.

4. Ibid., 56.

5. Alfred North Whitehead, *Process and Reality* (New York, The Free Press, 1978), 346.

6. Ibid., 342f.

7. Alfred North Whitehead, *Adventure of Ideas* (New York, Macmillan, 1933), 214.

8. Ibid., p. 214.

9. See the title essay in Stephen Gould, *The Panda's Thumb* (Norron, 1980).

10. *Process and Reality*, 346.

Essays in Theology and Philosophy of Religion

- Clark Williamson
- George Nordgulen
- Donald Wayne Viney
- Theodore Vitali

The Authority of Scripture After the *Shoah*

Clark M. Williamson

I. Introduction

Entirely apart from the perplexing problems raised for Christian theology by the *Shoah*, the issue of the authority of scripture was already sufficiently puzzling. The collapse of authoritarian ways of doing theology in the modern and post-modern eras in itself poses the question of whether scripture can any longer be regarded as authoritative, and if so how and in what sense, with enough rigor to require a carefully considered response. Further, the awareness of the thoroughgoing historicity both of scripture and its interpreters requires the abandonment not only of traditional but of most modern responses to the question of scriptural authority. A convincing and affirmative answer to the question of scriptural authority is not easily found.

The effort to rethink Christianity after the *Shoah*, in the light both of the *adversus Judaeos* mode of interpreting scripture and of claiming its authority and in the light of the reality of Judaism and the Jewish people, understood in ways categorically removed from inherited and pejorative views of Judaism, compounds the problem of scriptural authority in ways not yet considered by most Christian theologians.

In this paper, no attempt can be made to offer a comprehensive solution to the question of the authority of scripture that would be adequate to the issues raised. What will be attempted is to show (1) how the problem continues to bedevil contemporary efforts to rethink the Christian witness in our time, (2) how traditional and revisionist views of the authority of scripture fail to be appropriate and credible after the *Shoah*, and (3) to offer a suggestion as to how scriptural authority might be reaffirmed by a Christian theology committed to affirm God's continuing covenant with the Jewish people.

II. The Continuing Problem

How the issue of scriptural authority, particularly the authority of the New Testament, is a continuing puzzle is aptly illustrated by two recent responses to the work of Paul M. Van Buren.

In a highly appreciative reply to Van Buren's work, Lloyd Gaston comments favorably on what he calls Van Buren's "most radical proposal" (Gaston, 58). Recognizing that anti-Judaism is to be found in the New Testament itself (Gaston, 55), Van Buren frees the New Testament from "an almost impossible bind" (Gaston, 59). How does he do this, that is: "By what criterion can one designate significant parts of the New Testament as no longer authoritative for the Christian Church" (Gaston, 59)?

The answer is ingenious. "By restricting the term 'Holy Scriptures' to *Tanakh*, and by consistently referring to the 'Apostolic Writings,'" says Gaston, "Van Buren solves many problems with a single stroke. Holy Scripture now becomes the criterion for determining what is authoritative in the Apostolic Writings" (Gaston, 59). The *Tanakh* now becomes the criterion for determining which parts of the Apostolic Writings are authoritative. The question here is not whether Gaston's interpretation of Van Buren is accurate (a case could be made for the authoritativeness of Paul in Van Buren's theology), but whether Gaston's view of the authority of the Apostolic Writings is adequate.

The strengths of Gaston's view are that the Apostolic Writings are now seen in continuity with Holy Scripture, that they are no longer set in antithesis to Holy Scripture, and that they speak directly to the situation of Christians in our post-*Shoah* era. These strengths are not to be minimized.

The weakness is equally glaring: it is simply that the Apostolic Writings are no longer Holy Scripture and therefore, it would seem, no longer authoritative. Authority is analytic in the name "Holy Scripture." If we decide no longer to use this name for the Apostolic Writings, we decide that they are no longer authoritative for us. If the problem for the post-Marcionite church was whether the Old Testament is biblical, for Gaston it is whether the New Testament is biblical.

The issue is nuanced and subtle. If scripture is authoritative but not authoritarian, then its authority must be a rule-conferred authority. The scriptures are a *norma normata*, a norm or criterion that is standardized by reference to a higher norm. That is, interpreters of the scriptures are not simply at the mercy of authoritarian scriptures; they can appeal to a higher norm, a *norma normans*, a norming norm that is not in turn normed. It is to this *norma normans* that we turn for what is authoritative and it is this that is "scripture" in the strict sense of the term. This determines what is derivatively authoritative in the scriptures. It is this that Gaston locates in the *Tanakh*, and not in the Apostolic Writings. Whatever in the latter might be authoritative is determined to be so by reference to the *norma normans*, the *Tanakh*.

Appealing as this may seem to Christians concerned to re-envision Christianity in the light of the reality of Judaism and the Jewish people, is it adequate? I do not disagree with Gaston that the Apostolic Writings are a normed norm. But it is worth pointing out that the norming norm can no longer be called Christian. Another way to make this point is to note that for him the Apostolic Writings are post-scriptural tradition and therefore not authoritative except insofar as they can be shown to be appropriate to the *Tanakh*. This looks like a Protestant view of scripture as preceding tradition and authoritative over against it, pushed back one historical step.

Alternatively, it is a view of the authority of the Apostolic Writings to which Jews might respond warmly, but which they would accept as applicable neither to the *Mishnah* and *Talmud* nor to the subsequent tradition of rabbinic decision-making down to today. The right of Rabbis to interpret and change the *Torah* is not authorized by the *Torah*, yet their tradition of doing so has its authoritative moments or diverse set of authoritative moments for different groupings within Judaism. How can we expect Christians to accept a view of the authority of Christian *midrashim* that Jews would not accept of Jewish *midrashim*? If we grant, with Gaston, that the Apostolic Writings constitute a normed norm, a rule-conferred authority, can we not find that rule within them?

Another response to Van Buren's work, also one that claims to appreciate his perception of "the need to reiterate the organic-covenantal linkage between Jews and Israel and to remind the church of the essential Jewishness of Christianity" (Glasser, 65), shows the problem of the authority of the Apostolic Writings from a radically different perspective.

Arthur F. Glasser claims that "the underlying issue" presented by Van Buren's work is that of "truth as revealed in Scripture" (Glasser, 65). That the truth is indeed revealed in the New Testament (Glasser does not use the term "Apostolic writings") is a point on which Glasser is not prepared to yield. He rejects Van Buren's reconstructed view of Jesus categorically and claims that Jesus is truthfully presented in the gospels: "Fortunately, the church has continued to believe that the mind of Jesus Christ is accurately portrayed in the Gospels. Indeed, there is no priori reason why this portrayal of Him may not be accurate nor why it may not correspond with His own self-understanding" (Glasser, 67). The crucifixion and resurrection account for the "data" of the New Testament, not some present-day reconstruction (Glasser, 67). For Glasser the truth about Jesus is found in the New Testament, a book "written by Jews within two brief generations of Jesus' death and when its details could be confirmed by Jewish eyewitnesses still living" (Glasser, 68).

Whereas Gaston is apparently willing to re-locate authority outside of the New Testament because of its anti-Judaism, Glasser is unwilling to admit that there is any anti-Judaism in it: "Down through church history some Jews and Gentiles, in their reading of the Scriptures, all too often poured into certain texts the accumulated prejudice and hostility of centuries to the neglect of their plain meaning" (Glasser, 68–69). Although he does not in this context use the word, the New Testament is clearly "inerrant" for Glasser, an inerrancy he attempts to justify with such historical-critical results, e.g., J. A. T. Robinson's dating of the gospels (Glasser, 68) as comport with his views.

The result is an incoherent blending of the traditional scripture principle with a conservative use of historical-critical method, not recognizing that such a method, regardless of its results, cannot get beyond probabilities on historical matters (Tillich, 227). Using a probabilistic method to support an absolutist position is an odd way of doing one's theological business.

The theological pay-off of Glasser's approach to the authority of the New Testament is the reaffirmation of a supersessionist interpretation of it:

> If there had been no resurrection, there would never have been a Christian Church, a gospel of life-transforming power through the resurrected Christ, a conversion-to-Christ experience untold millions have subsequently experienced, the subsequent *replacement* of the Jewish Sabbath by the Lord's Day and the existence of the New Testament (Glasser, 71; emphasis mine).

The Lord's Day here displaces the Sabbath. It is probably fair to take these two as standing for two religious systems and peoples, one of which replaces the other. Not only is this clearly supersessionist, carrying the implication that the replaced religious system should no longer exist because it has been replaced by God, but it calls into serious question Glasser's opening affirmation of the "organic-covenantal linkage" between Israel and the church. Is it intelligible to speak of an organic-covenantal linkage between the church and a *replaced* Israel?

There we have the continuing problem posed between two positions, one of which affirms continuity between Israel and the church but denies the authority of the New Testament and the other of which affirms the authority of the New Testament without qualification, yet also affirms the supersession of Israel by the church. The question this stand-off poses is whether and how Christians can claim both God's continuing covenant with Israel and the authority of the Apostolic Writings or New Testament.

III. The Scripture Principle

A. Its Traditional Form

We turn now to look at alternative models for construing the authority of the New Testament, with the purpose of seeing if any one or more can lend warrant to the claim of post-*Shoah* Christian theology that God remains faithful to the covenant with Israel.

The oldest model of scriptural authority in Christianity is called "the scripture principle." Here I shall summarize Farley and Hodgson's account of it. This principle apparently originated among Jews in the Diaspora subsequent to the Babylonian Exile. No longer having the land, temple or priesthood, they created in their place the synagogue and the written Torah (Farley and Hodgson, 63). While representing a tremendous advance in Israelite religion, this development was not totally lacking in ambiguity.

With it the idea of scripture came to entail a written deposit of complete and definitive revelation that functioned to authorize cultic and moral regulations. According to Farley and Hodgson, the scripture principle exhaustively locates revelation in the past and claims that the text is "totally and equally valid in all its parts and details" (Farley and Hodgson, 63).

The scripture principle periodizes history, which unfolds through discrete stages with revelation fixed in the past. The past epoch is normative, there can be no new revelation. Although Christianity claimed that there had been a new revelation of God in Jesus Chrsit, it nonetheless adopted the scripture principle but, in doing so, had to reperiodize salvation history (Farley and Hodgson, 65).

The scripture principle presupposes an *identity* between what God intends to communicate and what comes to expression in scripture. Hence the text and its content are regarded as possessing the "qualities of inerrancy, infallibility, and absolute truthfulness . . ." (Farley and Hodgson, 65). Consequently, the contents of the text are *leveled*, the inerrant truth being distributed equally throughout it. Further, this truth is *immutable*, universally valid for all future generations (Farley and Hodgson, 66).

Farley and Hodgson overlook that the power of the scripture principle was broken in Judaism by the Pharisees, who laid the Oral Torah alongside of the Written Torah and developed an exegetical method ("you have read, but the meaning is") allowing them to revolutionize the immutable meanings deposited in the past (Rivkin, 209–311).

The church eventually adopted the scripture principle, in spite of some misgivings (Tertullian complained that "the Holy Spirit was chased into a book") and in spite of some modifications the principle had to undergo at Christian hands. The changes included: a shift from *Torah* to gospel as the genre of scripture, and a hyphenated scripture composed of an Old and a New Testament, with the former having only provisional validity. Such shifts would seem to invalidate the claims of the scripture principle to immutability and the fixing of revelation in the past, but the church nonetheless adopted it and its associated apparatus: "a canon of officially recognized authoritative writings, atomistic exegesis and proof-texting, and the establishment of revelation as the foundation of theology contained in human-historical deposits regarded as inspired and infallible" (Farley and Hodgson, 68). The work of the theologians, on the terms of the scripture principle, is to translate the truth of scripture for the present age. There is no room for critical inquiry into the scriptures.

Not surprisingly, the scripture principle is at work in Glasser's response to Van Buren. Glasser therefore rejects critical efforts to get behind the texts of scripture, and defends both the supersessionism that is built into the reperiodization of history presupposed by the Christian development of the scripture principle and the triumphalism involved in thinking of God in the mode of an in-the-world-being who intervenes in the world process with infallible communications.

Theologians who defend the scripture principle formally, no matter how much they might transcend it in their exegetical or hermeneutical work, can not help address the task of Christian theology after the *Shoah*, because the scripture principle is itself too large a theological claim on behalf of the church's supersession of Judaism and the Jewish people to be overcome.

The great theologians in the history of the church manifest a tension between their ways of interpreting scripture and their insistence on

130

retaining the scripture principle, a tension no less evident in Luther and Calvin than in Augustine. Luther implicitly challenged the scripture principle but would not do so explicitly, and Calvin disallowed any challenge to the scripture principle, in spite of the fact that his covenantal theology went far to undermine it. Consequently, the principle was hardened in the era of Protestant scholasticism and remains so in contemporary representatives of that movement, for whom the scriptures remain the *norma absoluta* of theological reflection.

B. Calvin's Metaphor

John Calvin used the metaphor of spectacles to explain how scripture functions as scripture. The knowledge of God that we can discern from the creation as such does not much help us, says Calvin:

> Just as old or bleary-eyed men and those with weak vision, if you thrust before them a most beautiful volume, even if they recognize it to be some sort of writing, yet can scarcely construe two words, but with the aid of spectacles will begin to read distinctly; so Scripture, gathering up the otherwise confused knowledge of God in our minds, having dispersed our dullness, shows us the true God (Calvin, 35).

Helpful as the metaphor of scripture as a set of spectacles is, it has one drawback. The church has no power to judge scripture; rather it "recognizes Scripture to be the truth of its own God [and] . . . it unhesitatingly venerates Scripture" (Calvin, 36). Calvin assumes that all distortions are in the lens of the natural eye, none in the spectacles. But what if the spectacles introduce distortions into one's vision, distortions of which one would never "naturally" have thought? We reach the limits of helplessness of Calvin's metaphor for the scriptures with the recognition that while without them we would not see things as we do, nonetheless they also introduce a profound nearsightedness into the Christian tradition—the nearsightedness of anti-Judaism.

C. Calvin Trumped

On two different occasions, many years apart, I tried to read *The Book of Mormon* and *The Divine Principle* of the Reverend Moon and the Unification Church. Each time I quickly gave up, because these two texts of holy scripture of their respective churches struck me as utter gibberish. I simply do not stand in the tradition of interpreting either of these texts. So with the Bible, if we had no tradition of reading and interpreting it in the church, of coping with it in historical-critical and hermeneutical ways, it too would be utter gibberish to us. Imagine walking on a beach one fine day, never having encountered a Bible before, and finding one washed up on the shore with some driftwood. Imagine picking it up and opening it for the first time. It makes no sense. You go on about your business.

Here we have the Catholic insight: "Look at the Bible through the spectacles of the Church" (Moehler, 40). It is ". . . better to contemplate the star with the aid of a glass than to let it escape your dull organ of vision and be lost in mist and darkness" (Moehler, 40–1). The argument goes something like this: scripture indeed is infallible, but its interpreters are not. Therefore the tradition of scriptural interpretation by the church constitutes the general sense of the meaning of scripture that must prevail against any merely individual interpretations. In the subjective meaning of the word, tradition is "the living word, perpetuated in the heart of believers" (Moehler, 39). In the objective sense, it is the *regula fidei*, the standard for interpreting scripture (Moehler, 39).

In some senses, this position is clearly right. We now know that tradition preceded scriptures (writings), that scriptures preceded canon, that tradition decided which scriptures were to be canonical, and that the canon was followed by an exegetical and interpretive tradition. Hard forms of the Protestant *sola scriptura* doctrine are no longer credible.

Yet a position such as Moehler's suffers from its own difficulties. It is authoritarian: the community, never the individual, has the truth (Moehler, 38–9). While Moehler has a high doctrine of scripture, in the last analysis, he has no need of it: ". . . when instruction through the apostleship, and the ecclesiastical education in the way described, takes place in the individual, the Sacred Scriptures are not even necessary for our acquisition of their general contents" (Moehler, 38). He therefore also overlooks that, if the tradition is so authoritative, then he should take seriously the fact that it was precisely the tradition that defined itself canonically. Lastly, the tradition also, no less than the scriptures, contains its own distortions, not the least of which is anti-Judaism. Never in the dogma, often in the doctrine, traditional anti-Jewish exegesis and hermeneutics heightens what anti-Judaism there is in the scriptures. This lens, too, is badly warped.

IV. Some Contemporary Options

A. Scripture "Authors" Identity

In what is probably the most influential proposal on the topic of scriptural authority on the current scene, David Kelsey argues the thesis that scripture is authoritative insofar as it operates ecclesiastically to form new human identities and to transform the life of individuals and communities. Says he:

> In a Christian community it is precisely the biblical writings which . . . provide the images, concepts, principles, parables, etc., that serve to evoke, nurture, and correct the dispositions, beliefs, policies, emotions, etc., that are basic to the identities of members of the community and to the identity of the community itself. When used in these ways they may be said often to "author" new personal identities (Kelsey, 51).

Kelsey's proposal has several strengths that recommend it for careful consideration. Obviously, (1) it unites scripture and tradition. The biblical writings can function as scripture only in tradition, i.e., only in the act of handing on (*actus tradendi*) from generation to generation "a promise and a call through the use of these texts" (Kelsey, 51). Further, (2) the claim that scripture is authoritative is empirically grounded. Biblical writings are authoritative because, in fact, they have operated in this way. The very meaning of scripture, the naming of biblical writings with this term, recognizes "that they are authoritative *de facto* in the church and that that authority is *functional*" (Kelsey, 52). Also, (3) these texts function authoritatively in a variety of ways, as addressing the affections, the needs for reflective thought, and for regulating behavior. And (4) because scripture "authors" identity it also "authorizes" theological proposals.

In fact, therefore, scripture is authoritative. Should it be? Noting that *de facto* authority is not enough (it could be merely an arbitrary claim), Kelsey contends that scriptural authority must be grounded *del jure*. He acknowledges the correctness of Schubert Ogden's claim that *de jure* authority is "rule-conferred authority," i.e., that authority has a right to be acknowledged "only when there are rules that govern legitimation of authority" (Kelsey, 54). Rule-conferred authority prevents any heteronomous authority from being exercised by or on behalf of scripture. Therefore, scripture is "normed norm" (*norma normata*).

Traditional ways of affirming the *de jure* authority of scripture (the scripture principle) isolated *Heilsgeschichte* from ordinary history, resulting in an "intellectually dishonest special pleading" with regard to historical study of the biblical writings and a docetic picture of God's involvement with the world (Kelsey, 56). More recent attempts by Barth, Bultmann, and Tillich to stress, respectively, "word," "kerygma," and "message" as grounding the *de jure* authority of scripture do not help, because these terms lack "any determinate content at all" (Kelsey, 56). They cannot be formulated as norms by which to assess the appropriateness of theological proposals.

What does Kelsey propose as an alternative to both the scripture principle and to recent efforts to substitute something else (the Word of God or the *kerygma*) for it? His constructive suggestion is that the *de jure* authority of scripture be grounded in God's role as transformer of human identity, i.e., in the Holy Spirit. Scripture is, he says, "a heterogeneous collection of images, parables, metaphors, principles for action, beliefs, emotion-concepts, etc., each of which is determinately particular and concrete" (Kelsey, 57). This heterogeneity elicits and demands a theological judgment about "what can serve as a norming norm [*norma normans*] by which to select, order, and interrelate the scripture to which appeal is made" (Kelsey, 58).

The content of this *norma normans* "is the actuality of the inauguration in and for the world of the eschatological rule of God in the resurrection of the crucified Jesus" (Kelsey, 58). Specifically, it is the narratives about Jesus' life, ministry, death, and resurrection that bring focus to the heterogeneity of biblical writings.

Kelsey's proposal is influential for good reasons; it has many strengths and represents an advance beyond major earlier 20th-century suggestions as to the nature of biblical authority. The scriptures must be a *norma normata*, and we do need to be able to specify the content of the *norma normans*. Granting all that (and more, for Kelsey's is a largely adequate statement), nonetheless we must ask how well it helps us address the theological task of developing a new theological proposal, one that overcomes the *adversus Judaeos* tradition and affirms the solidarity of the church with the synagogue.

Here it seems not quite adequate, for the following reasons. While it is true that, *de facto*, scripture has authored Christian identity, one of the chief ways in which it has done this has been anti-Jewish. That is, the chief function of the *adversus Judaeos* tracts and sermons was to use the scriptures in the shaping of Christian identity by telling Christians who they are. They are not Jewish, they are anti-Jewish, they are better than Jewish. They are a new people, not old, Gentile, not Jewish, spiritual, not carnal, ruled by grace, not by law, etc. Any *de facto* authority that scripture has must be derived from its *de jure* authority, not vice versa, because the character of its *de facto* authority has been at the heart of the problem.

Also, to define scripture in the strict sense (the *norma normans*) as the "actuality of the inauguration in and for the world of the eschatological rule of God in the resurrection of the crucified Jesus" is, once again, to make of the *Tanakh* merely a preparatory authority, one that anticipates but does not celebrate the *actuality* of God's rule. What it hopes for is inaugurated in Christian scripture, in that to which the New Testament attests.

There are two problems here. One is the question of credibility. Is it plausible to claim that God's rule was actualized or inaugurated in the resurrection of Jesus, even if this rule is defined as eschatological? What it might credibly mean to talk of God's rule is one issue. Whether this rule is effective only after the resurrection is another. In whatever sense it is credible to speak of God's rule, that rule can have been no less evident to Israel than to the church. Unless some credible way of talking of this rule is devised, a sober regard for the butcher block of human history will either falsify it or cause it to be viewed as meaningless.

The other problem is supersessionism. If the rule of God as attested to by Christian scripture is understood now to be actual, inaugurated, then all earlier witness to it will be regarded as standing in relation to the New Testament as mere possibility stands to actuality or as shadow to reality. I doubt very much that this is Kelsey's intent, but it does seem that it is the pay-off of his position. Farley and Hodgson are closer to the truth in their affirmation: "Faith in Jesus Christ is not a substitute for Israel's faith but a new universal availability of divine presence" (Farley and Hodgson, 85).

B. Scripture Re-presents God's Grace

At this point Schubert Ogden's proposal for construing scriptural authority promises to be of greater help to Christian theologians attempting to rethink the Christian witness in the light of the reality of Judaism and the Jewish people. Scripture, as Ogden approaches the matter, can be authoritative only with respect to the appropriateness of Christian theological assertions, "with respect to the end of bearing the distinctively Christian witness of faith" (Ogden, 1976: 245), not with respect to the intelligibility of those assertions.

Scripture is the norming norm for all theological proposals, yet even its normative character is rule-conferred. Although it is normative with regard to all other theological norms, "it itself ultimately stands on the same level as those who are subject to its authority *vis-a-vis* Jesus the Christ" (Ogden, 1976: 246). That is, we who are subject to its authority are not thereby deprived of our theological freedom. As with any authorized authority, we can appeal over the head of scripture to the one who authorizes it. Its authority is not authoritarian, but governed by that to which it is the authoritative witness.

Ogden tries to get at scripture as *norma normans* by reconsidering the issue of the canon. In one sense, canon refers to a collection of writings recognized by the early church. In this sense it is an invention of the post-Marcionite church, although its contents were previously available (Ogden, 1976: 250). In the proper sense of the term, canon is "whatever of or in those writings [that] is in fact authorized by Christ through the church's continuing experience under the guidance of the Holy Spirit" (Ogden, 1976: 250). The true test is whether these writings are genuinely apostolic, which is the criterion to which the tradition itself appealed in the establishment of the canon. In establishing the canon, however, the early church applied the criterion of apostolicity (whether a writing was authored by someone in turn authorized by Christ himself) ambivalently. It decided questions of apostolicity by reference to the content of books. Orthodox content implied apostolic authorship.

But if one insists on using the early church's own criterion, then it must be the apostolic witness to Jesus Christ itself that is the canon, the *norma normans sed non normata*. In relation to which the New Testament is to be scrutinized. That is, one task of theology is to criticize the Christian witness in the light of the norm of appropriateness, the canon. The New Testament is criticizable Christian witness. The canon, accessible only through historical reconstruction from the New Testament, is the apostolic testimony to Jesus (Ogden, 1976: 252). Therefore, merely to show that an assertion is found in the scriptures fails to authorize it as theologically appropriate. One must further establish that this scriptural source "is itself authorized by the apostolic witness of faith" (Ogden, 1976: 257). It is the stratum of witness, the earliest that can be reconstructed, that "is itself the norm of appropriateness" (Ogden, 1982: 63).

The content of this apostolic witness lies behind the New Testament, but can also be found in it, in Paul and elsewhere. Paul succinctly formulates the Christian witness: "Yet for us there is one God, the Father, from whom are all things and for whom we exist, and one Lord, Jesus Christ, through whom are all things and through whom we exist" (1 Corinthians 8:6). Ogden interprets Paul to say that "what it means to have God as our Father is existentially the same as having Jesus Christ as our Lord" (Ogden, 1966: 201). God the Father is "the covenant God of Israel who has disclosed himself in Israel's history, and thence through the law and the prophets, to be the God of a unique promise and demand" (Ogden, 1966: 201). Hence Paul's intent is to affirm that the revelation of God in Jesus Christ "is the decisive revelation to all mankind of the same promise and demand re-presented by the Old Testament revelation (cf. Romans 3:21)" (Ogden, 1966: 202). The word spoken to us in Jesus Christ is "precisely the *same* word" that was earlier "re-presented through 'the law and the prophets'" (Ogden, 1966: 203).

The strength of Ogden's proposal, particularly in relation to the task of constructing an appropriate post-*Shoah* Christian theology, lies in its total avoidance of the works-righteousness inherent in all forms of supersessionism. The "new" knowledge of God of which Christians can lay hold, for Paul, is exactly identical with the primordial revelation of God previously re-presented in the faith of Israel. Our salvation does not "become possible" in Christ—a statement that the New Testament nowhere affirms—but in him what was always possible now "becomes manifest" (Ogden, 1961: 143). This view comports with a thorough-going acceptance of the principles *sola gratia—sola fide*: When "the event of Jesus becomes a condition apart from which God is not free to be a gracious God, the heretical doctrine of works-righteousness achieves its final and most dangerous triumph" (Ogden, 1961: 145). In other words, Paul rightly affirmed that Abraham is "the father of us all" (Romans 4:16) not because Abraham believed in Jesus Christ, but because he "believed God and it was reckoned to him as righteousness" (Romans 4:3; Ogden, 1961: 142–143).

Ogden's understanding of scriptural authority renders explicit the theocentric basis of the Christian witness—that "we are Christ's," but that "Christ is God's" (1 Corinthians 3:23; 11:3)—and makes the only condition of salvation one that can be formulated without reference to Jesus Christ, as stated in the parable of the Last Judgment (Matthew 25:31–46). The only demand we must meet to receive salvation is that we accept God's love for ourselves and thereby become freed to respond to the concrete needs of the neighbor (Ogden, 1961: 144). All Christian triumphalism and exclusivism are hereby rejected.

There are two reasons for wondering, however, whether Ogden's view of scriptural authority, helpful as it is, is quite adequate to the needs of a post-*Shoah* theology. One is that the earliest witness of Christian faith, the *norma normans*, must be reconstructed from behind the writings of the early church by historical-critical method. This earliest witness, the "Jesus-kerygma," will be subject, as a result, to the variableness of historical-critical method itself. Historical-critical method can never claim to reach results that are more than probable and that are not subject to further correction. We are left peering over the edge of an archaeological dig, hoping that what is dug up will not be an exclusivistic witness. But what if it is? Do we then take our medicine and admit that exclusivism is inherently Christian?

The other difficulty is that the authority of the Hebrew Bible may not be adequately stated on this proposal. Obviously, Ogden does not subject it to the Apostolic Writings. They are subject to the Jesus-kerygma, as is the Hebrew Bible. Ogden's view of the authority of the Hebrew Bible is that it "document[s] the particular linguistic form of the question of human existence ... to which the Jesus-kerygma presents itself as the answer" (Ogden, 1976: 260). The meaning of the Jesus-kerygma is that it is a development of the understanding of existence "variously expressed in the writings of the Old Testament" (Ogden, 1976: 260). The Hebrew Bible, therefore, stands in relation to the Jesus-kerygma as question to answer or presupposition to assertion. This does not deprive it of theological authority, because "the authoritative answer to a question must endow the question itself with an equivalent authority" (Ogden, 1976: 261).

Here Ogden seems to have fallen into an inconsistency. If the Christian witness is a re-presentation of precisely the same word that was earlier re-presented through the law and the prophets, as Ogden has said it is, how then can this witness stand in relation to its earlier identical re-presentation as an answer to a preceding question? If the same word is in each place re-presented, is it not in each place an answer to the same question? The Hebrew Bible is not just a question, however important a question we may regard it as being. It is also an answer, an answer which, as Ogden rightly claims, has lately been re-presented to us. On these two points, then, the locus of the *norma normans* of distinctively Christian scripture and the affirmation of the authority of this Christian scripture without regarding it as the answer to the Old Testament's question, we have more work to do.

C. Observing Scripture's Hermeneutical Axioms

The suggestion offered by canonical criticism is that we look at the scriptures as distillates from a living tradition, something on the following order. At any point on their historical trajectory, we find the people Israel confronted with a hermeneutical task. They have a tradition and the new experience of the contemporary generation. They must interpret the new experience in the light of the tradition in order to understand it and to incorporate it in the living tradition. But to do this, they must reinterpret the tradition if it is to incorporate this new experience and be credible in face of it. They must do both in order to pass on their faith to the next generation. Hermeneutics is generational joining. "Process," as Sanders says, "was there from the start and continues unabated through and after the periods of intense canonical process of stabilization" (Sanders, 31).

Every time Israel interprets its faith it re-interprets it. We never find it simply luxuriating in uninterpreted experience (aside from the autobiography of a stone, as Whitehead once said, there is no uninterpreted experience). There is no need for Israel always to say the same thing that it said before, although its foundational commitments will be constant, and sometimes the re-interpretation will have to deny what was earlier claimed: "As I live, says the Lord God, this proverb shall no more be used by you in Israel" (Ezekiel 18:2).

Our attention therefore must be given to what we might call Israel's hermeneutical principles, the axioms in terms of which it interpreted and reinterpreted its tradition. This turn, it is hoped, will provide a clue to the norm of appropriateness or canon for Christian scripture. With Ogden, I take it that we do not look to scripture to find norms of credibility.

To look for the hermeneutical axioms of the biblical tradition is a move associated with canonical criticism. The relevance of canonical criticism to this discussion is noted by James A. Sanders: "Christianity has become so systemically Marcionite and anti-Semitic that only a truly radical revival of the concept of canon as applied to the Bible will, I think, counter it" (Sanders, xv).

Some of the hermeneutical axioms used in the canonical process, as Sanders analyzes them, are directly pertinent to our discussion. (1) The Bible is a monotheizing literature, i.e., it regularly struggles "within and against polytheistic contexts to affirm God's oneness" (Sanders, 52). (2) It reflects a broad theocentric hermeneutic, expressed in two hermeneutical axioms, the prophetic and the constitutive. The former stresses that God is the God of *all*, the latter that God is the particular Redeemer of Israel or the church. The constitutive axiom bespeaks promise, the prophetic challenge (Sanders, 53). Each gives voice to the grace of God. In situations that require it the prophetic mode is stressed, and Israel is reminded of God's love for Egypt and Assyria (Isaiah 19:25). At other times the constitutive mode is stressed and Israel is reminded that she is the first among God's beloved.

These same hermeneutic modes can be used to read a passage of scripture today. "No one comes to the Father but by me" (John 14:7) can be read in a quite exclusivist way. "In fact," states Sanders, "reading the Bible exclusively in the constitutive mode can issue in a totally denominational, if not tribal, reading of the whole Bible" (Sanders, 66). In an exclusivist reading, it denies to God the freedom to be gracious apart from Jesus Christ, thereby turning God's gift into a condition apart from which God is not free to be gracious. It can also be read prophetically in the light of John 10:16, "I have sheep not of this fold," to show that an exclusivist reading is self-serving and "canonically false" (Sanders, 67).

A difficulty with canonical criticism is its insistence that "everything is a gift of God" (Sanders, 55). While in an ultimate sense it is possibly true to say this, since without God we would receive no gifts whatever, nonetheless the proposal to monotheize, as Sanders expresses it, forgets that some gifts are not from God. Was the *Shoah*, Hitler's attempt to make the earth *Judenrein*, a gift of God? Such a claim suffers from being incredible as well as being inappropriate to the prophetic axioms that God is the gracious, all-inclusive God of everyone for whom God commands justice. The deeper problem with canonical criticism seems to be, therefore, that it collapses criteria of intelligibility into criteria of appropriateness.

V. A Proposal

My proposal for the scriptural authority of the New Testament, therefore, is that it is authoritative where it struggles to monotheize the Christian witness, where it theocentrically articulates the all-inclusive, free grace of God, proclaiming also the constancy of God's faithfulness to God's particularly beloved people. However much the New Testament may reinterpret Israel's faith and in it surely we find many attempts to interpret this new event of Jesus Christ in the light of the traditions of Israel ("according to the scriptures," they said) and to reinterpret that tradition in the light of this new event, it does so appropriately where it monotheizes its new interpretations, thinks theocentrically, and balances a constitutive hermeneutic with a prophetic once.

Paul the apostle, e.g., shows us all these moves in one passage: "For we hold that a man is justified by faith apart from works of law. Or is God the God of Jews only? Is he not the God of Gentiles also? Yes, of Gentiles also, since God is one; and he will justify the circumcised on the ground of their faith and the uncircumcised through their faith. Do we then overthrow the law by this faith? By no means! On the contrary, we uphold the law" (Romans 3:28–31). As Sanders reads it, Paul "monotheized constantly in his reading of Scripture for his churches and pursued a theocentric hermeneutic in working out his understandings of Christology and ecclesiology" (Sanders, 58).

Where the New Testament uses biblical hermeneutics to interpret the Christian witness, it is as biblical as the Old Testament, no more, no less. Where it is supersessionist (or is interpreted as supersessionist), it or its interpreters fail to interpret their witness theocentrically, and turn God's promise of free grace offered to each and all and God's command that justice be done to each and all into a divisive and destructive idol.

What canonical criticism enables us to do is to locate Ogden's norm of appropriateness within the scriptures, not behind them, and to see this norm as the same hermeneutical axioms that were also Israel's. Additionally, it enables us to interpret scripture as it interpreted itself, certainly not a move inappropriate to scripture. This is true, provided scripture functions as canon only to provide a norm of appropriateness for Christian theology. Norms of credibility—such matters as width of illumination and coherence—must be kept distinct from norms of appropriateness.

The situation that faced the people Israel and that faced the apostle Paul also faces us: we must interpret the new events of our time, particularly the attempt in the most deeply Christian part of the world to see to it that not another Jew lived on planet earth, in the light of the Christian tradition, and we must reinterpret that tradition if it is to be credible and morally plausible after that event. Doing so is painful, if only because one discovers how deeply the Christian tradition was an accomplice to that crime. Radical change necessitates radical reinterpretation (Odgden, 1971: 173). The question faced by this essay is whether the New Testament can still function authoritatively in this process of Christian reinterpretation or whether it must be abandoned for it to take place. I hope to have made a case for the former position. Unless we can do so, the logical conclusion points to the abandonment of the tradition, not its reinterpretation.

References

Calvin, John
1985 "With the Aid of Spectacles." In *Readings In Christian Theology*, ed. Peter C. Hodgson and Robert H. King. Philadelphia: Fortress Press: 31–37.

Farley, Edward and Hodgson, Peter C.
1985 "Scripture and Tradition." In *Christian Theology: An Introduction to Its Traditions and Tasks*, ed. Peter C. Hodgson and Robert H. King. Philadelphia: Fortress Press: 61–87.

Gaston, Lloyd
1986 "Jesus the Jew in the Apostolic Writings." *Religion & Intellectual Life*, III: 55–59.

Glasser, Arthur F.
1986 "Truth As Revealed In Scripture." *Religion & Intellectual Life*, III: 65–71.

Kelsey, David
1985 "The Function of Scripture." In *Readings In Christian Theology*, ed. Peter C. Hodgson and Robert H. King. Philadelphia: Fortress Press: 50–59.

Moehler, Johann Adam
1985 "Tradition As The Living Word." In *Readings In Christian Theology*, ed. Peter C. Hodgson and Robert H. King. Philadelphia: Fortress Press: 37–41.

Ogden, Schubert M.
1961 *Christ Without Myth*. New York: Harper & Brothers.
1966 *The Reality of God*. New York: Harper & Row.
1971 "Toward a New Theism." In *Process Philosophy and Christian Thought*, ed. Delwin Brown, Ralph E. James, Jr., and Gene Reeves. Indianapolis: Bobbs-Merrill: 173–187.
1976 "The Authority of Scripture for Theology." *Interpretation*, 30: 242–261. Republished in Schubert M. Ogden, *On Theology* (San Francisco: Harper & Row, 1986): 45–68.
1982 *The Point of Christology*. San Francisco: Harper & Row.

Rivkin, Ellis
1978 *A Hidden Revolution: The Pharisees' Search For The Kingdom Within*. Nashville: Abingdon Press, Sanders, James A.
1984 *Canon and Community: A Guide to Canonical Criticism*. Philadelphia: Fortress Press.

Tillich, Paul
1967 *Perspectives On 19th and 20th Century Protestant Theology*. New York: Harper & Row.

The Resurrection in Judaism and Christianity

George Nordgulen

Eugene was my seminary teacher in philosophical theology. It was he who introduced me to process thought, to Whitehead and Hartshorne. In 1983, at the Society of Christian Philosophers Conference, I organized a section on neoclassical and classical theology. I invited Eugene to be the main speaker. While at this meeting we talked about developments in process theology. I indicated that I had become interested in exploring world religions in the light of process thought. Though he himself had not done this, he felt that it was an important project. This paper is the attempt to carry out that exploration in terms of Christianity and Judaism.

An interesting development over the past fifty years or so has been the renewed and sustained dialogue between Judaism and Christianity. That there has been a family quarrel between the two for almost 2000 years has been recognized by both; that the child has mistreated its parent is also a shameful but needed confession. The parent, Judaism, mistreated its child, Christianity, early. There was debate, persecution, rejection, and before the destruction of the temple of Jerusalem there was some success in relationships. But after A.D. 70, at least from the Christian side, Paul's letter to the Romans, chapters 9–11, was not heeded. Rather, it was the case that enmity and bitterness grew between the two. The Crusades and the Holocaust are sad commentaries on this tragic family relationship. But there has been renewal. Today there is a healthy and vibrant dialogue that is being carried out between Jews and Christians. For example, Pinchas Lapide, a Jewish scholar, has met with and discussed themes of common interest with Christian theologians: Hans Küng from the Roman Catholic tradition, Wolfhart Pannenberg from the Protestant tradition, and Jurgen Moltmann have discussed the Trinity with Lapide, while Peter Stuhlmacher has discussed the role of Paul in Christianity with him. Hence, there seems to be the dawn of a new day in which discussions toward reconciliation can take place between the two. The purpose of this paper is to examine the dialogue between Lapide and Pannenberg on the resurrection of Jesus. Though Pannenberg and Lapide have had discussions on issues that separate and unite Christianity and Judaism, they did not directly address this topic. And yet it is a very natural one for them to discuss since the resurrection is so fundamental for Pannenberg's theology and since Lapide has written a book on *The Resurrection of Jesus*. I shall raise and seek to answer four questions concerning this topic between the two men: (1) What is the resurrection of the dead? (2) How can we apprehend the resurrection of the dead? (3) What are the evidences for the resurrection of Jesus? (4) What are the consequences of the resurrrection of Jesus? Finally, I shall evaluate this dialogue from the standpoint of process theology.

I. The Resurrection of the Dead

One issue that both Lapide and Pannenberg agree on is that the resurrection of Jesus must be understood in the context of Jewish history. I find it strange that Lapide never mentions Pannenberg nor does he place him in the bibliography at the end of the book on *The Resurrection of Jesus*. Nevertheless, I will seek to show that they are in striking agreement concerning the importance of Jewish history for the understanding of Jesus' resurrection. But our first question is: What is the resurrection of the dead? I shall first set forth Lapide's position and then turn to Pannenberg's.

Lapide begins his exposition by rightly claiming that the crucifixion and the resurrection are the two fundamental events in Christianity. (*RJ*, p. 32) In all of the gospels there is a single line of tradition that leads to these events. But it is through the resurrection that God exalts and glorifies the life and deeds of Jesus. Without the experience of the resurrection, the crucifixion of Jesus would not have been significant and, as Lapide says, it probably would have been forgotten. He also quotes from Paul, "If Christ has not been raised, then our preaching is in vain and your faith is in vain." (1 Corinthians 15:14) Hence, the centrality of the resurrection and the resurrection faith needs to be explained. We have noted that for Lapide this can be done in terms of the history of Judaism.

What is the understanding of the resurrection of the dead in Judaism? Here Lapide raises and answers two questions: (1) Was Judaism before the time of Jesus acquainted with individual resurrection? (2) Was the hope of the resurrection from the dead already a part of the Jewish faith in the time of Jesus? His answer to both of these questions is yes. (*RJ*, p. 46) Beginning with the first question, Lapide catalogs the following incidents from the Jewish scripture: there is the translation of Enoch, Genesis 5:24. The argument is that whoever walks with God is not because he is taken by God. Enoch walked with God. Therefore, Enoch was not because he was taken by God. The second instance is the ascension of Elijah recorded in 2 Kings 2:11. Whoever is a faithful servant of God is taken by God. Elijah was a faithful servant of God. Therefore, Elijah was taken up by God. A third instance is the transformation of Saul. After the anointing by Samuel, Saul is told that the spirit of Yahweh will "seize" him and that he will be put into "ecstacy" and "changed into another man." (1 Samuel 10:6) So the argument is that whoever is seized by the spirit of Yahweh is transformed into another person. Saul is seized by the spirit of Yahweh and so Saul is transformed into another person.

The next three instances are records of resurrection from the dead. The first concerns Elijah's raising up the son of the widow at Zarephath. The son had become very ill and the illness was such that life left him. Elijah prays to God to allow the "soul" of the boy to return and Yahweh hears. Whoever receives the spirit of life, the soul, receives it from Yahweh. The widow's son received the spirit of life. Hence, the widow's son is resurrected to life by Yahweh. A second instance concerns Elisha who finds the son of a wealthy woman dead on his bed. Since the woman had given hospitality to Elisha, he prays to God and the son is awakened to life. God is the giver of life after it has departed from the body. (2 Kings 4:18–37) The last instance Lapide mentions is the dead person who is buried where Elisha's bones are deposited and when the body comes in contact with the bones, it is revived. (2 Kings 13:20–21) The author notes that none of these instances is ever questioned in the history of Israel and that all are accepted as a demonstration of the power of God to resurrect the dead. (*RJ*, p. 49) Hence, the tradition of Judaism is acquainted with the resurrection of the dead and it is this that gives them a hope in the resurrection, which answers the second question.

We shall be concerned with two questions in Pannenberg's procedure: (1) What is the meaning of the conception of the resurrection of the dead? (2) How is this to be understood in terms of Jesus' resurrection? As to the first question, Pannenberg is as convinced as Lapide that the proper understanding of the phrase must be gleaned from Jewish history. But it is postexilic Judaism rather than the whole history of Judaism from Enoch through Elisha that gives a very definite meaning to the resurrection of the dead. In the first place it must be noted that the resurrection from the dead is a metaphor. (*JGM*, p. 74) This is revealed in the inner logic of the concept itself for it suggests one who awakens from sleep and rises. Yet we really cannot know the resurrected life since it lies on the "other" side of our experience. Hence, "sleep" serves as a metaphor of the unknown destiny of the dead.

Pannenberg gives many illustrations of this. (*JGM*, p. 75) He notes that the first biblical evidence for the resurrection hope mentions "resurrection and waking" in parallel in Isa. 26:19. Dan. 12:2 speaks of those who "sleep" in the dust of the earth as awakening at the end of time. The Ethiopian Enoch, 93:3, speaks of "the just man who will arise from sleep." The Syriac Apocalypse of Baruch, 30:1, claims that "Then all those will arise who have gone to sleep hoping in him (the Messiah)." In the New Testament Paul speaks in 1 Thessalonians 4:13ff of "those who are asleep" in reference to the future resurrection. He also uses this imagery to refer to the dead in 1 Corinthians 15:6, 51. Finally, Paul calls the resurrected Jesus the "first fruits of those who have fallen asleep." (1 Corinthians 15:20) Pannenberg draws the following conclusions from this: (1) "the intended reality and the mode in which it is expressed in language are essentially different." The point is that the intended reality is beyond the experience of the person who lives on this side of death. Hence, the only language one can use is metaphorical. The true essence of the event is still hidden from us. (2) Nevertheless, in primitive Christianity they had experienced one who was resurrected and this at least qualifies the metaphorical language. (*JGM*, p. 75)

Lapide uses resuscitation and resurrection synonomously. Does Pannenberg follow him in this? Lapide, when dealing with the illustrations from Elijah and Elisha, notes that all three are "resurrections or resuscitations which God carried out through the hands of his prophets." (*RJ*, p. 46) Each dealt with a dead person who was resuscitated and restored to life. But presumably all three died again. In the New Testament we have the same power of God demonstrated in Jesus who raises Jarius' daughter, Mark 5:35–43; the raising of the man from Nain, Luke 7:11–17; and the calling forth of Lazarus out of the tomb, John 11:11–44. These are properly called resuscitations and presumably each died again. But at least the resuscitation of Lazarus points to the resurrection of Jesus: I am the resurrection and the life. (John 11:25) But Pannenberg claims that the resurrection of Jesus is different from the mere resuscitation of a dead body. In interpreting Paul he claims that "resurrection means the new life of a new body, not the return of life into a dead but not yet decayed fleshly body." (*JGM*, p. 75) The resurrected body of Christ is a spiritual body and those who belong to Christ will be resurrected in the same manner. Hence, the resurrection of the dead is not to be understood as the resuscitation of a dead corpse that stands up and walks on the analogy of waking and sleeping, but rather it is to be understood as the resurrection of a new, spiritual body that will not return to death. This also means for Pannenberg that the resurrection of Jesus and that of the Christian is essentially parallel. The conclusion, then, is "that one must sharply distinguish the resurrection of the dead in the Christian hope for the future from those resuscitations of corpses which are otherwise reported occasionally in ancient litera-ture" and also from the resuscitations accomplished by Jesus such as the young man from Nain (Luke 7:11–17), the daughter of Jarius . . . or Lazarus." (*JGM*, p. 77) Nevertheless, in the Apocalyptic literature there was also the teaching that the resurrection means transformation and not simply resuscitation. (*JGM*, p. 80) Lapide does not make these distinctions in his discussion. Hence there is a substantive, not merely terminological, difference between the two at this point. We shall see if this carries over to the resurrection of Jesus. I now turn to the second of our questions, namely, how we can apprehend the resurrection of the dead?

II. Apprehending the Resurrection

Perhaps the most Jewish characteristic of faith is faith in the resurrection of Jesus, "a faith which, in the unsearchable ways of God for salvation, led to the birth of Christianity." (*RJ*, p. 30) What is faith and what is the faith experience for the Jew? According to Lapide, it is the total commitment to and acceptance of the God who revealed himself to people. The Jewish faith is in the covenant God who acts in the events of history. Whatever is a covenant act of God in history is open to the eyes of faith. We have already seen that for Lapide the resurrection is an act of God in history and therefore the resurrection is open to the one of faith. The word of God is effective in history and yet is hidden; God reveals himself to the weak and feeble and often in distorted statements of people. (*RJ*, p. 94) The response of people to God's gracious revelations opens one to new dimensions of life. Lapide finds this faith crucial to the apprehension of the disciples in their experience of the resurrection of Jesus. He notes several points.

First, it is women who report the empty tomb and they are the first to witness the resurrection of Jesus. The point is that the testimony of women was considered invalid in rabbinic Judaism. He illustrates this in terms of Monah, the mother Samson, and Sarah, the mother of Isaac.

(*RJ*, p. 95–96) Hence, it is only out of faith that one could accept that God had acted in terms of the resurrection of Jesus to which the women gave their testimony. Furthermore, one of these women, Mary Magdalene, was said to have been possessed by demons which would further discredit her testimony. Hence, only in terms of the faith experience that is prominent throughout Jewish history can the resurrection be apprehended. For no human being saw, let alone understood, the manner and nature of the resurrection. (*RJ*, p. 97) A third point is that the resurrection of Jesus was not disclosed to all people. Those who experienced the resurrection of Jesus were those who had learned "unconditional believing" from God. (*RJ*, p. 97) This subjectivity of the reality of the resurrection is particularly discerned in the experience of Paul. It is only in this context that one can understand the repeated doubt, disbelief, and hesitation of the first disciples. In short, it is the unquestionable power of faith through which the resurrection of Jesus is apprehended. The resurrection of Jesus is a "single grandiose effort to unriddle the death of Jesus in the sense of faith." (*RJ*, p. 111) Since the disciples were not concerned with the historical, they were open to the metaphysical reality of the resurrection. If one experiences the resurrection then it is because of an in-spite-of faith that they apprehend it. (*RJ*, pp. 111–118) It provides a basis for hope, a hope that arises from an anticipation of that incomprehensible infinity and final reality which we call God; a hope that death is not the end; a hope that has confidence that looks upward and ahead. One knows that God has revealed himself in history and one knows that through the power of God he reveals himself again. Hence, the resurrection stands in the history of God's revelation which is apprehended through faith.

For Pannenberg, the resurrection is an historical event and as such can be understood through reason. "Whether or not Jesus was raised from the dead is an historical question insofar as it is an inquiry into what did or did not happen at a certain time. Such questions could only be answered by historical argument . . . (*TH*, p. 128) History refers to what actually happened at a certain time and in a certain place. Whatever happened as factual and meaningful in history can be examined by historical reason. Pannenberg will have nothing to do with those positivists who split up facts and evaluations; every event brings its own meaning and admittedly some events are vague in meaning while others have more clarity. But it is only when the original unity of event and meaning is grasped together that one can deal with the historicity of Jesus' resurrection. (*TH*, p. 127) It follows that all talk about the presence of Jesus in the church is based on the conviction that Jesus was resurrected from the dead. Hence, in the first instance, the facticity and meaning of the resurrection is historical in nature and therefore reason settles one way or the other that it did or did not happen.

But does this mean that faith is superficial and that God's revelation in Christ is a matter of knowledge? Pannenberg rejects such an alternative, faith or knowledge. One cannot know God's revelation in Jesus Christ without believing but faith does not take the place of reason. Rather, faith has its basis in an event that is a matter of knowledge, and acquisition of such knowledge requires adequate information. Truth requires as much; hence, the logical presupposition of the knowledge of Jesus' resurrection from the dead is the basis of faith. The historical resurrection of Jesus is a matter to be settled by reason, but such reason leads on to faith: "Knowledge is not a stage beyond faith but leads into faith and the more exact it is the more certainly it does so." (*TH*, p. 124) Again, in the knowledge of Jesus' history one is led to faith, to trust in God's future. But then is salvation dependent on reason or knowledge? Not so, argues Pannenberg. If one understands through historical knowledge or reason the resurrection of Jesus then one can accept this act of God's grace and by faith be drawn into God's future which imparts salvation. In short, "faith can breathe freely only when it is certain, even in the field of scientific (historical) research, that its foundation is true." (*TH*, p. 131)

Pannenberg would insist that this is a continuation of the Old Testament understanding of history and that the resurrection is to be known in the same way. It is through the events of history that God has made himself known. Thus, as reason can understand the historical events of the Torah, so it can understand the historical events of the resurrection. It was the conviction of Israel that "all history is wrought by Yahweh and that through reason one could come to recognize the revelatory action of God." (*TH*, p. 131) Hence, Pannenberg would be more circumspect than is Lapide in the relation of reason and faith and would not claim that the resurrection is to be apprehended by faith only but rather reason can establish the historical event of the resurrection and salvation grows out of that event. It is here that we encounter a deep difference between the two and this is revealed in our third question, namely, what are the evidences for the resurrection of Jesus?

III. The Evidence of the Resurrection

Of the two fundamental events, the cross and the resurrection, it is the resurrection that is most important, for, as we have noted, Lapide says, "without the experience of the resurrection, the crucifixion of

Jesus would most likely have remained without consequences and forgotten" like so many other Jews had experienced. Yet it is precisely this event that generates so much skepticism, and the reason is the "conflicts" that lie in the accounts themselves. What are these conflicts and how do they affect the overall credibility of the resurrection?

For Lapide, the empty tomb is typical of the incongruities that surround the account of the resurrection. While Matthew tells of a guard at the tomb, Mark is silent at this point. In Mark the women meet an angel who sits quietly in the empty tomb; however, in Matthew the angels come down from heaven and cause the guards to fall down as dead. In Mark three women come to the tomb; in Matthew there are only two. (*RJ*, p. 28) In Matthew they meet the angels in front of the tomb while in Mark they encounter the angel inside of the tomb. (*RJ*, p. 38) Again, all four gospels record that it was women who found the tomb open and empty and report this to the apostles. But Jewish tradition claims that women are incapable of valid testimony, as we have noted before. Furthermore, the women were "amazed, astonished, excited" and their words seemed an idle tale. (*RJ*, p. 96) Finally, Paul, the earliest author of the New Testament does not seem to have knowledge of the empty tomb. With this criss-cross of testimony concerning the historical resurrection, the reporting at least diminishes the evidence. Add to these that not fewer than a dozen "nature deities, heroes, philosophers, and rulers who, all long before Jesus, suffered, died, and rose again on the third day so that the skepticism of most non-Chrisitians can be easily understood . . . Oris dies on 17 Athyss; the discovery and revivification of his body follows in the night of the 19th; . . . the death of Attis is celebrated 22 March, his return to life probable on 25 March; . . . the day of the resurrection of Adonis is not certain, but the third day is probable." (*RJ*, pp. 40–41) In short, the case for the resurrection of Jesus rests on very tenous historical grounds.

The second line of evidence concerning the resurrection is the appearances of the resurrected Christ to individuals. Again, the conflict of evidence stands out: in Luke 24:34 the disciples speak of an appearance to Peter but in Matthew the appearance took place in Galilee. Luke has the appearance to the disciples in Jerusalem on Easter Sunday. Paul seems to think that all of the appearances were from heaven but Luke has the risen Lord walking on the earth. (*RJ*, pp. 35–36) The resurrection picture of the appearance is indeed a varied one. Jesus appears to individuals, a couple of disciples, a small group, a large crowd, to mostly men but also women. Again, the locations vary: in the open air, now in a house, before the gates of the city, in Jerusalem, a Judean village, on the shores of Lake Gennesaret, in the hill country of Galilee, one even outside Palestine. The earliest accounts are the shortest; Paul gives four sentences whereas Mark, decades later, gives eight; Matthew expands this to 20 verses and Luke to 53 verses while the fourth gospel devotes two chapters to it. Lapide concludes that the later the report the more the narrative and the more colorful becomes the description. (*RJ*, p. 39) Furthermore, Jesus seems only to appear to Jews; why did he not appear also to outsiders and opponents and especially the people as a whole? argues Celsus. (*RJ*, p. 40) Hence, there has never been a lack of plausible, historical objections to the resurrection.

Because of the irregularities, the conflicts, and the incongruities in the historical record, Lapide wishes to point out against these purely "logical" counter-arguments that this is to view the evidence in too restricted a manner. It is to overlook the Jewish way of seeing reality and of understanding facticity. In short, it overlooks faith and lacks empathy with the Jewish locus of the Easter event. He then catalogs the resurrections in Judaism, which we have already noted, and insists that faith in the resurrection is as old as Judaism itself. (*RJ*, p. 55) All of Israel shares in the future world. The Pharisees had a lively faith in the resurrection and it was this faith that prepared the Jews for the acceptance of the resurrection of Jesus. Furthermore, there was a connection between the verified resurrections of Judaism, which we have noted, and the hoped for resurrection of all the dead. (*RJ*, p. 61) This was the precondition of Paul on the road to Damascus. (*RJ*, p. 62) It was not the Sadducees or skeptics or atheists that prepared the way for the acceptance of the resurrection, but the Pharisees. Hence, it is faith that lies at the heart of the Jewish religion, the faith in God who acts in the events of history and the faith in the resurrection of the dead that points to and confirms the resurrection of Jesus.

We now turn to Pannenberg with the question: What are the evidences of the resurrection of Jesus? For Pannenberg, the Easter tradition divides into two different traditions: the discovery of the empty tomb and the appearance of Jesus. (*JGM*, p. 88) The gospel tradition seeks to draw these traditions together: Mark still holds to the account of the empty tomb; Luke has both the empty tomb and the appearances; John allows the appearances to take place at the tomb. But it stands that Mark has only the empty tomb and Paul has only the appearances; hence, they are separate traditions. The earliest literary account is Paul's, but the earliest historical event is the empty tomb. I shall follow Pannenberg's procedure in dealing first with the appearances and then the empty tomb.

The earliest record we have of the appearances of the resurrected

Christ comes from Paul, 1 Corinthians 15:1–11, where he enumerates six appearances: to Peter, to the twelve, to five hundred Christian brethren, to James the brother of Jesus, to all the apostles and finally to Paul himself. (*JGM*, p. 89) Why does Paul give this catalog of appearances? Because he wishes to give proof of the facticity or historicity of the resurrection. Furthermore, the Pauline report has two unique qualities: (1) the person of Paul and (2) the age of the formula. (*JGM*, p. 90) First, if Paul's conversion is to be dated, from the information in Gal. 1, in about A.D. 33–35 and if Jesus' death is to be put about A.D. 30, then Paul was in Jerusalem between six and eight years after the resurrection events. (*JGM*, p. 90) Hence, Paul is very close to the events themselves and his reference to James may come from this period. Secondly, Paul uses formulations that were coined previously, perhaps within five years after the resurrection. It is through these collected formulations that Paul intends to prove the resurrection. Was Paul influenced by the cults of the dying and rising gods? No. There is not the slightest trace of such mythology in first century Palestine. (*JGM*, p. 91) Paul assumes that the appearances that he experienced were the same as those that were experienced by the others. What elements were involved in the appearances to Paul?

There was first the appearance of Jesus to Paul, "God was pleased to reveal His son to me." (Galatians 1:16) The appearance of the man Jesus was very clear to Paul, and he witnessed him as the Lord Jesus Christ. Secondly, Paul witnessed a spiritual body, a *soma pneumatikon*, on the road to Damascus, not an earthly body. Thirdly, the appearance was from "on high," in heaven, and the encounter did not take place on earth; hence, the resurrection and Jesus' departure into heaven coincide. Fourthly, Paul's account and the Acts account are not identical. Hence, where both speak of Paul's experience, then we should accept Paul's own account over the secondary material of Acts. Lastly, the experience included audition. (*JGM*, pp. 92–93) In every case Paul recognized Jesus of Nazareth. Hence, the conclusion is that Jesus has been raised from the dead.

Paul does not mention the empty tomb; hence, this constitutes a separate tradition. The empty tomb belongs to the fate of the crucified one. The shortness of the time between the burial and the resurrection had little interest to Paul, even if he was aware of the tradition. But it did have interest to the Jerusalem Christians. How could Jesus' disciples proclaim the resurrection if they could be refuted merely by viewing the grave in which his body was interred? In short, the resurrection kerygma could not have withstood the Jerusalem audience for a "single day, a single hour" if the emptiness of the tomb had not been established as an historical fact. (*JGM*, p. 100) The trustworthiness of the report of the empty tomb is confirmed by the silence of the Jewish polemic. If the tomb was not empty then the Jewish polemic would have had every interest in preserving that fact. But it shared the conviction of its Christian opponents that Jesus' grave was empty. (*JGM*, p. 101)

The conclusion Pannenberg reaches is: "If the appearance tradition and the grave tradition came into existence independently" they mutually complement one another in the assertion of the reality of Jesus' resurrection. Furthermore, one can argue that the discovery of the empty tomb was the cause of the disciples going to Galilee. (*JGM*, pp. 105–106)

We may draw the following conclusions: whereas for Lapide the conflicting historical testimony weakens the evidence and this must be taken into account; for Pannenberg the overwhelming positive evidence deduced speaks for the resurrection of Jesus. Lapide's emphasis is on the conflicts and irregularities; Pannenberg's is on the positive power of the traditions of the appearances and the empty tomb to confirm the resurrection of Jesus. For Lapide this would confirm that the acceptance of the resurrection is a matter of faith; for Pannenberg reason can examine the historical evidence, the appearances and the empty tomb, and confirm from this the historical resurrection of Jesus upon which faith itself can rest. The proof of Paul in 1 Corinthians 15 seems to follow this procedure. Since the resurrection is an historical event, then reason can and must ascertain the historical evidence. Faith, in the Jewish-Christian tradition of a God who acts, who reveals himself in the events of history, calls for such confirmation. Lastly, it is to be noted that whereas Lapide places his emphasis on the gospels with their conflicts and irregularities, he places secondary importance on Paul's account. Pannenberg does just the opposite. It is Paul's account that is primary and the gospel accounts are secondary.

Both Lapide and Pannenberg accept the resurrection of Jesus. Their sharpest difference is in the interpretation of the significance of the resurrection. If Jesus has been raised from the dead, then of what significance and importance is this to Lapide? And the same question can be asked of Pannenberg. We now turn to our final question: What are the consequences of the resurrection of Jesus?

IV. The Consequences of Jesus' Resurrection

Lapide has argued that the resurrection of the dead is to be understood in Israel's covenant with God and that we apprehend the resurrection through faith in the God who acts in history. It is the "unquestionable power of faith" (*RJ*, p. 106) that allows one to hear and accept the resurrection of Jesus. The whole burden of the New Testament is "but a single grandiose effort to unriddle the death of Jesus in the sense of faith" and through the resurrection God has the last word. But what are the consequences of believing in the resurrection? What cash value does it have in God's plan for salvation? Lapide holds that Jesus belongs to the *preparation messianica* (*RJ*, p. 153) Like all the other resurrections in the history of Israel, the resurrection of Jesus belongs to that messianic preparation for the full salvation of people that lies in the future. Put otherwise, whatever belongs to the messianic preparation belongs to the history of the final salvation of God. The resurrection of Jesus belongs to the messianic preparation and there-fore, the resurrection of Jesus belongs to the history of the final salvation of God. So the messianic expectation of salvation is not connected to the resurrection of Jesus.

In other words, the resurrection of Jesus does not make Jesus the Messiah for Israel. Nor does the testimony of the resurrection give any proof of the messiahship of Jesus. Lapide's confession is clear: "I therefore can accept neither the messiahship of Jesus for the people of Israel nor the Pauline interpretation of the resurrection of Jesus." (*RJ*, p. 153) Hence, Lapide can say yes to the resurrection of Jesus, but he also says no to the messianic claim of Jesus. Here there is a definite parting of the way, even more serious than the conflict over faith and reason. Lapide looks forward to the coming of the Messiah, for if Jesus was the Messiah, then how do we explain the world in which we live? Where is the golden age of the Messiah in our world today? How can people continue to hope for goodness and justice in a world that remains inhumane and alienated from God? "Indeed, this world remains un-saved and we are still suffering in it." (*RJ*, p. 146) But then is there no significance in the resurrection of Jesus and have Christians been fooled all these years? Not quite! God has used the resurrection of Jesus as a means of preaching to the Gentiles or the whole world.

"The experience of the resurrection is the foundation of the church that has carried faith in the God of Israel into the whole Western world and must belong to God's plan for salvation." (*RJ*, p. 142) In other words, whatever message of God reaches the whole world is a part of God's plan for world salvation. The resurrection of Jesus reaches the whole world through the missionary work of Christians and therefore the resurrection is a part of God's world plan for salvation. Hence, the salvation that Christianity offers is a valid way of salvation but it is also a "preparation messianica" in agreement with "Isaiah (42:6, 49:6),

Jeremiah (4:2), and Zephaniah (3:9) which would result in the universal conversion of all people to God . . ." (*RJ*, p. 143) Since the foundation of Christianity is based on the resurrection and since this is a part of the salvation history of Israel than the Easter faith has to be recognized as part of God's providential plan. Hence, there is a common hope between the Jews and Christians but there is also separation: the Jews can accept Good Friday and the resurrection of Jesus, but they cannot accept that the resurrected Jesus is the Messiah. The Christian on the other hand believes that the resurrected Christ is the Messiah. Let us now turn to Pannenberg's position.

Pannenberg has argued that the self-revelation of God is brought about indirectly by means of the historical acts of God (*TH*, p. 125) and that the resurrection of Jesus is a self-revelation of God and therefore the resurrection is an historical act of God's. Furthermore, the historical revelation has a universal character open to anyone who has eyes to see. (*TH*, p. 135) The resurrection is an historical event and as such can be examined as all other historical events. The universal revelation of God is first realized in the fate of Jesus since in Jesus the end of all events are anticipated. (*TH*, p. 139) Since the resurrection of Jesus is a universal revelation of God, then the fate of Jesus and the resurrection of Jesus anticipates this summing up of history in God. But the Christ event reveals God as a part of the history of Israel (*TH*, p. 145) and therefore the resurrection is to be understood in the light of the history of Israel. Indeed, it is a part of that history. But another step is needed, namely, the universality of God's self-vindication in Jesus Christ comes to expression in the Gentile Christian Church. (*TH*, p. 149) The resurrection is God's self-vindication in Christ and therefore, the universality of the eschatological revelation of God in the resurrection of Jesus comes to actual expression in Gentile Christianity. In terms of this history of revelation, what significant conclusions does Pannenberg draw for the resurrection of Jesus?

"If Jesus has been raised from the dead, then the end of the world has begun." (*JGM*, p. 67) This means that the universal resurrection of all has been anticipated in Christ for the same spirit of God that dwelt in Jesus now dwells in Christians. Whoever participates in the spirit of Jesus participates in the resurrection of the new age. Christians are those who participate in the spirit of Jesus and therefore they participate in the resurrection of the new age.

A second consequence of significance concerning Jesus' resurrection is, "if Jesus has been raised, this for a Jew can only mean that God himself has confirmed the pre-Easter activity of Jesus." (*JGM*, p. 67) The Jew cannot take this event as one that happens apart from the will of

God. Whatever, therefore, is of the character of the resurrection comes about in terms of the God of Israel. The resurrection of Jesus occurred and therefore it came about as the result of God's power. This also suggests that the life of Jesus is to be read backward, that is, in light of the resurrection the life and the ministry of Jesus is to be understood.

Through the resurrection the man Jesus will come again since in the resurrection Jesus is identified as the Son of Man. (*JGM*, p. 68) The fullness of the resurrection revelation does not take place until the end. There is a difference in the disciples apprehension of Jesus as the Son of Man before and after the resurrection. Before Jesus is the teacher, the healer, the Messiah walking upon the earth but afterward Jesus is the Son of Man that is in heaven and is expected in the future. Hence, through the resurrection Jesus as the Son of Man takes on a new role.

A fourth significance of the resurrection is that "if Jesus has been raised from the dead, is ascended to God and if thereby the end of the world has begun, then God is ultimately revealed in Jesus." (*JGM*, p. 69) We have seen that in the resurrection the end of history is prolyptically revealed. In Jesus as the Messiah, God has appeared to people with salvation. Whoever shares in the resurrection of Jesus shares in the universal salvation at the end-time of God. Christians, and implicitly all people, share or can share in the resurrection and therefore all can share in the universal salvation at God's end-time. It is this hope that gave motivation to the Gentile mission where the eschatological resurrection of Jesus, the resurrection of the crucified one, provides a meaningful universal salvation history. It is the fulfillment of the universalistic line of the Israelite tradition that the resurrection of Jesus is or continues to be the good news of God to all people. The words of the risen Christ get their meaning and significance from the resurrection of Jesus. (*JGM*, p. 72) The unifying factor of the revelation of God in the resurrection of Jesus brings about the actual possibility of universal salvation.

V. Summary and Evaluations

It may be well briefly and succinctly to draw together the various points of comparisons so that we might see wherein there is agreement and, more importantly, wherein there are differences between Lapide and Pannenberg. The last point is important in pointing us forward into further dialogue with one another. We shall follow the outline above.

The first question we dealt with was in terms of the notion of the resurrection of the dead. Both of our authors show that resurrection is part of the Israelite covenant history with God although there is some variation. Whereas Lapide tends to equate resuscitation and resurrection, we noted that Pannenberg makes a distinction: A resuscitated body presumably dies again, but the resurrection of Jesus brings with it a new spiritual body for the new age. Hence, resuscitation and resurrection are not synonymous for Pannenberg. But both of them feel that resurrection is an act of God and thus dependent on God. And whereas Lapide dealt with the early history of Israel, Pannenberg stresses Israel's eschatological history after the return from Exile. Though there are differences here, they can be overcome. Pannenberg does mention the resuscitations in the New Testament and would presumably accept the ones that Lapide enumerates. Also, Lapide is aware of the eschatological expectation around the time of Jesus. Both agree that the resurrection is an historical event wrought by God. On the first question, then, the agreement is significant, and the differences, with the exception of the spiritual body, are not serious.

The second question concerning the apprehension of the resurrection showed more serious divergences. For Lapide, the resurrection is a matter of faith, faith in the God who acts in history. One may interpret that faith, but faith stands as the first response to the historical action of God. For Pannenberg the resurrection is an historical happening and as such is open to the investigations of historical scholarship. Reason can establish whether or not such an event happened, and faith must base itself upon what did or did not happen. This is not a matter for faith; faith flows out of the answer to the rational question of the meaning and truth of the historical event. Yet for both men faith and reason are important, although they place them differently—Pannenberg claiming that reason can examine the historical evidences and reach reasonable conclusions of what did or did not happen, and Lapide claiming that faith is the first response to the event, at this point the event of the resurrection. Here, I think, Pannenberg gives the more persuasive case in that he is able to show *where* reason is to be used and *how* faith is to be based. Lapide gives the overwhelming weight to the role of faith in historical investigation. One accepts what has happened and then one reasons about it. But what happened is the question. Reason can come to conclusions about just that question independent of a faith commitment to the record. This leads to the third question concerning the evidences of the resurrection.

We noted that the evidences for the resurrection were the empty tomb and the appearances. Lapide concentrates his attention on the conflict of evidence in both cases. He examines the gospel accounts and is able to point up the variations, but he does not have the same argument with Paul. Most of the times he lumps Paul's account with the gospels. He is more severe in terms of the evidences of the empty tomb than he is of the appearances. But the conflicts and variations for Lapide speak against the power of the historical evidence. Such a confused evidence does not speak with power to the mind. But beyond these "logical methods," Lapide insists that the Jewish way of faith stands out as the way of accepting God's action in the resurrection. Because the resurrection cannot rest on reason, it must rest on faith. The must of the resurrection is grounded in faith of the God who acts in history. One can accept the act of God in history—and the resurrection is such an act—and then one can think or reason about it. Here, faith precedes reason.

For Pannenberg, since the resurrection is an historical event, then reason can examine the objective evidence of this event. It can examine the evidence of the empty tomb and the evidence of the appearances of Jesus. He is careful to lay out Paul's case for the resurrection and to claim that they are historically more reliable than the gospels. Paul appeals to eye witnesses and his own life comes very close to the resurrection of Jesus. Hence, the historical evidence of the resurrection appearances is very strong. And the case for the empty tomb is also strong. The Jews (and here Lapide would agree) do not deny the empty tomb. In short, the methodological difference of faith and reason between Pannenberg and Lapide shows up strongly here. And more work needs to be done in order to resolve this difference. It will be a matter of determining what is historical evidence, how it is to be critically examined, and what conclusions can be reached.

It is in terms of the consequences of the resurrection that the greatest differences arise, namely, for Lapide the resurrection of Jesus occurred, but Jesus is not the Messiah nor is salvation connected to Jesus' resurrection. For Pannenberg, the resurrected Christ is the Messiah whose message is universal salvation. Lapide does give recognition to the missionary role of Christianity, but this is to proclaim the God of Israel and the Messiah is yet to come. For Pannenberg there is a second coming, the general resurrection, but this is already proleptically revealed in the resurrection of Jesus who is the Messiah. So it is a Jew who stands between Judaism and Christianity, Jesus.

But we must press further. What can the Christian learn about the expectations of the Messiah from the Jews? And what can the Jew learn about the Messiah from Christians? If we are in earnest about our transcreative dialogue with the Jews, then we must learn to listen to what they understand in terms of the messianic hope and the same would apply to the Jews hearing Christians. It is not a question we can take lightly and one that must be explored seriously if progress between the two concerning the resolution of differences that block mutual understanding on the different perspectives of the Messiah is to be adequately dealt with. Due to the rhetoric between the parent and the child, much has been screened out and here the child is mostly at fault. But what is it that we can learn as Christians and what is it that Jews can learn through a mutual dialogue that will lead to transcreation? I would suggest two things: the Messiah and salvation. I would further suggest that both of these leads us to learn something about God. And it is here that I think process thought can help us to clarify what we mean by God, how we might re-think the notion of the Messiah and further understand salvation, incarnation, and resurrection.

Throughout the history of the Jews there had been a powerful affirmation of the God who works in their history. Paul noted that "God has not deserted his people" and that to them belong the "covenant, the promises, the law, the patriarchs," in short, they are "God's chosen people." (Romans 9:4–5) As Christians we need to learn again that God is a faithful God and that the covenant is grounded in God. Whatever meaning in relation to death, whatever power there is to overcome that death in history is to be seen in the resurrection that belongs to God. The resurrection of Jesus is the resurrection by God. In other words, the resurrection calls forth faith in a God that even raises the dead— remember the words of Jesus to the Sadducees that God is a God of the living, not of the dead, Mt. 23:32—but it also calls forth reason to examine what did or did not happen in history, such as Paul's account of the resurrection in 1 Cor. 15. Now here process thought can help us, for it holds that God is active in every event in history and each event is provided its initial aim from God. (*PR*, pp. 224, 244) That aim can be resisted, rejected, or followed by persons. Since novelty of aims are given by God to each occasion and since this is to be understood within the events of history, then the question of the resurrection cannot be ruled out *a priori*. The historical course of events has an indeterminacy, an emergence of something new that is not traceable to previous events. It is in light of novelty, newness that one understands the resurrection, and the surprise, the amazement, and the puzzlement—as well as the doubts—of the disciples.

But what do the Jews expect in the Messiah? There were many interpretations to this, both in the days of Jesus and now. Some felt that the Messiah would be a political leader like David and that the nation of Israel would be restored to the golden age. Some looked for a Messiah that would destroy the earth and set up the new kingdom and felt that man would assist in this process such as believed by those at Qumran or the zealots at Mazada. There were others who looked for a golden age in which suffering would be done away with and in which God's rule would right wrongs. There is a utopianism, expressed by both Lapide and Pannenberg, that I feel is incongruent with the nature of God. If God is essentially creative and creates creators as process theology holds, then the tragedies in life, which are also in God, result from the conflicting decisions of beings.

In a society of free individuals in conflict, we must add that it is the "bad" decisions that good people make that constitute the greatest evil, the most tragic of wrongs. Hence, both the cross and the resurrection must be taken together if we are to understand the Messiah and the salvation that he brings. But according to process thought these tragedies are also tragedies in God, and God would be happier if, for instance, Pilate had not made the final decision to crucify Jesus or Hitler had not made the decision to kill the Jews. And God suffered the loss and tragedy more than we.

But can the Jews learn something from the messianic understanding of the Christians? Ultimately, they must answer this question for themselves. In Christianity, there have been a variety of understandings from "heaven beyond the grave" to the experience of the presence of the spirit of Christ now. There have been all too many exclusive theories that have bred a sense of privilege.

In process thought God and the world constitute the final interpretation. (*PR*, p. 341) It is the understanding of the nature of God and the nature of the world in mutual relationship that is called for. The religious problem is how can order in novelty fail to add up to loss or how can process not entail ultimate perishing? God and the world constitute the final evaluation bearing on this question. The various elements in this answer would include God, salvation, incarnation, resurrection, and the kingdom of God. A brief word on each of these will show how process theology transforms the question as well as the answer of the resurrection.

How are we to understand the nature of God? The nature of God, analogous to all actual entities, is dipolar. (*PR*, p. 345) God is primordial and consequent. The primordial aspect of God's nature is conceptual and it embraces "the unlimited conceptual realization of the absolute wealth of potentiality." (*PR*, p. 343) In terms of this side of God's nature, deity is the "lure for feeling," the "eternal urge of desire" which constantly confronts the creative advance of the world. For each occasion of experience God provides an initial aim which determines for that occasion what possibilities are relevant and what actualities are appropriate. Hence, the subjective form is determined by the subjective aim. Each occasion also has a subjective aim and it is the interaction and integration of the two that finally provides the satisfaction of the occasion of experience. This is God's primary action on the world. But God is also consequent, hence, deity is not only the beginning but also the end of the creative act. But in between the beginning and the end, there is room for the self-determination or creation of the individual entity. When each occasion is complete it perishes or becomes a part of the immediate past and that immediate past is the consequent nature of God. The moment dies, the present perishes and yet lives forevermore in the consequent nature of God.

It is in this way that God saves the world. The deeper tragedy of life would be that what perishes is lost forever. But in the consequent nature of God this problem is solved for God cherishes the creations of the world. Each value event, whatever that value may have been, whether trivial or great, is preserved. Hence, the salvation of each event is incarnated in the nature of God. As incarnate in God it lives forevermore. It becomes a living reality and loss is not the last word. God becomes incarnate in the world through the deity's aims, lures for feelings and eternal urge of desire to achieve more and more value. But the world, and more particularly, each event of each society of actual occasions of experience becomes incarnate in God, hence, to be a part of the divine nature forever.

But there is another element in this divine operation, namely, resurrection. We die and yet are resurrected to newness of life that is everlasting. In terms of our topic, Jesus died on the cross, but was resurrected by God never to die again. The resurrection is to be understood in light of the nature of God, God's incarnation and God's preservation of each individual in the supreme's nature. In this way the resurrection is the resurrection by God of that which perishes. In this way, the resurrection is completed by the incarnation of life in God. Both resurrection and incarnation are understood as historical. Both happen in history, but they also go beyond the empirical limitations of history. Hence, historical evidence for the resurrection of Jesus the Christ are important for the evaluation of that event. And both resurrection and incarnation can be understood in terms of reason and faith, faith and reason. In terms of reason and faith we look to the historical occurrence of the resurrection and evaluate the evidence. In terms of faith and reason we look to God who is absolute yet everlasting in nature.

This is the kingdom of God which is not simple future but is with us today. As Jesus indicated, the kingdom of God is within us now. (Luke 17) Within the kingdom all values are preserved and neither rust nor moth can degenerate them. What is accomplished lives forevermore. Each value that is created out of the possibilities and the physical actualities or the future and the past is resurrected into the kingdom of God where it is incarnated forevermore. What is done is done and nothing can erase it. But more can be actualized. The creative phases of actuality show that God is the "conceptual origination" which is "infinite in its adjustment of valuation." (*PR*, p. 350) There is then the temporal phase of physical origination from the past which is determined by the first phase. Thirdly, there follows integration and actualization in which the "many become one everlastingly." The fourth phase is the completion or satisfaction. It passes into God's consequent nature or the kingdom of God. This reality then passes back into the world. This is the love of God for the world. Hence, what is resurrected into the kingdom of God passes back into the world and qualifies it. (*PR*, p. 350–351)

The kingdom of God is present, but we also look to a future hope of its coming. The presence of God furnishes the ground of hope, both in the present and future, that evil or destruction is not the last word. And within the kingdom of God we can understand the resurrection. All individuals live and die and yet are resurrected to a newness of life forevermore in the kingdom of God. It seems to me that this is a fruitful direction for spiritual speculation to take. The Messiah is not to be conceived in a utopian way, but rather, as realized now and in the future. So if there is a tragic element in God's love, and if perfection means perfectability, then there is no final goal, no once-for-all achievement. For every value achieved, more value *can* be achieved. This supplies a hope for every future moment. Again, "what is done in the world is transformed into a reality in heaven, and the reality in heaven passes back into the world. By reason of this reciprocal relation, the love of the world passes into the love in heaven, and floods back again into the world. In this sense, God is the great companion—the fellow-sufferer who understands." (*PR*, p. 351) The resurrection is a vital part of the incarnation of God in the world and the world in God. This is a part of what is meant by the resurrection joy in the messianic salvation brought about in the kingdom of God.

One can hope that the dialogue between the parent and the child may increase and that it will bear much fruit toward mutual understanding and transcreative value. Discussion of the event of the resurrection and the resurrection faith is a giant step in the right direction. May we be given time to persist, patience to endure, reason to search and faith to hope that new understandings and new forms of reconciliation are not merely dreams or wishful thinking, but a living reality within the family of God.

References

The references in this paper are abbreviated as follows:

RJ — Pinchas Lapide, *The Resurrection of Jesus*. Minneapolis, Augsburg Publishing House, 1983.

JGM — Wolfhart Pannenberg, *Jesus: God and Man*. Philadelphia, Westminister Press, 1968.

TH — Edited by James M. Robinson and John B. Cobb, Jr., *Theology as History*. New York, Harper & Row, 1967.

PR — Alfred North Whitehead, *Process and Reality*, Corrected Edition. New York, The Free Press, 1978.

Faith As a Creative Act: Kierkegaard and Lequier on the Relation of Faith and Reason

Donald Wayne Viney

Soren Kierkegaard (1813–1855) is well known for his contributions to philosophy. Jules Lequier (1814–1862), a French contemporary of Kierkegaard, attracts less scholarly attention than the Dane, but displays a comparable genius in his philosophy. Lequier has been called "the French Kierkegaard," indicating that there are striking parallels between these thinkers (OC ix-xi).[1] The parallels are the more remarkable in light of the fact that neither of these men knew of the other's work. While such comparisons are interesting, this paper examines the dissimilarites between their views of the relation of faith and reason.* Specifically, I argue that Kierkegaard's insistence on the primacy of passionate inwardness in faith is not incompatible with some degree of objective certainty about God. Lequier provides the model for the reconciliation of reason and a passionate faith by seeing faith as a creative act. This view opens the way to reasoned knowledge of God, while allowing for the passionate inwardness stressed by Kierkegaard. Thus, I am as much concerned to compare Kierkegaard and Lequier as to "maintain a proper balance between reason and faith and delimit their domains" (PJ 197).

---

*The position on the relation of faith and reason which I attribute to Kierkegaard is found mainly in the *Philosophical Fragments* and the *Concluding Unscientific Postscript*, both written under the pseudonym of "Johannes Climacus." For those who heed, with more caution than I, Kierkegaard's warning that "not a single word" in the pseudonymous works are his (CUP 551), it is necessary only to substitute "Johannes Climacus" for "Kierkegaard." It is enough for my purpose that the views expressed in the *Fragments* and the *Postscript* are interesting and important and therefore bear examination.

Kierkegaard on Faith and Reason

Kierkegaard's views of the relation of faith and reason were forged in the philosophical climate of Hegelian Idealism. It is in terms of this backdrop that the Kierkegaardian opposition of faith to reason must be understood. For it is not reason *per se* that Kierkegaard opposes to faith, but only reason as embodied in idealist philosophy (KE). Kierkegaard resisted the Hegelian ambition to subsume Christianity within idealistic metaphysics. Although in some moods Kierkegaard praises the accomplishments of speculative philosophy and even holds Hegel in admiration (CUP 54), he argues that Christian faith is neither inferior to nor secondary to reason. According to Kierkegaard, Christianity is the opposite of speculative philosophy.

> Christianity is not a doctrine, but an existential communication expressing an existential contradiction. If Christianity were a doctrine, it would *eo ipso* not be an opposite to speculative thought, but rather a phase within it. Christianity has to do with existence, with the act of existing; but existence and existing constitute precisely the opposite of speculation (CUP 339).

Christianity is not, for Kierkegaard, a series of propositions to be understood, but a call to live in light of what is scandalous to reason, that is, that the eternal came into being in time—the incarnation. For this reason, it is "the highest pitch of misunderstanding" to attempt to understand Christianity speculatively (CUP 339).

SUBJECTIVE TRUTH. This is not say that Kierkegaard denies the truth of his religion. But the truth is not embodied in formalized creeds or in idealist philosophy. For Kierkegaard, truth in religion "requires that the individual should existentially venture all." To venture all is to take a risk, even when the chances of success are small. To venture all *existentially* is to commit one's life, not merely one's intellectual assent, on the chances for success (KA). Christianity involves this risk but it also involves something more. What sets Christianity apart from other religions is that it requires the individual to "believe against the understanding (CUP 384). The central message of Christianity is the incarnation, which Kierkegaard believes to require the contradiction that the eternal came to be in time.* The truth of Christianity must be the antithesis of what can be grasped intellectually by the speculative philosopher.

Kierkegaard elaborates on the concept of truth in his celebrated distinction between being "in the truth" objectively or subjectively (CUP 179-180). To be "in the truth" objectively is to give one's assent to a true proposition. The objectivity of the truth stems from the irrelevance of the knowing subject. Thus, objective truth concerns the WHAT of what is believed. One cannot be "in the truth" objectively unless the WHAT—the object of one's belief—is true. To be "in the truth" subjectively is to be directed toward the object with what Kierkegaard calls "the passion of the infinite." According to Robert Adams, this means that one's interest in something is so strong that it leads one to make the greatest possible sacrifices in order to obtain it on the smallest possible chance of success (KA 223). What is important for subjective truth is the strength of interest; it concerns the HOW of the relationship between knower the object known.

In religion it is subjective truth which is paramount. Objectively one may be concerned, for example, to find the most coherent and religiously satisfying concept of God, one is concerned with the WHAT of worship. Subjectively one is concerned with one's relationship to God (however God is conceived); the HOW of worship becomes important. For Kierkegaard, speculation about God is insignificant when compared to a passionate faith in God. It is better, he says, to worship an idol "with the entire passion of the infinite" than to worship God in a "false spirit" (CUP 180). A passionate paganism is better than an indifferent orthodoxy.

Objectively, there are two categories, the true and the false, or theologically, the true God and idols. Subjectively there is also a true and a false; one may worship with "the entire passion of the infinite" or in a "false spirit." The following diagram illustrates the possibilities.

Subjectivity (HOW)	*Objectivity* (WHAT)
(1) passion of the infinite	The true God
(2) false spirit	
(3) passion of the infinite	Idols
(4) false spirit	

---

*Kierkegaard speaks freely of God's having come to be in time as a contradiction (PF 108-109). Elsewhere he distinguishes (a) the contradiction within immanence of basing one's eternal happiness upon the relation to something historical and (b) the contradiction that the eternal "comes into existence in time, is born, grows up, and dies" (CUP 513). This second meaning of contradiction is a "breach with all thinking." I take this to mean that it is a logical contradiction to assert both that God is eternal and that God comes to be in time. Thomas Morris' *The Logic of God Incarnate* is an interesting, albeit unkierkegaardian, attempt to circumvent this apparent contradiction (LI 62-70).

Kierkegaard's example of the passionate pagan makes clear that he believes that (3) is better than (2). It is better to worship a false god in a true spirit than to worship the true God in a false spirit. It follows that (3) is better than (4). If subjectivity is what counts in religion, then one is better off worshiping a false god in a true spirit than in a false spirit. Similarly, (1) is better than (2). The principle Kierkegaard implicitly adopts is that it is always better to be subjectively in the truth, even if the object of one's worship happens to be an idol. Nothing in Kierkegaard's discussion, to this point, demands a preference of (1) over (3). However, Judaism and Christianity prohibit the worship of idols and the believer is enjoined to worship not only in spirit, but also in truth (Exodus 20:3 and John 4:24). This would seem to be the natural place where, in Kierkegaard's thought, speculative thought might find a humble niche. But Kierkegaard allows faith its rational partner only, as it were, through the back door.

THE USE OF REASON. There are two ways, in Kierkegaard's thought, that reason can be of service to Christianity. First, any object of worship about which one can gain objective certainty is, for that reason, an idol. The "knowlege" of God acquired through the efforts of natural theologians could be used to show what God is not. Kierkegaard could find use for the *via negativa*. Second, the Christian doctrine of the incarnation, as Kierkegaard understands it, demands the use of reason to see that it involves a contradiction (cf. PF 46-60). To understand that something is a contradiction requires the use of reason. Thus, Kierkegaard says,

> Instead of the objective uncertainty, there is here a certainty, namely, that objectively it is absurd; and this absurdity, held fast in the passion of inwardness is faith (CUP 188).

Reason may thus be allowed a place in the sphere of religion. According to Kierkegaard, "it will be the function of this speculation more and more profoundly to grasp the impossibility of understanding Christianity . . ." (CUP 338).

Reason serves Christianity by making it certain that the central doctrine of the faith is an absurdity. This is a service to the believer insofar as it shows that Christianity is not something to be understood speculatively. Moreover, the fact that objectively Christianity is absurd, makes possible the subjective inwardness of faith. According to Kierkegaard,

. . . without risk there is no faith, and the greater the risk, the greater the faith; the more objective security, the less inwardness (for inwardness is precisely subjectivity), and the less objective security, the more profound the possible inwardness (CUP 188).

Insofar as it produces objective certainty, speculation destroys the need for faith. Thus, as far as religion is concerned, the more objective uncertainty there is, the better. Since a contradiction is, so to speak, the limit of objective uncertainty, Christianity, being founded on a contradiction, allows for the greatest possible inwardness. Precisely because the incarnation is a scandal to reason, it is the most appropriate object for faith.

Kierkegaard is commonly criticized for his claim that there is an inverse relation between inwardness and objective certainly (RB 433). Many things about which one is objectively uncertain are a matter of indifference (for example, the average number of feathers on a pigeon), and many things that are matters of deep concern are objectively certain (for example, the knowledge that one has a terminal illness). However, such criticisms are not to the point. Kierkegaard is not offering an empirical generalization about inwardness and objective certainty; he is providing an analysis of the logic of faith. According to Kierkegaard, faith requires risk (CUP 182). Objective uncertainty is the corrolate of risk—the greater the uncertainty, the greater the risk. When an objective uncertainty is "held fast in an appropriation-process of the most passionate inwardness," there is truth (or faith), "the highest truth attainable by an *existing* individual" (CUP 182).

Kierkegaard's stress on a passionate faith is well founded. Where he is vulnerable is in the claim that objective uncertainty must be grounded in speculative doubt. To be more specific, there is good reason to deny that the possibility of passionate faith is guaranteed by the absurdity of the incarnation. There is nothing more certainly false than a contradiction. If, as Kierkegaard urges, the incarnation is a contradiction, then reason dictates that it is false, as certainly false as a tautology is certainly true. The very certainty of its falsity would destroy the passion that is the mark of genuine faith. The certainty of its falsity eliminates the risk that is necessary for faith. If the objective uncertainty required by faith cannot be vouchsafed by a contradiction, then Kierkegaard's argument that what is scandalous to reason provides for the greatest possible inwardness fails. However, objective uncertainty can be purchased elsewhere, and it does not cost the sacrifice of speculation. To see how this is possible, let us turn to the philosophy of Lequier.

Lequier on Faith and Reason

Lequier is more sympathetic than Kierkegaard to the claims of speculative reason but is no less emphatic in defending the passionate leap of faith. Indeed, much of Lequier's philosophy is reminiscent of Kierkegaard's. Like Kierkegaard, he found Hegel's philosophy incompatible with the existence of the free individual (EK 430), and inadequate as a vehicle for the expression of Christian ideas. The freedom required by the leap of faith he called a "scandalous rock" and a "paradox" (OC 411). Lequier cites the example of Abraham as the father of faith. In a Kierkegaardian turn of phrase, Lequier marvels at God's command to Abraham to sacrifice Isaac, "Oh subversion of all things human and divine" (OC 232). The inwardness stressed by Kierkegaard pervades Lequier's thought. As Jean Wahl says, "At the bottom of Lequier's work is the feeling of a sort of vertigo which is not unlike Kierkegaardian anguish" (EK 430).

Lequier's emphasis on subjectivity does not prevent him from speculating on the nature of God and engaging in natural theology. Here there is a parting of the ways between Lequier and Kierkegaard. For all of his aversion to Hegelianism, Lequier believes that reason can discover truths about God, truths that are at once compatible with and complementary to what Lequier took to be revealed truth (for example, the Incarnation and Redemption). For Lequier, there is a reciprocal influence between Christianity and philosophy. Jean Grenier summarizes Lequier's position.

> Metaphysics throws light on religion and this, no doubt, is the work of theology. For its part, religion confirms metaphysics since the truths laboriously proved by reason are made certain by revelation. Philosophy is itself insufficient . . . because of the stain of Adam. Faith comes, without contradicting it, to complete the work of reason (PT 197).

It is difficult to imagine Kierkegaard endorsing this kind of reconciliation of faith and reason.

CREATIVITY. Although Lequier distinguishes between the truths of reason (philosophy) and the truths of faith (Christianity), he believes that each domain requires an act of faith (PJ 196). It is beyond the scope of this paper to dwell on the dialectic that leads Lequier to this conclusion. Other commentators have ably followed Lequier's reasoning (cf. LJ, JL, and PJ). For our purposes, it is enough to note that, fundamentally, the act of faith is an example of and belief in the individual power of freedom or creativity. This is the heart of Lequier's philosophy. As Grenier says, "The philosophy of Lequier is nothing but a serious meditation on the word *create*" (PJ 210). Faith, then, is a creative act. And it is this creative act around which the whole of Lequier's philosophy and religion turn.

For Lequier, freedom or creativity (the two concepts are equivalent in Lequier's view) is the power to actualize real possibilities. Lequier is careful to explain the sense of possibility required by the free act. He distinguishes the sense of possibility that results from an ignorance of causal factors, and the kind of possibility that results from a real indetermination in the nature of things. With Lequier, let us call these two kinds of possibility, respectively, fictive and real. Says Lequier, "It would be the greatest of errors to confuse such different meanings" (OC 180).

Lequier illustrates the difference between fictive and real possibilities as follows (OC 187). Suppose a shepherd is passing the time on a hill throwing rocks. Down below a man sleeps, unaware that he might be in danger of being struck by one of the shepherd's missiles. An observer of the situation might say that the man might or might not be hit. However, if the observer had the relevant information concerning the man's position on the hill and the rock's course as determined by the laws of physics, he or she would know whether it is really possible for the man to be hit. Once a rock is thrown, its course is determined by nature's laws. The observer's ignorance permits him or her to say that the man's being hit or not hit are equally (i.e. fictively) possible. If the arc of the rock's path as described by physics ends at the man's skull, then it is a fictive, not a real possibility, that the rock will miss the sleeping man (assuming the man is not a sleep walker and remains where he is). If we think now of the shepherd's decision, we can say that he might or might not hurl the rock. In this case, there *may* be more than fictive possibilities. He throws the rock or he does not throw the rock—both really possible. In this case, it is not ignorance that makes either alternative seem possible. It is a real indetermination in the situation. The shepherd has not decided whether to throw the rock and thus the future opens onto more than one real possibility.

Lequier's account of the creative act depends on real possibility. He says, "If it is a question of a free act, we know that it is really possible not to do it" (OC 192). Fictive possibility may preserve a feeling that one is free, but it cannot insure real freedom. Lequier says that a man imprisoned in a dungeon precisely his own size might think of himself as free to go for a walk as long as he doesn't decide to take a step (OC

135). However, because he cannot budge, he is not free. Fictive possibilities only insure that one can imagine being free. For Lequier, real freedom requires real possibilities (OC 75). "I can take this determination or not take it; in this I am free" (OC 155).

Lequier says that we should guard against the temptation to ascend to the antecedents of a free act looking for the precise causes why it occurred. This kind of investigation represents a misunderstanding of freedom. Suppose a choice is made between two really possible alternatives. Why was the choice made? Because I willed one rather than the other. Why did I will one rather than the other? Because I willed one over the other. Why precisely one rather than the other? Because precisely I willed one over the other. "But that is no answer," the determinist may say. "But that is no question!" replies Lequier (OC 47). If Lequier is correct, a free act cannot, by its very nature, be exhaustively explained by antecedent conditions.

It is in this context that Lequier speaks of freedom as a miracle, in the vulgar sense of the term, as something not governed by the laws of nature (OC 400). Or again, he says that the only thing to comprehend about freedom is that it is incomprehensible (OC 401). The point is that one does not grasp the meaning of freedom by trying to understand it deterministically. The free, creative act is not merely a link in a causal chain, it sets in motion new causal chains. Thus, he says, "To act is to initiate" (OC 43).

THEOLOGY. Lequier's theology, developed in light of his philosophy of creative freedom, provides fresh insights into the concepts of divine power and knowledge. For much of classical theology, creativity, in the proper sense of the term, was a divine prerogative. God was the creator, anything else was a creature (ISA 243). Lequier says, God "has created me creator of myself" (OC 70). As Teilhard de Chardin would later say, omnipotence is not so much the power to make; it is the power to make things make themselves (CE 28). The doctrine of *imago dei* is reinterpreted accordingly. Lequier says that we are made in the image of God in the sense that "we are creators. We are more than kings [or queens]; we are Gods" (OC 398). God creates by making beings who are themselves capable of creation. Creation is a joint effort between God and the creatures.

An important consequence of Lequier's concept of omnipotence is that the creatures, by their creative acts, have effects on God. Lequier may have been the first to state unambiguously that to create something in oneself is also to create something in God. Creative freedom, if it is not illusory must have real effects, including effects on God. Human beings, by their free decisions "make a blot on the absolute which destroys the absolute" (OC 74). Again, we find Lequier denying the claims of classical theology, according to which God is unaffected by creaturely decisions (HP 83). Against the Thomists and the better part of classical theology, Lequier claims that the "relation from God to the creature is as real as the relation from the creature to God" (OC 73).

The idea of creative freedom also has consequences for the concept of God's knowledge. As we have seen, in Lequier's view, to be free is to face an indeterminate future, composed of real possibilities. Since these possibilities have yet to be actualized, not even a perfect knower could know them as already, or eternally actual. Knowledge of a free being's future can at best consist of a knowledge of the possibilities open to that being, and of the likelihood that some among those possibilities will become actual. According to Lequier, God has "conjectural" knowledge of future free decisions. Thus, he says, "Dreadful prodigy: man deliberates and God waits" (OC 71).

It would be a misunderstanding of Lequier's position to say that he believes in a God whose knowledge is limited. Lequier's God is omniscient in the most robust sense of the word. As Charles Hartshorne says,

> The point is not that God is first ignorant and then knowing, but rather that first there is no definite fact of the kind to know and then there is the fact . . . "knowing all truth" is entirely compatible with "acquiring new truths" as new realities come into being (CAP 60).

Precisely because God's knowledge is perfect, it conforms perfectly to its objects. Lequier says that God knows the past *as* past, the present *as* prsent, and the future *as* future (OC 123). The difference between divine and nondivine awareness of real possibilities is that the latter is "limited, obscure and full of errors, whereas God knows them perfectly" (OC 205).

FAITH. The consequence of Lequier's theology for the concept of faith is that faith is viewed as much more than a free leap beyond sensible evidence. It is a creative act—creative of oneself, the world, and God. This is not to say that God's existence (or the existence of oneself and the world) depends on human decisions. With Hartshorne one can distinguish existence and actuality (IO 98-99; HA 44). The fact of God's existence is unaffected by the act of faith; but God's actuality, or the particular manner in which the divine existence is realized, is affected by creaturely decisions. Although Lequier never makes the Hartshornean distinction explicitly, it provides a natural reading of his meaning. Thus, Harvey Brimmer finds three aspects of the divine distinguished in Lequier's work: the abstract and essential nature, the necessarily existent entity with this nature, and the concrete states of this being (JL 288; cf. PJ 208). It is in the concrete states of God that human creativity has an effect on the divine being.

It is evident that, for Lequier, the act of faith is no mere intellectual exercise. As for Kierkegaard, so for Lequier, faith is a movement of one's entire being in which one ventures all. What is at stake in the act of faith is nothing less than one's destiny. This is illustrated in Lequier's story of "Abel and Abel." The identical twins, Abel and Abel, are tested as to their response to the possibility of God favoring one over the other. Lequier imagines three possible outcomes to the test. In the first, the chosen Abel is puffed up with pride while his brother is jealous and angry. In the second, the chosen Abel refuses his election out of concern for his brother. In the third, the Abel who was not chosen rejoices in his brother's good fortune. Whichever outcome occurs, the two Abels discover that God's favor is based upon their responses to the test. As Lequier says, the "Book of God" is a stone engraved thus: "Your name is: What you were in the test" (OC 276). Only in the last two scenarios are the Abels triumphant, and their destinies secured. As George Seailles says, divine grace is a "call made to the freedom of those who are its object" (PI 145). In this way, Lequier develops the idea that God creates us creators of ourselves.

The momentousness of the act of faith derives from faith's creative nature, not only for one's own destiny, but also for the consequences of one's acts. In "The Hornbeam Leaf" (a short autobiographical piece that was to have been the introduction to a major work) Lequier describes a childhood experience in which he reaches for a leaf. A little bird is frightened, and takes flight only to be seized in midair by a sparrow hawk (OC 13-17). The innocent act had dire consequences of which the child could not be aware beforehand. Moreover, the consequences are forever thereafter part of the world. "Henceforth it will be eternally true that this thing is . . . (OC 210). What is done, for better or worse, is done for all time. Lequier says,

What do we know of that which is open or of that which is closed for us in the future for each of our acts, and I speak even of the least of them? No more than I know if this movement, of my hand transmits a movement, and what movement, to the extremities of Asia. How our being escapes us, especially as it expands more and more (OC 210).[2]

174

It is because of this uncertainty of what will be and the certainty that what is done cannot be undone that Lequier says that one wills only with audacity and passion (Ek 431).

Lequier and Kierkegaard

There are echoes of Lequier's vision of an open future and of a God affected by human decisions in Kierkegaard's sermon on the unchangeableness of God. Although Kierkegaard holds to the unchangeableness of God's will, he says, that God is "moved" by the most "insignificant trifle" (AKA ;470). Nothing escapes God's notice. Kierkegaard speaks of the divine memory as a perfect reservoir of accomplished fact, good and bad, "Aye, and if you do not will as [God] will, [God] remembers it unchanged for an eternity" (AKA 477). God is affected by what we do, and what we do is written permanently in the memory of God. Despite this, Kierkegaard did not take the step Lequier found necessary of saying that the future is open for God. As Kierkegaard argues in the *Postscript*, system and finality belong together, but "Existence itself is a system—for God; but it cannot be a system for an existing spirit" (CUP 107). This view is also hinted at in the sermon when he says, "everything is for God eternally present . . ." (AKA 479). But Lequier asks, "Try to conceive that what is eternally all present, is not eternally, and that what is eternally is not eternal?" (OC 125). For Lequier, this is an absurdity. Future free decisions cannot be present to God except as real possibilities.

John D. Glenn Jr. argues that Kierkegaard's claim that existence is a system for God is incidental and is not central to his thought (HN 55). He cites a footnote in the *Postscript* in which Kierkegaard acknowledges that insofar as the religious life is concerned with the intensification of inwardness, it is "sympathetic with the conception [that God is moved or changed]" (CUP 387). Thus, according to Glenn, Kierkegaard did not intend "to assert doctrines concerning the divine being, but to accentuate the existential condition of the human being" (HN 55). If Glenn is correct, then Kierkegaard and Lequier are not so distant as might first appear. Like Lequier, Kierkegaard could allow for change in the divine being if this concession would deepen the inwardness necessary for faith.

Glenn's reading of Kierkegaard is plausible without being entirely convincing. It may be true that Kierkegaard was not promoting a doctrine of divine timelessness. However, the point of calling the incarnation the absolute paradox is lost if God is not conceived as timeless. Moreover, Kierkegaard may well have believed that the admission that God could be moved or changed is compatible with existence being a system for God.* The sermon on the unchangeableness of God invites this interpretation. As we have already noted, the sermon says both that God is moved *and* that everything is eternally present for God. If this "compatibilist" view is correct then the fact that God is moved carries no implication that the future contains real possibilities. Therefore, it is still the paradox of the incarnation that, for Kierkegaard, must serve as the ground for faith's passion, and not the uncertainty of the future.

What is important for our purposes is that, for Lequier, the openness of the future, for God and the creatures, is what provides faith with the objective uncertainty that Kierkegaard postulates as the necessary corrolate of inwardness. Whereas Kierkegaard locates objective uncertainty in the paradox of the incarnation, Lequier places it in the existence of real possibilities. Lequier's avenue is not open to Kierkegaard since, for the Dane, the uncertainty of the future concerns, at best, fictive possibilities. From God's point of view there could be no uncertainty, no "shadows." For Lequier, the future is uncertain in itself because it depends for its formulation on the self-creativity of divine and nondivine creators.

Because Lequier was willing to engage in theological speculation, he was less inclined than Kierkegaard to imagine a paradox in the nature of God. Kierkegaard spoke of God's *existence* only when referring to the Incarnation (MK 147). Once God enters time, God is subject to the conditions of becoming. In Kierkegaard's mind this can only be a stumbling block to reason. For Lequier, God participates in the temporal flow precisely because God's relations to the world are real. Lequier found no paradox in this. While Lequier did not believe that the doctrine of the Incarnation could be rationally proved, he would never have called it a contradiction (PJ 212). It was Lequier's theology that led him to say that God is affected by human decisions and faces a partly open future.

Lequier's philosophy provides an alternative to Kierkegaard's by emphasizing the importance of theological speculation without sacrificing faith to reason. Credit must go to Kierkegaard for his special emphasis on inwardness, his identification of objective uncertainty as the necessary corrolate of inwardness, and his idea that a doctrine of

---

*Such a view was recently suggested by William Alston as a way of mediating Thomistic and Hartshornean theism (EA 89-90). Hartshorne's reasons for rejecting Alston's proposal are similar to Lequier's arguments: "Futurity and real possibility are one" (EA 99).

God should, at least in part, be judged on its contribution to faith's passion. There is no gainsaying these insights. What is not clear—and what Lequier's philosophy shows to the contrary—is that these insights must issue in Kierkegaardian fideism.

For Kierkegaard, the "passion of the infinite" is possible because of the paradoxical nature of the object of faith. For Lequier, there is nothing especially paradoxical about God. Lequier retains the "passion of the infinite" by drawing out the theological implications of his philosophy of creative freedom. In accordance with this philosophy, Lequier argues for the concept of a divine being for whom possibilities are real. This brings God into time. Not, however, in such a way as to make the concept of God a scandal to reason. Moreover, this concept of God enhances faith's intensity by forcing men and women to face an open future and to shoulder part of the responsibility for creation, being co-creators of the world with God.

References

1. All translations from French works are mine.
2. A somewhat humorous illustration of Lequier's point: Victorian Sardou, the French playwright and *salon* figure, knocked over his wine glass at a dinner party. The lady next to him sprinkled salt on the stain. Sardou tossed some over his shoulder to ward off ill fortune, straight into the eyes of a waiter who was about to serve him chicken. The man clutched his eyes and the platter crashed to the floor. The family dog, rising from his post by the fire, attacked the fowl so greedily that he began to choke. The son of the house jumped up to wrestle the bone out of the dog's throat. The dog savagely bit the son's finger. It had to be amputated (TR 29).

Bibliography

KA   Robert M. Adams, "Kierkegaard's Arguments Against Objective Reasoning in Religion," in *Contemporary Philosophy of Religion*, Steven M. Cahn and David Shatz eds., New York: Oxford University Press, 1982, 213–228.

RB   William P. Alston, ed., *Religious Belief and Philosophical Thought*, New York: Harcourt, Brace & World, 1963.

EA   William P. Alston, "Hartshorne and Aquinas A Via Media," in *Existence and Actuality Conversations with Charles Hartshorne*. John B. Cobb Jr. and Franklin I. Gamwell, eds., Chicago: University of Chicago Press, 1984, 78–98.

AKA   Robert Bretall ed., *A Kierkegaard Anthology*. New York: Modern Library, 1946.

LJ   Harvy H. Brimmer, "Lequier, Jules," in *The Encyclopedia of Philosophy*. Paul Edwards ed., New York: Macmillan, 1967, volume 4, 438–439.

JL   Harvy H. Brimmer, *Jules Lequier and Process Philosophy*. Dissertation, Emory University, 1975.

MK   James Collins, *The Mind of Kierkegaard*. Princeton, N.J.: Princeton University Press, 1983.

HP   Frederick Copleston, *A History of Philosophy*. Volume 2, part 2, Garden City, N.Y.: Image, 1962.

HN   John D. Glenn Jr., "Hartshornean Panentheism and Kierkegaardian Paradox," in *Hartshorne's Neo-Classical Theology*. Forrest Wood Jr. and Michael DeArmey eds., *Tulane Studies in Philosophy*, volume XXXIV, 1983, 53–64.

PJ   Jean Grenier, *La Philosophie de Jules Lequier*. Paris: Presses Universitaires de France, 1936.

IO   Charles Hartshorne, *Insights and Oversights of Great Thinkers*. Albany, N.Y.: State University of New York Press, 1983.

CAP   Charles Hartshorne, *Creativity in American Philosophy*. Albany, N.Y.: State University of New York Press, 1984.

CUP   Soren Kierkegaard, *Concluding Unscientific Postscript*, translated by David F. Swenson and completed, with introduction and notes by Walter Lowrie, Princeton, N.J.: Princeton University Press, 1941.

PF   Soren Kierkegaard, *Philosophical Fragments*, translated by David F. Swenson and revised by Howard V. Hong, Princeton, N.J.: Princeton University Press, 1962.

OC   Jules Lequier, *OEuvres Complete*. Jean Grenier ed., Neuchatel, Suisse: Editions de la Baconniere, 1952.

LG   Thomas V. Morris, *The Logic of God Incarnate*. Ithaca and London: Cornell University Press, 1986.

ISA   Anton C. Pegis ed., *Introduction to St. Thomas Aquinas*. New York: Modern Library, 1945.

KE   Robert L. Perkins, "Kierkegaard's Epistemological Preferences," *International Journal for Philosophy of Religion*, 4, 4 (Winter 1973), 197–217.

PI   Gabriel Seailles, "Un Philosophe Inconnu Jules Lequier," *Revue Philosophique de la France et de L'Etranger*, 1898, Tome XLV, 120–150.

CE   Pierre Teilhard de Chardin, *Christianity and Evolution*, translated by Rene Hague, New York: Harcourt Brace Jovanovich, 1971.

TR   *True Remarkable Occurrences*. Compiled & annotated by John Train, New York: Clarkson N. Potter, Inc. 1978.

HA   Donald Wayne Viney, "How to Argue for God's Existence: Reflections on Hartshorne's Global Argument," *The Midwest Quarterly*, XXVIII, 1 (Autumn 1986), 36–49.

EK   Jean Wahl, *Etudes Kierkegaardiennes*, Paris: Librarie Philosophique J. Vrin, 1967, 3e edition.

Norris Clarke and the Problem of Divine Relativity

Theodore Vitali

Among those philosophers and theologians engaged in the dialogue between Thomists and/or classical theists (those who hold a monopolar view of God) and process theists (those following the dipolar theism of Alfred North Whitehead, or more recently, John Cobb and Charles Hartshorne), Norris Clarke SJ is conspicuous as one of the most critical, knowledgeable, and productive. Self-denied as a "creative Neo-Thomist,"[1] Clarke has tried to meet the major thrust of criticism leveled against monopolar theism by process philosophers, *and* at the same time, retain the fundamental principles of Thomistic ontology, especially as applied to God. Clarke makes this attempt by emending the traditional theory of divine non-relativity by way of a Thomistically acceptable doctrine of divine relaitivity. In so doing, he has virtually built a bridge of dialogue between the two schools of thought. Furthermore, Clarke believes that a theory of divine relativity, if suitably explained by way of an appropriate doctrine of creation, could form the basis for philosophically legitimating Whiteheadian cosmology, that is, could form the basis for developing an adequate theory of unity which Clarke believes is absent in Whitehead's philosophy.

In this paper I will discuss 1) Clarke's reservations in regard to process ontology (especially its theistic implications); 2) his metaphysics of participation founded upon the so-called "thin-essence" view of the essence-existence distinction; 3) his emendation of the traditional theory of divine non-relativity on the basis of his theory of participation; 4) Thomistic and Whiteheadian points of reservation in regard to the adequacy of Clarke's theory; and 5) some possible directions that the dialogue could and should move in.

I. Unresolved Pluralism in Whiteheadian Ontology

In general, it can be safely said that Norris Clarke is sympathetic to and in overall agreement with the creative *cosmology* found in Whitehead's philosophy. There are strong reservations with respect to the atomistic account of actual occasions as is evidenced by his concern over the problem of explaining the emergence of new occasions. But, the idea of self-creation (*causa-sui*), at least in part, has appeal to him.[2] The problems Clarke perceives, however, concern the ontology, not the cosmology found in Whitehead. He is also seriously concerned with the theological implications of the ontology.

The problems with the theology will not concern us here, although from a Christian perspective they are serious. At this time, I will simply mention them. The principal difficulties are these: Whiteheadian dipolar theism entails an unresolvable dualism between God and the world, thus conflicting directly with official church teaching concerning the divine creation going back to at least Theophilus of Antioch in 181 AD. Furthermore, and as a result of this unresolvable dualism, the traditional doctrines of divine omnipotence, omniscience and providence are undermined. Clarke's concern is that Whitehead may well have turned our clocks back to an early Manichean dualism long rejected by Christianity.

The ontological problems that concern us are reducible to two fundamental issues: 1) the inadequacy of the Category of the Ultimate, i.e., creativity, as a philosophically satisfying principle of unity, and 2) the inadequacy of creativity as a normative principle of explanation for the everlastingness of creativity itself, the ever-ongoing emergence of new occasions of creative activity.

The first difficulty may be described as the problem of affinity between God and the world. The second may be described as the problem of explaining "why there are events rather than nothing."

Clarke draws upon his Neo-Platonic interpretation of St. Thomas' *De Potentia* 3, 5 when he challenges Whiteheadian metaphysics to provide a theory of unity that is capable of resolving its apparent radical dualism. Clarke writes:

> ... all of the great metaphysicians of the past, East and West, except Plato and Aristotle, have agreed on at least this: that *every* many must ultimately be grounded in some more primordial and ultimate one. *A many makes no sense at all unless there is some common ground or property* (existence, goodness, actuality, crea-

tivity) *shared by each, without which they could not be compared or correlated at all* [italics added].[3]

Further,

> Nor can many be intrinsically oriented toward order and synthesis unless some ultimate unitary/ordering mind first creatively thought up within itself this primordial correlation and affinity and implanted it in the many from one source.[4]

Clarke's criticism is aimed at the very heart of Whitehead's own understanding of creativity, his ultimate principle. Clarke correctly understands that for Whitehead creativity, apart from actual occasions, is merely a highly generalized abstraction, not an entitative principle. Therefore, *in concreto*, "creativity" is merely a descriptive generalization (and thus non-normative) with respect to what is believed to occur in all events, namely, the "many become one and are increased by one" (*Process and Reality,* Revised ed., 1978, 32; hereafter PR).

Furthermore, Clarke also recognizes that Whitehead's dipolar theism requries that the God-World relationship remain mutual and thus unresolved as to some ultimate causal derivation (*PR* 528).

Given his accurate understanding of Whitehead's dipolar view of God and the world, and further, Whitehead's radical pluralism, Clarke aims his criticism at the adequacy of such a view to render the world intelligible. Clarke argues in this way. The intelligibility of a pluralistic universe, precisely insofar as it is pluralistic, needs a) a principle of unity by which the many are somehow one, since plurality and difference cannot explain why they are at the same time one and the same, and b) a theory of affinity between the many and the one in order to explain the orderliness and proportionality that the many exhibit but cannot explain. Clarke states:

> . . . an infinitely fragmented force of creativity cannot be an authentic ultimate, precisely because it is actually a many, and only abstractly one.[5]

Furthermore, he asks:

> What then is the ultimate source of the explanation of the unity of the universe, or why its two correlative poles, God and the multiplicity of the world, are *attuned* to each other so as to make up a single system, since neither one ultimately derives all its being from the other.[6]

Clarke's second line of criticism deals with the problem of explaining the emergence of new events, since no causal explanation is given for their emergence. He asks why events continue to "bubble up unfailingly and inexhaustibly all over the universe through endless time," without any ultimate causal explanation as to their appearance.[7]

The point of this criticism is heightened when one recalls that creativity apart from concrete occasions is merely an abstraction. Therefore, whatever explanation that can be given, must be given in and through actualities (Whitehead's Ontological Principle, *PR* 36). But these actualities are in themselves finite, "drops of experience, complex and interdependent" (*PR* 28). Within this schema, then, there can be no explanation beyond the actualities themselves because finitude would have to be the reason for its own finitude. Somehow or other the perishing, finite occasions would have to be the reason for their own successor occasions, even though they, *qua* temporal and finite, perish upon their own completion or satisfaction.

Whitehead's own response to the issue is that it is simply "in the nature of things that the many enter into complex unity," (*PR* 31), in other words, that the process *in fact* goes on. Its epistemological validation is an appeal to intuition (*PR* 32).

Clarke and others, friends and critics alike of the Whiteheadian philosophy, find this appeal to mere fact and intuition unsatisfying. If creativity is to be the final metaphysical principle for explaining the order and structure of events in the world, it must be more than an abstraction, no matter how generalized, and more than an instrance itself of what is to be explained.[8]

Clarke's own solution to the problem of unity and affinity rests upon the traditional theory of divine creation of the world *ex nihilo*. He is aware of recent work by such Neo-Whiteheadians as Jorge Nobo and Marjorie Suchocki in which the problem of emergent occasions is handled through a revised view of Whiteheadian efficient causality. In their view, new occasions arise because of the overflow of transient energy from past to present occasions. Upon satisfaction, the transient energy evokes new occasions of creativity.[9]. Clarke finds this theory appealing. But, he also sees that transient energy itself requires ultimate explanation. The doctrine of *creatio ex nihilo* is thus brought in to handle this. Clarke's solution then contrains a principle of affinity *and* an explanation for the new occasions.

In his theory of creation, Clarke is also aware of the concern by process philosophers that the traditional doctrine of creation annihilates any way in which finite creativity can occur. God becomes in their view the total author of both agent and act because, in the process perspective, there is no agent apart from the act. If God created the agent, creative freedom would be a mere illusion since God could also be the creator of the act.

Clarke responds that there is a distinction between agent and act in Thomistic anthropology and metaphysics. God, in creating the world, creates agents who exercise secondary causalities. In some cases, such secondary causality is contingent or free. The traditional doctrine affirms that God creates agents who exercise their proper causalities. Therefore, Clarke feels Thomists and Whiteheadians need not argue this point if both recognize that the traditional doctrine does not entail the loss of self-creation on the part of creatures since the *terminus* of divine causality is the agent whom God has also willed to act freely or contingently.[10]

> The fact that all creatures are totally dependent on God both in their being and in their action does not therefore mean that God *determines* their actions from without. He communicates to creatures their own being and their own native power and supports them in its use, so that without Him they could neither exist nor act. But since He really has given them a share in His own power, they determine the use to which this power is put, even to use it against the express conditional will of God (= *sin*). This is a free self-limitation inherent in every notion of participated perfection and hence part of the very logic of participation.[11]

II. Clarke's Thomistic Theory of Participation and the Essence/Existence Distinction

In an early paper, written in the 1950s, Clarke defined and then further explored St. Thomas' theory of participation. At that time he was concerned with developing what might be called a neo-platonic or Plotinian interpretation of Thomas' existentialist metaphysics. It was and remains Clarke's view that the doctrine of participation, neo-platonically interpreted, provides the best key to understanding Thomas' later, more Aristotelian thought.

In this early paper entitled "The Meaning of Participation in St. Thomas," Clarke defines the theory of participation as

> the theory for rendering intelligible a 'many' in any order in terms of a higher one, in other words, for explaining the common possession in the logical or the ontological order, by reference to a higher source from which all receive or participate in some way the perfection they possess in common.[12]

Clarke finds in Plotinus' theory of emanantion a new dimension to the idea of the "infinite as a plenitude of positive perfection, indetermination by excess, instead of defect." Furthermore, with this idea of participation as emanation, the "principle of illimitation of an unparticipated perfection and its limitation by reception in a participant" is introduced. Clarke sees in Plotinus' theory of emanation how *form as limit* can have a "double role." It perfects what it informs, that which is below it in the emantionist scheme, but it also contracts the plenitude above it.[13]

For St. Thomas, or at least the St. Thomas which Clarke neoplatonically interprets, participation requires 1) "a source which possesses the perfection ... in a total and unrestricted manner; 2) a participant subject which possesses the same perfection in some partial or restricted way; and 3) which has received this perfection in some way from, or in dependence on, the higher source."[14]

The source must possess the perfection essentially, not derivatively or participatively, because the lack of essential identity of perfection and subject would entail their composition. Composition in turn would require a more fundamental causal explanation. Therefore the source must be its own perfection.

The identity of subject and perfection, an identity in "perfect purity and simplicity,"[15] also means that the source must be unique and infinite. It must be unique because two sources having the same essential perfections would be indistinguishable. And it must be infinite, because the identity of essence and perfection precludes a limit to the perfection.[16]

With respect to the participant, the possession of the perfection cannot be essential but only derivative or participative. The perfection, in other words, must be received. Furthermore, the reception of the perfection must occur through contraction and limitation of the otherwise unlimited plenitude of the perfection. The participant, therefore, has to be viewed as an existing composite whose principle of contraction, i.e., whose essence as a principle of limitation, also functions as the ontological principle of finitude.

The full implications of this theory of participation for the discussion at hand can be better appreciated if we take his study of the essence-existence distinction into account. It is his "thin-essence" view of the use of a theory of participation as a foundation for a creative ontology that does not beg the unity question.

In the Preface to William Carlo's fine book *The Ultimate Reducibility of Essence to Existence in Existential Metaphysics*, Clarke gives us an insight into what he calls the "thin-essence" view of the essence-existence distinction. He writes:

> Thus each particular new existent . . . will, because of its internal *negative-limiting principle*, contain only a certain determined qualitative "quantum" . . . of the unique all-embracing perfection of *esse*. Each new particular finite existent will be thought of, accordingly, not so much as an essence receiving, or being actualized by, an act of existence, as though the essence itself were the subject, actualized from without, but rather as a limited, determined, particularized act of existence, which *becomes a new subject precisely by being fixed through its internal negating principle at one determinate enduring mode of esse, becoming a new center and source of its own action, a new limited expression of the total perfection of esse*. [italics added][17]

Further on in the text, Clarke concludes:

> Nor does the essence/existence relation lend itself with ease to explication in terms of reciprocal causality since it is hard to apply the name "cause" in any meaningful way to a *negative limiting principle all of whose positivity lies not in itself but in that which it limits*. [italics added][18]

Within the existential metaphysics of St. Thomas according to Clarke, "all perfection resides in the act of existence itself."[19] So in this view, existence is not an external actualizer of some other positive reality, namely, the essence, but rather existence must be considered the "whole inner core of all perfection the being contains." Essence, then, can only be understood as "nothing but the interior limiting principle, the inner limit or partial negation . . . of the perfection which resides properly within the act of existence itself."[20] Only the act of existence, therefore, has true positivity. The essence is only the *limit* or *negation* of the perfection.

Returning to the theory of participation, essence as limit means that finite perfections are only modes of the plenitude of the perfection, the perfection under negatized conditions. In a strong sense, then, this "thin-essence" view entails that creatures are "relative-non-beings," channels and/or limits of that which is truly and solely positive, the divine infinite plenitude of being and perfection.

III. Clarke's Theory of Divine Relativity

One of the most important contributions Clarke has made to the dialogue has been his attempt to reformulate the traditional doctrine of divine nonrelativity. After years of dialogue with process philosophers, he has conceded that the traditional doctrine of nonrelativity, though not intrinsically false, nevertheless ought still to be emended or revised. He feels that the traditional position is simply not worth defending. Rather, it would be more beneficial to admit some form of divine relativity if it is properly understood, that is, if the new theory of divine relativity does not impinge upon or impair the sound doctrine of divine immutability and simplicity.[21]

Clarke is clear from the outset that the revised theory of divine relativity has as its subject, not the divine being *in se*, nor the divine perfection. Rather, it has as its subject the divine consciousness. He writes:

> . . . our metaphysics of God must certainly allow us to say that in some real and genuine way God is *affected positively by what we do*, that he receives love from us and experiences joy *precisely because* of our responses: in a word, that His consciousness is contingently and qualitatively *different* because of what we do. All this difference remains, however, on the level of God's *relational consciousness* and therefore does not involve increase or decrease in the Infinite Plenitude of God's *intrinsic inner being and perfection*—what St. Thomas would call the 'absolute' (non-relative) aspect of His perfection. God does not become a more or less perfect being because of the love we return to Him and the joy or its absence He experiences therefrom. [italics his and mine][22]

The maximally relative aspect of the divine consciousness (Clarke follows Hartshorne at this point quite closely) is the living out of His primordial perfection as perfect person. But, Clarke contends, He is perfect person only because God is also infinite being. Because God is infinite, personal being, God can, in His relative consciousness, "be said to be different as so affected *because* of whatever creatures do. . . ."[23] He is the "*Supreme Receiver* gathering in His consciousness all that creatures do" and responds accordingly and appropriately to it.[24]

But, even after having made this strong assertion concerning the divine relativity, Clarke reminds the reader that he is not abandoning his traditional metaphysics of divine immutability and simplicity, i.e., the metaphysics of pure actuality. He warns us that we should not mistake his theory of relativity to imply that God is somehow passive to creatures in the same way as an effect is passive to its causes.[25] God does not need creatures, in his view, and thus cannot be affected positively or negatively by what creatures do. The infinite intensity of God's being precludes such a possibility of "increase or decrease in the Infinite Plenitude of God's intrinsic inner being and perfection."[26]

At this point, Clarke seems to have thrown himself onto the horns of a rather painful dilemma. In one text he describes God as being "the Supreme Receiver"; in another text, he tells us God is incapable of increase or decrease in the inner intensity of His being. What can divine relativity mean if Receiver does not entail "increase or decrease" in God's inner being and perfection?

Clarke's theory of participation and its foundation on the "thin-essence" view of the essence/existence distinction is intended to get him off the hook, or at least, so he hopes.

Creatures make a difference to God only insofar as they specify, determine, channel, and/or limit God's causality, thus modifying God's knowledge, power, and being. Clarke writes in this regard:

It is that God is constantly working in and through us with His supportive and collaborative power, supporting both the being and action of every creature. But he allows this power to be determinately channeled by the respective natures, especially the free-will decisions of creatures. *Thus God knows what we are doing by how we allow His power*, in *itself indeterminate, to flow through us*; by how we determinately channel this flow of power, according to our own free initiatives. *Thus He knows not by being acted on, but through His own action in us*. He knows what we are doing by doing with us whatever we are doing, except that it is *we who supply the determinations to specify in-itself-transcendent (and thus indeterminate) fullness of His power*. (Italics added)[27]

The theory of participation is clearly evident in this text. Creatures contract and limit the divine plenitude of power and as such participate in and are a result of that power. The positive perfection is the power, God's infinite plenitude of being. The negative dimension is the constriction of God's power by creatures. The object of God's consciousness and love is thus God's own power (positive) as channeled by us (negative). In such a view, then, there is no composition in God because the object of God's knowledge and love remains the same, God's own positivity. But, creatures are real insofar as they limit. Thus they are known and *loved* (*sic*) insofar they are relative non-being. They affect God's consciousness insofar as they limit it as negatives, not insofar as they are positive entitative realities independent of God in their own right. This is an extremely subtle point which Clarke needs to clarify. He does.

> I still insist . . ., that all such 'novelty' and enrichment in God (new joy and so forth), authentically new as they are, can only be new *determinate modalities of expression* of the already infinite intensity of the actual interior joy in God, and hence can never rise higher in qualitative intensity of perfection than the already infinite Source of which all finite modalities are only limited participations (italics his).[28]

If his theory of essence as negation should hold true, then Clarke's theory of participation would seem to allow him to hold a theory of divine relativity without sacrificing divine immutability and simplicity. He also would avoid the problem of causal determinism because his theory of divine relativity would open the door to genuine novelty.

IV. The Inadequacy of Clarke's Theory of Divine Relativity

The inadequacy of Clarke's theory lies not so much in the explicit theory of participation but in the "thin-essence" theory that underlies it. If the "thin-essence" view of existential metaphysics cannot be sustained, then Clarke will have to abandon his theory of divine relativity altogether or else espouse much more radically the process view of divine relativity in which God is an effect in the literal sense.

John Wippel recently provided what I feel to be an extremely damaging criticism of the "thin-essence" theory of the essence/existence distinction. He writes:

> As I see it, to reduce essence to a *mode* of *esse* would be to rob the essence principle of a given substance of any *positive content* in distinction from that of its existence principle [italics added].[29]

Beyond the problem of accounting for the role of essence in receiving and determining existence, if it is merely a mode or channel of existence, the problem of the ontological status of the non-being of the essences looms even larger. Wippel writes:

> . . . according to Aquinas, *act as such is not self-limiting*. This is especially true of the act of existence. *Esse* as such is not self-

limiting. If we do find finite instances of being and therefore of existence, this is because in every finite substance its existence principle is received and limited by its correlative essence principle. While differing from *esse*, therefore, *essence must enjoy some positive content if it is to receive and limit esse. Essence will be unable to fulfill this function either if it is reduced to absolute non-being or if it is regarded as nothing but a mode of existence*. [italics added][30]

Wippel clearly sees that this "thin-essence" view, what he calls the theory of essence as "relative non-being," cannot account for the principle of limitation which is central to Clarke's form of participation metaphysics.

To reduce the essence principle within created beings to absolute non-being, or even to regard it as nothing but a mode of existence, will seriously compromise Thomas' understanding of participation. To put this in the most summary fashion, the essence principle within a given substance receives and limits that same substance's *esse* and thereby enables the substance to participate in *esse* without being identical to it. But it is difficult to understand how an essence which is nothing but a given degree of existence (*esse*) or which is understood as absolute nonbeing can fulfill this function. [31]

Wippell's argument might be summarized in this manner. If essence is merely a mode or limitation of existence, then its positivity must lie precisely in its existence. But if its positivity is its existence, how can it, precisely as limited *existence*, be its own limit? It would have to be either identical to its existence, and thus in no way a limit, or it would have to be a form of non-existence. In the latter case, it would either have to be *nothing*, and thus incapable of limiting anything, or it would have to be something. But if it is something, then its positivity would have to lie in whatever something it is, and not in its existence.

But if Clarke were to accept this criticism and thus buy into the "thick-essence" view, as it is sometimes called, he would be caught on the horns of his own dilemma. He would have to claim (if he would intend to hold onto his theory of divine relativity) that creatures do in fact make a differences to God. Something would have to go: either divine relativity or divine immutability. He could not retain both once his "thin-essence" view was abandoned. Creatures would simply have too much positivity in the "thick-essence" view to allow for divine relativity without divine mutability.

Clarke's theory is also vulnerable to attack from the process view. If creativity means anything, it means genuine increase in value. Clarke accepts this view. He also agrees that such a view requires some form of relativity in the divine consciousness. Without such relativity, novel values would be meaningless. The values would lack ontological status, i.e., they would make no significant and important difference to God. God must be "affected" in some way.

But, Clarke's "thin-essence" view voids created values of any meaning. Created beings exist insofar as they are limits! Their value is in their limitation, in their "relative non-being." Creatures are valuable to God's relational consciousness precisely and solely insofar as they are the existent non-beings which contract that alone which is valuable, God's own self-being. Creative novelty in the finite order would be ontologically impotent because in fact such novelty would be nothing positive.[32]

For creativity to be a meaningful concept, novelty must be genuine. Real positive values must be constantly increasing in the universe. This can only be possible if in fact God were to be affected by these new values. An eternal, immutable, utterly simple God can never be an adequate philosophical concept from the process point of view. Divine transcendence, understood as pure eternal actuality, precludes the possibility of any form of relativity on the part of God, and thus, of any real values beyond God. Clarke implies this when he tries to develop a theory of divine relativity. His introduction of the personalist dimension to infinity was an attempt to work out the kinks in a traditional concept of God which also affirmed some form of relativity. But, in the end, as I hope I've shown, it fails. In my judgment, divine relativity and true emergent novel values require a dipolar form of theism in which God is really related to the world and as such really an effect as well as a cause.

V. Concluding Remarks

Clarke's project may well have failed, and, as I have just stated, I believe it has. But, Clarke has provided an enormous service to the theological discussion now taking place. He has focused our attention on some critical issues, *and* he has made some major contributions.

Though I reject Clarke's final solution to the problem of affinity and the emergence of novel occasions, I believe he is correct that the problem of affinity requires a theory of unity not immediately available in standard Whiteheadian philosophy. Robert Neville has also focused on this "normative" dimension of Whiteheadian philosophy—that is, the "non-normative" character of creativity.[33] Both he and Clarke are clearly aware and are correct that descriptive generalizations of creativity simply cannot provide an ontologically normative basis for *why* there is affinity between God and the World, and *why* there are new occasions rather than nothing. Some ontological theory of unity is essential, in their view, if Whiteheadian cosmology is to have a sound ontological foundation. In this challenge to process philosophy, I concur with Neville and Clarke.

In recent years, as Clarke indicates in his writings, a number of neo-Whiteheadians have had similar reservations about Whitehead's ontology. Nobo and Suchocki have attempted to rework the theory of efficient causality in Whitehead in order to handle the problem of new occasions. Lewis S. Ford has developed the theory of God as the future of all actual occasions to meet the problem of unity in Whiteheadian metaphysics.[34] More recently, Nancy Frankenberry has attempted to emend the theory of efficient causality, following Suchocki, in order to build a theory of unity, though one based on the unity of God as the "totality-of-the-past."[35]

The important point to note in these recent writings is the agreed upon concern for meeting the question of unity and the problem of why occasions arise. The weakness of the new attempts, even though in some instances the unity question is handled through efficient causality, is that the problem of "normative affinity" is not really addressed. Ford and Frankenberry stay close to the original Whiteheadian thesis that metaphysical concepts are empirical generalizations—though the most universal. This means that the normative question simply gets by-passed. Both Ford and Frankenberry call the readers' attention to the Whiteheadian text in which the final appeal is to "intuition." This simply will not wash for people like Clarke and Neville. Some ontologically normative principle must be the final basis for the unity of the universe, the final affinity between God and the world, and for the *why* of the necessity that finite occasions of experience continue everlastingly to "bubble up."

In an earlier paper of mine,[36] I argued that the normative character of creativity could be discovered through an analysis of the idea of necessary existence found in Hartshorne's version of dipolar theism. I argued that the normativeness of creativity may well be due to the dialectical relationship between God and the world insofar as the divine necessity requires the "ever-on-goingness" of finite creative events. In this regard, there can never be a state of affairs in which novel occasions cease to occur—cease to "bubble up." If occasions would cease to occur, God's experience of the world would be utterly repetitive and boring—would cease, in other words, to be creative. But that is impossible, if the above aesthetic dialectic between God and world *and* God as necessary existent obtains, since then God *must* be creative. Therefore, creativity is as normative as the divine existence itself.

References

1. Norris Clarke SJ, *A Philosophical Approach to God*. Winston-Salem: Wake Forest University Press, 1979, p. 92.
2. *Ibid.*, p. 82.
3. *Ibid.*, pp. 70–72.
4. *Ibid.*, p. 75.
5. *Ibid.*, p. 72.
6. *Ibid.*, p. 73.
7. *Ibid.*
8. *Ibid.*, p. 72.
9. *Ibid.*, pp. 76–78, 81–83.
10. *Ibid.*, pp. 85–86.
11. *Ibid.*, p. 85.
12. Clarke, "The Meaning of Participation in St. Thomas" in *Readings in Metaphysics*, Ed. Jean Rosenberg. Westminster: Newman Press, 1964, pp. 238–239.
13. *Ibid.*, p. 238.
14. *Ibid.*, p. 240.
15. *Ibid.*
16. *Ibid.*, p. 241.
17. Clarke, Preface, *The Ultimate Reducibility of Essence to Existence in Existential Metaphysics*, by William E. Carlo. The Hague: Martinus Nijhoff, 1966, p. viii.
18. *Ibid.*, p. xii.
19. Clarke, "St. Thomas' Essence-Existence Doctrine," *New Scholasticism*, Vol. 48 (Winter, 1974), p. 36.
20. *Ibid.*
21. *A Philosophical Approach to God*, p. 91.
22. *Ibid.*, p. 92.
23. *Ibid.*, p. 93.
24. *Ibid.*

25. *Ibid.*

26. *Ibid.*, p. 92.

27. *Ibid.*, pp. 96–97.

28. *Ibid.*, p. 98.

29. John F. Wippel, "Thomas Acquinas on the Distinction and Derivation of the Many from the One,"*Review of Metaphysics*, Vol. XXXVIII, No. 3 (March, 1985), p. 587.

30. *Ibid.*, pp. 588–589.

31. *Ibid.*, p. 589.

32. See Vitali, "Creativity, God, and Creation," *Modern Schoolman*, Vol. LVII, No. 2 (January, 1985).

33. Robert Neville, *Creativity and God*. New York: Seabury Press, 1980, pp. 44–45.

34. Lewis S. Ford, "The Search for the Source of Creativity," *Logos*, 1/80, pp. 47–48; "God as the Subjectivity of the Future," *Encounter*, 41/3 (Summer, 1980), pp. 289–291; "The Divine Activity of the Future," *Process Studies*, Vol. II, No. 3 (Fall, 1981), pp. 169–180.

35. Nancy Frankenberry, "The Power of the Past," *Process Studies*, Vol. 13, no. 2 (Summer, 1983), pp. 132–142; "The Emergent Paradigm and Divine Causation," *Process Studies*, Vol. 13, No. 3 (Fall, 1983), pp. 207–217; "The Logic of Whitehead's Intuition of Everlastingness," *Southern Journal of Philosophy*, Vol. XXI, No. 1, pp. 31–46.

36. "Creativity, God, and Creation," especially, pp. 92–93.

Philosophic Method

- George W. Shields

Hartshorne and the Analytic Philosophical Tradition

By George W. Shields

Introduction

When most of us think of the "analytic philosophical tradition," Charles Hartshorne does not readily come to mind as one of the figures to be associated with it. Yet, if anything has been made clear by the burgeoning Hartshorne scholarship of the past fifteen years or so, it is that his philosophy is an original synthesis of both personal insights and quite variegated influences, influences not restricted to Whitehead or Peirce. Eugene Peters, for one, has done a very effective job of showing the importance for Hartshorne of the idealistic tradition of Royce and Hocking (see MMCH). In this essay, I wish to show the importance for Hartshorne of the analytic tradition and to make a beginning at charting his explicit and implicit relationship to that tradition. More specifically, it is my purpose in this essay to show that, despite some rather common presumption to the contrary (or perhaps lack of awareness), Hartshorne has been very concerned with developments in twentieth century analytic philosophy, to an extent that it would not be foolhardy or inappropriate to suggest that he stands *somewhere* within the intellectual currents of the analytic tradition broadly conceived. Perhaps more cautiously stated, what I wish to argue is that, while Hartshorne is a thoroughly independent philosopher with wide interests, he has been at the least a "para-traveler" with the analytic tradition, who has employed its tools and some of its vocabulary, while keeping a critical distance, especially, for example, to any claims of methodological definitiveness on the part of some proponents of ordinary language philosophy and to certain dogmas such as verificationism and falsificationism.

I will proceed by, first, making some general observations about Hartshorne's style and the analytic tradition, and, second, by discussing his relationship to the earlier work of G. E. Moore and Bertrand Russell, to logical positivism, to Wittgenstein and ordinary language analysis, and to the more recently influential work of Quine and Kripke. My notions of the "analytic tradition" will be standard ones, informed by the historical categories of Urmson and Weitz.[1] That is to say, I will consider the "analytic tradition" to be that body of philosophical activity which considers formal logic and/or the analysis of language or conceptual frameworks (including and especially frameworks in the special sciences) to be fundamental tasks of philosophy, as is exhibited in a lineage of thought having four roughly discernible periods: (1) The period of Moore and Russell in their "emancipation" from idealism to the logical atomism of Russell and the Tractarian Wittgenstein (approximately from Moore's turn of the century "Refutation" to Russell's 1918–19 *Monist* papers on logical atomism). (2) The period of so-called logical positivism, beginning with the meetings of the Vienna Circle in the early twenties to the "death knell" sounded in A. J. Ayer's 1946 "Introduction" to the Second Edition of his influential *Language, Truth and Logic*, or perhaps Carl Hempel's 1950 admissions in his "Problems and Changes in the Empiricist Criterion of Meaning" published in the *Revue Internationale de Philosophie*. (3) The period of ordinary language analysis, having roots in G. E. Moore's analysis of ordinary language and defense of common sense beliefs, but gaining momentum only in the early fifties after the appearance of the English translation of Wittgenstein's *Philosophische Untersuchungen* in 1953. (4) The current "pluralistic" period, in which the limitations of ordinary language analysis have been recognized, and the views of Rorty, Quine, and, on the other hand, Kripke, are more in the ascendancy.

I.

Before I get to the details of my interpretation and argument, I wish to make some observations about the general tenor and style of Hartshorne's philosophical work *vis-à-vis* the analytic tradition, which will enhance the overall plausibility of my interpretive claims. I would suggest that Hartshorne's philosophy exhibits the following methodological and stylistic features which also broadly characterize much philosophizing in the analytic tradition:

(1) A concern for clarity of written expression and a concomitant avoidance of neologisms and pretentious or obscurantist termi-

nology (such as in the lengthy hyphenated expressions of some European writers).

(2) A concern with attaining maximal clarity and rigour in the exposition and analysis of argument by employing formal logic and conceptual analysis of language.

(3) A concern with integrating developments in the natural sciences into one's philosophical positions, or at least being cognizant of and responsive to such developments.

Concerning (1): Students of Hartshorne's writings will no doubt find the first item completely uncontroversial. As Lewis Ford once put it aptly, "Hartshorne's clarity of presentation and argument, coupled with a freedom from Whitehead's neologisms, has made him a most influential exponent of process thought."[2] Hartshorne himself has explicitly stated that he considers both clarity and readability to be important criteria by which a philosopher should be judged (CSPM 41-42). Also note that, while Hartshorne has been appreciative of certain insights of continental thinkers such as Heidegger, Sartre, and Berdyaev, he finds their rhapsodic style and sometimes obscure language both unappealing and unnecessary (see for example CSPM 84). Indeed, there is in Hartshorne's writing a quality of elegant simplicity, and an apparently deliberate omission of pretentious terminology, which makes him refreshing to read. His style is, I submit, exemplary of the best tradition of Anglo-American philosophical writing. If one is put to a comparison, I would suppose that his writing compares favorably with Brand Blanshard's (albeit, without Blanshard's vivid turn of phrase), or perhaps, Richard Taylor's in such works as *Metaphysics* and *With Heart and Mind*.

Concerning (2): From Eugene Peters' informative *résumé* of Hartshorne's intellectual development (HNM 5), we learn that Hartshorne received formal training in logic at Harvard from two masters: he took H. M. Sheffer's course in Symbolic Logic and C. I. Lewis' in Advanced Logic. No doubt he learned in this area from editing the Peirce papers, and there is evidence of study in *Principia Mathematica* during his graduate student days at Harvard (WP 1). It is not surprising then that Hartshorne would employ formal logic throughout his career to elucidate a number of philosophical topics. The extent of his employment of and/or appeal to such formal tools in fact goes well beyond his celebrated modal formalization of the ontological argument at LP 49-68: For example, note his reflection on the Sheffer functions and the semantic tableaux of sentential logic as they bear on the theory of relations (CSPM 205-219), his sentential formalization of a *reductio ad absurdum* applied to the Thomistic theory of deity (DR 12-15), and his contribution to the Sheffer *Festschrift*[3] on strict and genetic-identity. Moreover, he discusses such matters as: the so-called "paradox" of C. I. Lewis' notion of strict implication and necessary propositions (AD 41-48), Jan Berg's extensionalist formalization of the ontological argument (AD 265-267), Frederic Fitch's view of properties, existence and classes (AD 287-297), and Carnap's *Meaning and Necessity vis-à-vis* the logic of relations (DR 100-115), Carnap's notion of "meaning postulates" as a way of introducing analytic judgments into formal languages (LP, 54). Finally, his writings contain persistent and numerous references to the literature of formal logic, including work by O. Becker, W. E. Johnson, C. I. Lewis, Alonzo Church, A. N. Prior, Storrs McCall, R. M. Martin, Norman Martin, Hans Reichenbach, Felix Kaufmann, William Werneck, the Kneales, Quine, and, of course, Whitehead and Russell. As a sample of his skills at the conceptual elucidation of language in *something* like Ryle's or Urmson's quasi-formal fashion, I submit his 1965 paper published in *Mind*, "The Meaning of 'Is Going to Be.'"

Concerning (3): It is not to be forgotten that Hartshorne has had an intensive engagement with the experimental sciences. He studied experimental psychology at Harvard under Troland, McDougall, and Langfeld (HNM 11), and continued in such inquiry most extensively while researching his first book, *The Philosophy and Psychology of Sensation*. He has also had a serious, lifelong interest in ornithology, culminating in his impressive *Born to Sing: A World Survey and Interpretation of Bird Song*. No one can read this work, with its mastery of ornithological data, evolutionary principles, and sophisticated computer-aided employment of statistical analyses, and fail to see Hartshorne as one who is intimately acquainted with the methods of the working experimental sciences. Moreover, he has shown a rather keen interest in physics and philosophy of physics, as can be judged from his many passing references to or discussions of Jordan, Frank, Einstein, Poincaré, Bohr, Heisenberg, Wigner, von Weizsäcker, Schrödinger, Stein, Capek, Wheeler, and his important recent article on H. P. Stapp's theory of space-time.[4] Thus, he can hardly be viewed as a sheer "armchair" philosopher, since he has in fact philosophized from a perspective at least informed by the special sciences. This feature he shares with a number of figures in the analytic tradition from Russell to Popper to Sellars.

Notwithstanding, Hartshorne's metaphysics has been judged by some as having a central weakness in its alleged claim to be "exempt" from criticism on grounds of "empirical fact" (for instance in its alleged incompatibility with relativity physics and Big Bang Cosmology).[5] However, I urge consideration of the following points: (i) Following Popperian distinctions, Hartshorne has never claimed that his metaphysics is in principle exempt from empirical *disconfirmation*, although it is "exempt" from the quite distinct notion of empirical *confirmation* (see BH 292, CSPM 278). (ii) The determination of the relevant "empirical facts" (or interpretations of them) which a philosopher is forced to accept is a subtle, highly theory dependent and disputable matter, especially in the case of relativity and Big Bang theory. For example, it is not at all clear or agreed upon that relativity physics entails that time is "relative" even in Newton's sense,[6] nor is it clear that Big Bang "proves" the finitude of time or creative process *as such*.[7] (iii) Hartshorne has been cognizant of the *prima facie* tensions between relativity and Big Bang theory and his neoclassical metaphysics, and he has at least offered plausible concilliatory suggestions, such as his embrace of Stapp's concept of a primordial world-line, and the notion of the impotence of Big Bang theory to establish more than contingencies of our present physical *chronometry* of time (OTM, 135). As Hilary Putnam has pointed out,[8] the procedure of offering "auxiliary hypotheses" in situations in which a theoretically simple or elegant model or law is challenged by recalcitrant data is not unusual in the special sciences, often producing successful results. For example, nineteenth century mathematical astronomers postulated a completely speculative planet X, rather than give up the elegant theory of universal gravitation, when they discovered surprising aberrations in the orbit of Uranus (of course, the planet turned out to be Neptune). Thus, I see nothing inherently, methodologically suspect in Hartshorne's so-called "evasive" appeal to, say, Stapp's view of space-time, in order to produce a more coherent process theory of reality. All claims about the "anti-empirical" thrust of Hartshorne's metaphysics stand, it seems to me, with the epistemically naive assumption that it is tolerably clear that there really do exist some *established* or *hard* empirical facts which are incompatible with neoclassical metaphysics. In effect, to hold that such metaphysics has been empirically *disconfirmed* is, at best, highly controversial, given the current state of physics and foundations of mathematics.

II.

1. *Hartshorne, Moore, and Russell*
    The philosophies of G. E. Moore and Bertrand Russell have played significant roles in shaping, albeit largely negatively, some of Hart-

shorne's distinctive positions and arguments, especially his theory of internal and external relations and his related arguments for objective or ontological idealism. He has written a number of papers on Russell,[9] and has discussed Moore at some length, e.g., in PPS 87-89 and 100, BH 182-187, and DR 62-63 and 195-197. Russell was for a short time his colleague in the Department of Philosophy at the University of Chicago. While Hartshorne has sharply rejected (among other doctrines) Russell's logical atomism and G. E. Moore's critique of idealism, in so far as it involved objective idealism, he finds both philosophers to be sound and important critics of Bradley's absolute idealism. Hence, Hartshorne concurs with at least the negative results of what many have viewed as the "inauguration" of the analytic movement—the emancipation from "Absolute" or "Hegelian" style idealism.

G. E. Moore. Most significant in Hartshorne's relation to Moore is Moore's paper on "External and Internal Relations" (reprinted in *Philosophical Studies*), which furnishes Hartshorne with his criterion for external relations: X is externally related to Y if X could be exactly the same with or without Y (DR 62). More rigorously stated:

(For some X of [description] P and some Y, X of P is externally related to Y) entails that (either X of P and not -Y, or, X of P and Y).

Indeed, as part of his case against F. H. Bradley in *The Divine Relativity*, Hartshorne follows Moore's basic strategy of maintaining that there are surely *some* things which fit the above formal pattern, and thus it is not true that, as Bradley put it in the Index to *Appearance and Reality*, "all relations are intrinsical." One of Hartshorne's favorite examples here is that the number two is, on Moore's criterion, externally related to one's act of thinking the number two (DR 62). For it seems quite intuitively clear that the number two would have exactly the mathematical properties it does have (e.g., being less than three while greater than one), even if I (or someone else) never thought of or contemplated the number two. However, notice that the converse relation *is* intrinsical. Some act of contemplating the number two is what it is because of the number two, and to "change" the object contemplated is to change the nature of *that* contemplative act. At any rate, Bradley's thesis of exclusive internal relations—whose consequence that relations are inherently absurd strikes us as paradoxical and eccentric in the first place—seems most untenable. Some relations are external.

But Hartshorne's analysis of the issue of relations runs much deeper than Moore's (and Russell's) in at least four philosophically significant respects*: (i) Hartshorne sees that the factor of temporality has an *essential* bearing on the issue of external and internal relations;** (ii) "externality" or "independence" can be discerned to the degree that the term in question is related to scopes of possibility (or futurity); (iii) external and internal relations are not *mutually* exclusive, but are complementary such that the terms of external relata are contained in the terms of internal relata (as objects are contained in subjects); and finally (iv) that all of the above supports objective idealism.

(i) and (iii). Moore's analysis seems to be a subtle but laborious treatment of the issue, which rests content in having shown that internal relations obtain in tautological contexts (such as P being internally related to the conjunction "P and Q"), while external relations obtain in what Moore defines as "contingent" contexts, where something might have been otherwise. Hartshorne goes beyond this to a brilliant and elegantly simple generalization. Since, as Moore sees clearly, *given* any totality or whole, its parts are constitutive of or intrinsic to it, then, applied to the temporal modes, it becomes clear that *the past*—that which is actual or fully determined—is always constitutive of or intrinsic to some new totality which becomes. Hence, in becoming what I am at the moment of writing this sentence, I cannot be exactly what I have become without the past I inherit or experience. On the other hand, the past remains exactly what it is whether or not I experience it. In other words, the past is externally related to or independent of any particular becoming subject, while any particular becoming subject is internally related to or dependent upon the past it inherits. It seems odd that Moore would have missed this generalization, since he defends the reality of temporal process, *contra* Bradley's monistic point of view, in his "The Conception of Reality" (published

---

*I see it as something of a scandal that one of Hartshorne's greatest contributions to technical philosophy—the intuitively penetrating, rigorous and systematically generalized account of relations in DR—was not so much as mentioned in Richard Rorty's review of the subject in *The Encyclopedia of Philosophy*, while Moore's and Russell's work was treated at considerable length. See Rorty, "Relations, Internal and External," *Encyclopedia of Philosophy* Vol. 7 (Macmillan, 1967).

**Curiously, Moore never once explicitly discusses temporal relations, although he does discuss spatial relations, in his "External and Internal Relations." He argues that in a given spatial whole, part of that whole, say, a parceled out patch of red, is intrinsic to the whole. However, the converse relation does not hold. The parcel of red can be what it is without the given spatial whole. See G. E. Moore, *Philosophical Studies* (Kegan Paul, 1922), p. 288.

in his *Philosophical Studies*). I say "odd" since if one is to maintain a logically consistent philosophical overview, then, being committed to the reality of temporal process would seem to mean being committed to an asymmetrical, not symmetrical, account of relations. Moore seems to have "compartmentalized" philosophical issues.

(ii). Hartshorne gives an interesting technical explication of Moore's definition of external relations when he connects it with C. I. Lewis' systems of "strict implication," where "P strictly implies Q" if and only if "necessarily, it is not the case that P and not-Q":

> external is the negative of internal, and internal relations are ontological correlates of logical relations of "strict implication" or entailment. This seems to agree with Moore's definition. For that which the conception of a thing entails is that without which the entity could not be itself, the entity conceived (DR 95).

An internal relation then is the ontological correlate of a Lewisian strict implication, while an external relation is precisely *not* the ontological correlate of a Lewisian strict implication. This allows Hartshorne to see with great clarity that the logical notion of "independence" or "externality" can be modally construed as a relationship to *open* possibility, since internality or dependence is seen as *restriction* of possible alternative—necessarily not, P without Q, if P is internally related to Q. This insight undermines any absolute idealistic retort that an alleged "external relation to P" is itself a relation which necessarily involves P as a term of the conceived relation. As Hartshorne puts it:

> ... the absoluteness [or externality] of [a] term ... is not, strictly speaking with respect to relation to [P], but with respect to a *kind* of relation, which can be defined, as logicians say, intensionally, or without mentioning [P]. Thus arithmetic is independent, not merely of my awareness of it, but of any particular awareness. Nothing is added to this attribution of independence by saying, "and also arithmetic is independent of my awareness." (DR 72)

(iv). The temporalistic generalization of relations discussed above has an important connection to the argument of Moore's celebrated "Refutation of Idealism." For, such a generalization, if properly understood, is tantamount to the position that every actuality is social in nature, and hence our descriptions of actualities must inevitably involve *some* sorts of psychological predicates. (Eugene Peters has seen this point with exquisite clarity. See HNM 83-84.) Every new (genuinely

individual) entity which becomes, becomes what it is (in part) because of past actuality (aggregates or swarms—such as tables as "swarms of atoms"—are not individuals in the way atoms are). In other words, every new actuality somehow grasps or inherits its past, which means grasping *other* entities, in the past, not identical to the becoming actuality. It is this "self-grasping of the other" which is social and psychological in nature, or is the fundamental conceptual intention or criterion *common* to all our psychological notions, such as "life," "sentience," "mentality," "experience," etc.

On the basis of this generalization, it seems correct to say that, Hartshorne's objective idealism is exempt from Moore's epoch-making critique of idealism, and for at least two reasons.

For one thing, Moore takes Berkeley's *esse est percipi* to be the crucial assumption in *all* idealistic arguments. Hartshorne's bone of contention here is that, while Moore's argument does hold against Berkeley's subjective idealism, and some other types of idealism, it does not at all hold against the very different doctrine of objective idealism or "societal realism" (BH 182-187). For, "societal realism" in fact represents a kind of reversal of the Berkeleyean dictum *esse est percipi*, since, on the social account of things, the being of an object is *not* (merely) in its *being perceived* or prehended, but rather in its having been a perceiver or prehender. Prehensions are the very ontological fabric of actual entities. It is because of the principle that an actual event is what it is by virtue of its prehensions that it is also true that every actual event is a potential for subsequent acts of prehension (RSP 70). Hartshorne has Berkeley's dictum nested, as it were, in a more fundamental proposition; "to be is to prehend" entails that "to be is to be prehended," if it is true that every event is a creative synthesis successive to and dependent upon past events.

Indeed, if E. D. Klemke[10] is correct in his analysis of the structure of Moore's argument, then Hartshorne's idealistic or societal realistic argument represents a fundamental alteration of that structure. According to Klemke, Moore's overall strategy was that P (P = *esse est percipi*) entails Q (Q = *esse est percipere*), and Q entails C (C = reality is psychic or mental in nature). But since Moore holds that P is false, this means that we cannot affirm Q, and if we cannot affirm Q we cannot affirm C. The main thrust of Moore's attack then is upon P. Hartshorne's argument for objective idealism might be formalized as follows: Q entails P and P entails C, but Q is the case, therefore C is the case. Hartshorne's initial premise is thus the *converse* of the initial premise in Moore's reconstruction of the idealistic argument. Since Moore does not consider all the relevant evidence in favor of Q, namely, the arguments in support of Whitehead's doctrine of prehensions, then it follows that he has not made a sufficiently strong enough case for his denial of P, and hence his reservations about C.

Secondly, in a penetrating passage (BH 182-183), Hartshorne identifies a main technical difficulty in Moore's argument. Moore makes much of the point, fully granted by Hartshorne, that the traditional idealists (such as Berkeley, Bradley, or Green) have not made the requisite distinction between awareness and the object of awareness. Indeed, without such a distinction, one is committed to "an absolute solipsism of the momentary act of consciousness," since one could only be aware of a contentless awareness if there is no distinct object of awareness (BH 182). However, it does not follow from this distinction that qualities, taken as objects of awareness, do not somehow become functions of awareness. For, if qualities are not somehow "in" awareness, by what criterion could we distinguish, say, awareness of blue from awareness of yellow? The possibility which Moore misses is *exactly* what Whitehead's doctrine of prehensions provides: an object can be an internal member of our system of consciousness, while also continuing to be a member of another system which can exist apart from us. Moore has simply assumed, "the Aristotelian notion of mutually exclusive substances, whose parts belong to no other wholes or which are *not* members one of another" (BH 183). This is just the notion that Whitehead's doctrine of prehensions plausibly challenges, and hence again, not *every* type of idealism has been adjudicated by Moore's argument.

Finally, no sketch of Hartshorne's relation to Moore would be tolerably complete without noting that Hartshorne has stated on a number of occasions that he finds Moore's paper, "On the Notion of Infinity" (published in *Some Main Problems of Philosophy*), to be a philosophical consolation (CSPM 125f, IO 167), since Moore defends the view shared by process philosophers that the past is infinite. While it is true that Moore does find the infinitist view a coherent one, I wish to point out that his central argument commits one to propositions which are clearly contrary to Hartshorne's neoclassical metaphysics. (Thus, it is somewhat puzzling that Hartshorne would appeal to it.) Moore argues that it is conceivable that an infinite process is completable, since one can and in fact does "traverse the infinite," for example, in stepping across the room! That is to say, Moore assumes that there are an infinite number of real points in any finite volume, and that common sense tells us that one does indeed traverse a finite volume. So, "traversing the infinite" is built into the very idea of real motion and hence "traversing an infinite past" as a species of "traversing the infinite" is not impossible. This is hardly a position that Hartshorne can consistently accept, since it involves the notion of actually infinite points. Indeed, Hartshorne follows Whitehead's method of extensive abstraction in viewing a point as a relative volume, not as an ideal Euclidean infinitesimal (WP 95).

Bertrand Russell. Russell, through his and Moore's analysis of relations, reached a point of view diametrically opposed to Bradley's monism—logical atomism. Russell states this doctrine very succinctly in his *Outline of Philosophy*, "pluralism . . . admits the existence of a great multiplicity of events, each minimal event being a logically self-subsistent entity."[11] One can readily see that this view is logically equivalent to the view that all relations are external (in Moore's sense). If P is an event externally related to Q, and Q is externally related to P, then, on the terms of Hartshorne's strict implication analysis:

not- (necessarily not, P without Q) and not- (necessarily not, Q without P) or taking the double negations into account:*

it is possible that (P without Q) and it is possible that (Q without P). If *every* event is to be analyzed in these terms, as Russell's pure external relations doctrine asserts, then every event can exist *without* any other event, and hence every event is a logically self-subsistent entity.

Hartshorne's critique of such an ontology is, in my view, quite effective. For one thing, it seems very odd on the face of it that there should exist internal relations *only* or external relations *only*, since our discourse about relational contexts seems to invoke both conceptions. It is almost bizarre that Russell did not see this point, since it has a strict formal analogy that one would surmise Russell would be quite aware of. The dilemma "either all internal relata or all external relata (strong disjunction), where internal relata are negates of external relata" is equivalent to the formally invalid dilemma, "either *all* terms are intrinsical or *no* terms are intrinsical." This is formally invalid in the sense that it claims to be exhaustive of the possible alternatives, yet leaves out of account propositions of the traditional "sub-alternative" type. Why is the possibility that, "some terms are intrinsical and some terms are not intrinsical" being ruled out? When we add to this the fact that, clearly there are instances of internal relations, namely, as stated

---

*The following Lewisian modal calculus states this more rigorously:

1. $\sim[N\sim(P.\sim Q)].\sim[N\sim(Q.\sim P)]$ Assumption
2. $\sim[\sim M\sim\sim(P.\sim Q)].\sim[\sim M\sim\sim(Q.\sim P)]$ From 1, Modal Definition.
3. $\sim[\sim M(P.\sim Q)].\sim[\sim M(Q.\sim P)]$ From 2, Double Negation.
4. $[M(P.\sim Q)].[M(Q.\sim P)]$ From 3, Double Negation.

above, a new event (such as my experience of typing this sentence in toto) is internally related to the past (such as my typing the first letter of this sentence), then it seems most unlikely that Russell could be correct in his claim that one must *choose* between absolute monism and absolute atomism.

A precisely analogous problem occurs in Russell's argument for the strict determinacy of the future, which he held (at the time) along with a related denial of the objective or ontological status of temporal process.[12] Russell argued, much akin to the famous Master Argument of Diodorus, that considerations of logic prove that the future is determinate. He holds that "X will occur" and "X will not occur" are exhaustive. Since these sentences can be formally generalized into the tautologous sentential function X v~X, it is a truth of logic that the future will be one way and not another, that is, since one or the other of these alternatives must obtain on pain of denying the tautologous status of X v~X. Hartshorne reports that he once got Russell to admit that such an argument amounts to no more than a *petitio principii* (CSPM 134). For the issue is, before one chooses an appropriate meta-language formalization of propositions about the future, is it the case that "X will occur" and "X will not occur" are exhaustive contradictories, rather than contraries? Again, we seem to have a formally invalid dilemma comparable to taking the traditional super-alternative type propositions as logically exhaustive, while leaving out sub-alternative type propositions. "All conditions of the future (to the occurrence of X) are such that X will occur" and "No conditions of the future are such that X will occur" are not logically exhaustive. For why not, "some conditions of the future are and some are not such that X will occur, and it is indefinite *now* as to which alternative obtains"? Russell's argument "works" only on assuming the conclusion, namely, that there cannot *be* any indefiniteness with respect to X at any time! That is to say, he just rules out, by omission, the possibility that there might *be* indefiniteness with respect to X at time t, or that at time t, X may be neither required nor excluded, but merely permitted (CSPM 135).[13]

However, there are some ideas in Russell's long philosophical career which Hartshorne has found amenable. I cannot go into an

---

*Bertrand Russell, *Our Knowledge of the External World* (W. W. Norton, 1929) pp. 170–171, 195. Here Russell argues that the idea of infinity is a property of classes and is only applicable to a series, such as the series of events forming the past, in a derivative sense. Yet classes are given all at once, and no "successive synthesis" is required. Hence, Kant's first antinomy involves a mistaken definition of infinity. For a recent defense of Russell here, see Quentin Smith, "Infinity and the Past," *Philosophy of Science*, Vol. 53, No. 2 (1986).

exhaustive list here, but a few items are worthy of mention. As in Moore's case, Russell found the idea of an infinite past logically admissible, and on different grounds than Moore.* Hartshorne has referred to this in a number of instances (e.g., CSPM 126, OTM 94). Also, Hartshorne has found Russell's reflections on classical theism and the "class of all classes" to be a telling indictment of the coherence of the classical model of deity. In effect, Russell asked: Can God be conceived as a unified individual, and yet as inclusive of an *absolute maximum of possibility*—like the problematic "class of all classes" is conceived as an absolute maximum of included items, including itself? (R. M. Martin has recently challenged such an argument.[14] Notwithstanding, there is still a lesson to be gleaned here irrespective of the merits or demerits of Martin's challenge: should we not try out an alternative, less complicating concept of God, which does not even suggest such paradoxes?) Finally, Hartshorne has concurred with Russell's indictment of William James' notion[15] that theistic belief might have a sufficient justification by virtue of its value to the living of life. Hartshorne's "global argument" for theism, in its pragmatic strands, is not based upon the Jamesian assumption that "what is valuable is true," but rather upon the converse assumption that "that which is true is valuable" (NTOT 47). The global argument for theism tries to explain why there should be *any* interest in the truth.

2. Hartshorne and Positivism

Hartshorne's position on logical positivism has been rather clearcut and persistent from the early period of his papers on the topic published in *Philosophy of Science* (1935, 1941) to his comments on the verifiability and falsification principles in the mature CSPM. His severe criticisms of positivism's arguments against "metaphysics," its emotive theory of value, its reduction of the class of meaningful sentences to the class of conceivable *human* observation-sentences and to the language of physicalism, are in my view, incisive and demolishing. Indeed, his "Logical Positivism and the Method of Philosophy" (BH Ch. XVI), authored in the 1930s hey-day of Carnap, Neurath, Schlick, Reichenbach *et al*, was a courageous anticipation of what would later become philosophical common sense. At the same time, there are elements in the positivistic tradition—its penchant for formalism (especially Carnap's modal logical systems in *Meaning and Necessity*), its insistence upon distinctions between analytic and synthetic, necessary and contingent propositions, its sense of the importance of the natural sciences, and its insistence upon a connection between experience and meaning—which are important features of Hartshorne's philosophy. In fact, Hartshorne concludes his chapter on the positivists in BH with the gracious acknowledgment that, "The new metaphysics has more to learn from the logical positivists than from any other group of contemporary thinkers" (BH 295). Thus, his relation to this second major stage in the history of "analytic" philosophy is, as I interpret it, a mixed one, involving neither wholesale rejection nor wholesale acceptance. Put one way, he could never accept any philosophy which claims to deny the possibility of metaphysical inquiry *as such*, but he could accept, especially by virtue of his editing and study of the Peirce papers,* those points of interface between positivism and Peirce's pragmaticist philosophy, namely, those "elements in the positivistic tradition" mentioned above.

The *locus classicus* of the hallmark doctrine of positivism—its rejection of any sort of metaphysical inquiry—is Carnap's much discussed, "Die Ueberwindung der Metaphysik durch logische Analyse der Sprache." [16] One of Carnap's main arguments in that paper could be stated as follows:

(1) All metaphysical theories "seek objects *behind* the phenomena" accessible to the empirical sciences.
(2) All inquiry which is cognitively meaningful seeks phenomenal entities accessible to the empirical sciences.
∴ No metaphysical theories are theories which are cognitively meaningful.

Hartshorne effectively argues that the first premise fails to account for counter-examples of metaphysical theories which seek precisely notions which are illustrated in phenomena. Carnap defends his initial premise by citing examples of obscure statements taken out of philosophical context, from merely two German "metaphysicians"—Hegel and Heidegger (Heidegger would of course demur this classification)— and two perhaps less obscure items of classical metaphysical theology. But these examples hardly exhaust the class of metaphysical theories and notions *as such*. Nor are they especially representative of much of

---

*Partial corroboration of this resides in the fact that, from BH 253-297, Peirce is referred to some nineteen times, edging out Whitehead as the most mentioned non-positivist philosopher. Surely, Hartshorne was thinking about the positivists with Peirce readily in mind.

the thinking found in "modern" metaphysics, e.g., James Peirce, Bergson, or Whitehead. Indeed, Whitehead's metaphysical categories are intended to be always somehow exhibited *in* the phenomena they seek to describe (AI 159-165), and Hartshorne even defines a metaphysical "error" as a notion which has *no* illustration in phenomena, and which is thereby "meaningless" in the strict sense, even if it is stated in grammatically or syntactically correct sentences (BH 274).[17] A prime example of such an error, in Hartshorne's view, would be the proposal that the *nihil absolutum* is a possible state of affairs, since the conceptual intention of such a notion is the very absence of phenomena of any sort. (*That* this is an error has positive implication for metaphysics, namely that it must be true in *any* possible world that *something* exists.) Hence, it is clear that a really consistent Carnapian, who embraces the second premise above, would be led to certain sorts of constructive metaphysical proposals in applying the second premise to a wide variety of metaphysical proposals submitted in the history of philosophy.

Another argument of positivists, which re-surfaced in the literature from time to time, is that metaphysical proposals make no discernible difference to our experience which could be tested. One important variation on this theme has come to be known as the "falsifiability" criterion of cognitive meaning. A.G.N. Flew has put the point this way: any proposition P has cognitive meaning only if a state of affairs denied by P is observable in principle.[18] Since metaphysical proposals, which are purportedly necessary truths holding on any condition, can have no such denials which might be observed, they are cognitively meaningless. The problem with this, as Hartshorne notes in concurrence with Popper's *Logiche der Forschung* (CSPM 21), is that this criterion of cognitive meaning simply begs the question of the meaningfulness of metaphysical proposals, or, proposed necessary truths having existential import. *If* there are such truths, they cannot by their very nature have an empirically discernible falsification, and thus to define the class of cognitively meaningful statements in this way is simply to declare, not to argue, that there can be no meaningful necessary existential statements. Besides, such a criterion seems to make very ordinary mathematical assertions "meaningless." For, on certain views of the foundations of mathematics at least, there are surely "mathematical existentials" which appear to be both cognitively meaningful and necessarily true—such as "there *exists* a number greater than seven"— and yet there is no consistently conceivable denial of this state of affairs which some mathematician might intuit or someday prove. Rather, Hartshorne suggests that we employ the falsifiability criterion to demarcate the class of meaningful "restrictive" empirical or observational statements (CSPM 21). Thus, any proposition P is a restrictive empirical proposition, if the denial of P is observable in principle. For example, (a) "My copy of the *Tractatus* is on the table" belongs to this class of statements, since it is a conceivable observation that I or other observers might perform such that, (b) "My copy of the *Tractatus* is on the chair next to the table." Given the appropriate background assumptions, such as my having one copy of the *Tractatus* and that both utterances apply to some time t, (b) would falsify (a).

Most of these disagreements with positivism are well-known to close students of Hartshorne's writings. What is perhaps less known, and is most certainly less emphasized, is Hartshorne's affinity for some essential aspects of positivism. In addition to the penchants for formalism and integration with natural science, and maintenance of the analytic/synthetic and necessity/contingency distinction (see our discussion of Quine below), Hartshorne holds explicitly to a very logically "weak" or liberalized variety of verificationism. As he puts this at CSPM 24: "verifiability (liberally enough construed) is valid as a criterion of meaning in general." The problem with previous positivistic versions of a verifiability principle has *not* been in the insistence upon an essential connection between "meaning" and "experience," but in the restrictions placed upon the possible modes of experience or observation. There are many things which we cannot intuit or imagine or directly observe, but which we can conceptualize, and to which we can attribute a suitable observation by non-human observers in principle. For Hartshorne, to conceptualize P means roughly that one can purpose a state of affairs P such that the adequate semantical explication of P contains no formal contradictions, and such that *some* suitable observer could observe it. The reason for the latter phrase about "suitable observers" is that, for Hartshorne, it is meaningless to speak of a concept which attaches itself to *no* notion of evidence whatsoever (any notion of evidence carrying with it an evidentiary experience).* As Hartshorne once put it in response to Eugene Peters, "If no experience could tell you what you mean, why suppose you mean anything?" (Response to MMCH, 15). Here perhaps Hartshorne is closest to the pragmatic disposition in contemporary philosophy from Peirce's "How to Make Our Ideas Clear" to Quine, Putnam and Rorty: any theory or notion which is submitted as being beyond evidence of any sort is, by definition, a theory or notion which does no intellectual

---

*This is not incompatible with Tarski's semantical definition of truth (see CSPM 287).

work. And a theory or notion which does no intellectual work is useless, and hence, in the strictest sense, cognitively meaningless.

3. Hartshorne and Ordinary Language

Hartshorne has long been concerned with ordinary language philosophy. Like the positivistic case, his relation to it is one of both warm acceptance of some elements and unembarrassed rejection of others. He seems to have made a beginning at the analysis of some aspects of religious language, instigated by the work of Ian Ramsey, as early as 1956,[19] and by the time of the "Preface" to CSPM (1970), states his concern with so-called "linguistic analysis" quite self-consciously:

> In this book, more than in others, I have attempted to find common ground with linguistic analysts, and to meet the demand of our time to use no technical philosophical or theological terms without taking care to explain them in words with standard non-philosophical uses. I have tried hard to say things sufficiently definite so that they could at least be right or wrong, and then if possible to eliminate what is wrong. (CSPM xiv)

He has published several papers on Wittgenstein, Ryle, Lazerowitz and Wisdom,[20] and one on the subject of "Whitehead and Ordinary Language" (reprinted as Ch. 12 of WP). He has also discussed P. F. Strawson's *Individuals* at some length (CSPM 186-189). In what is to follow in this section, I will focus on Hartshorne's general remarks on ordinary language in CSPM, his relation to the referential theory of meaning, and his recent study of Wittgenstein (IO 293-305).

The Uses of Ordinary Language. Hartshorne's general position on ordinary language is that the analysis of ordinary language is a viable resource for and required task of philosophical reflection, since "philosophical puzzles have large syntactical and semantic components" (CSPM 71). His guiding methodological principle here seems to be that, philosophers should not use technical linguistic formulations unless there are clear extenuating reasons for doing so, although a sound case can be made for such appropriate extenuating reasons. In effect, he concurs with the spirit of ordinary language philosophy in maintaining that there is a "sanity embodied in [ordinary] language" from which philosophers should draw, but he thinks that some legitimate philosophical purposes "transcend ordinary human discourse" (CSPM 71). The justification for the occasional use of technical language in philosophical contexts is the same as it is in scientific contexts: we need special language only for the special purposes of science and philosophy, such as dealing with the extremely large or extremely small, or the extremely general or abstract, issues which simply do not (or very seldomly) arise in ordinary life. Any such "justifiable" technical language must, of course, not be taken as immune from criticism, or as license for obscurity.

A good example of how, for Hartshorne, ordinary language can furnish appropriate evidence in philosophical disputes is afforded by his brief essay on, "Sensory Qualities and Ordinary Language" (CSPM Ch. 15). He points out that ordinary language stands against the orthodox psychological doctrine that sensory qualities are value-neutral or lacking in emotive tone, although emotive tones are associated with sensory qualities, probably by contiguity (CSPM 298). On the contrary, ordinary language assumes that adjectival expressions, employed to indicate tertiary or emotional quality, are grounded in sensation, e.g., sweet and "my sweet" or blue and "the blues" or bright and "brightly" or dim and "a dim view of . . ." etc. (CSPM 299). This is evidence against the orthodox view, since, if the basis for this linguistic phenomenon is association by contiguity, we should expect personal differences in association to create difficulties in communication; yet, despite personal differences we readily understand what it means to have, e.g., "the blues." (Nor is it clear that there is a cultural basis for any "associations." See PPS, 170-171.)

On the other hand, a good example of how, for Hartshorne, ordinary language can be inappropriately used in philosophical disputes is afforded by P. F. Strawson's defense of the concept of "substance" in his *Individuals* (CSPM 186-189). Strawson argues that the notion of an "event," as opposed to that of "substance," is not compatible with requirements of ordinary language, and hence the only world about which we can talk meaningfully is one constituted by substances. For example, Strawson points out that the spatio-temporal orientation of ordinary language requires more than mere "events" or "happenings" ("bangs" are his paradigms here), that is, since such "events" have neither shape nor adequate continuity or sequentiality. However, "bangs" are not unit-events in the sense of Hartshorne's event ontology, but are rather abstract aspects of concrete individual events, such as micro-events of a chemical explosion from which a "bang" is detected. Indeed, ordinary language considerations may not, in this case, have any particular or decisive ontological significance, for quantum microphysics seems to suggest that "substances" are macro-scopic constructions of more fundamental micro-level, discrete events. This cannot be dismissed *simply* because it disagrees with ordinary language, or correlatively, common sense.[21]

Wittgenstein's Critique of the Referential Theory of Meaning. One of the major developments within ordinary language philosophy, especially powerful in the work of the later Wittgenstein, is its critique of the referential theory of meaning. At least one philosopher has seen in this critique the basis for an indictment of Hartshorne's philosophy.

In a doctoral dissertation,[*] L. Bryant Keeling has advanced the thesis that Hartshorne's seventh proof-step in the LP version of the ontological argument, $\sim N \sim q$, is faulty because it is grounded upon a "mistaken theory of meaning."[22] According to Keeling, it is a major presupposition of Hartshorne's metaphysics that the "meaning of a predicate word is that to which it refers."[23] However, he submits, ordinary language philosophers such as the later Wittgenstein, J. L. Austin, William Alston *et al* have successfully shown that the meanings of words are not equivalent to the referents of words. Such philosophers show that there are many things which can be said about objects that are the referents of words when used in certain ways, which cannot be said about the meanings of those words. As Wittgenstein once put the point:

> Let us first discuss *this* point of the argument: that a word has no meaning if nothing corresponds to it. It is important to note that the word "meaning" is being used illicitly if it is used to signify the thing that 'corresponds' to the word. That is to confound the meaning of a name with the *bearer* of the name. When Mr. N. N. dies one says that the bearer of the name dies, not that the meaning dies. And it would be nonsensical to say that, for if the name ceased to have meaning it would make no sense to say "Mr. N. N. is dead."[24]

Moreover, if meaning were reducible to reference, then words having different meanings could not have the same referent. However, there are many cases in which words have the same referent, and yet they are

---

[*]L. Bryant Keeling, *God-Language and Metaphysics: A Study in the Philosophy of Charles Hartshorne with Special Emphasis on the Ontological Argument*, 1971 Ph.D. Dissertation, The University of Chicago. In this section we will treat only Keeling's attack on Hartshorne's "theory of meaning" and its relation to the theory of modality. Also see his, "Feelings as a Metaphysical category: Hartshorne from an Analytical Point of View," *Process Studies*, Vol. 6, No. 1, 1976, pp. 51–56, and Hartshorne's response in the same issue.

clearly distinct in meaning, or rather have different "senses." Frege's "the evening star" and the "the morning star" is a classical illustration of this.

The implicit criticism of Hartshorne at this point is hardly decisive as Keeling admits.[25] Hartshorne's crucial move in the theory of modality—his exploitation of the insight that "definite thought is always about something" (AD 106)—is simply not threatened by the doctrine that meaning cannot be reduced to reference. All Hartshorne needs to establish is that meaning and reference are in some way or to some extent *connected*. The referents of words may or may not be the same across variant sentential contexts, and the shifts in meaning across variant sentential contexts may be due to variant "usages" of words resulting in different senses. But this is clearly distinct from altogether denying a referential dimension of language, or to speak with Alston, that aspect of language which provides "context identity."[26] "Mr. N. N." is not an expression occurring in a vacuum, having no connection to anything other than itself.

The problematic concerning "reference," which Keeling does think offers a serious challenge to Hartshorne, resides in the fact that one encounters difficulty in specifying the exact linguistic conditions which accompany the act of referring.[27] This is especially acute in the case of "value" words like "love," "hope," "justice," "beauty," "power," etc., but it persists even in the case of "object" words. Keeling offers Alston's analysis of object words and reference as justification for his view:

> There is no doubt that 'pencil' is related in some important way to the class of pencils, but does it *refer* to that class? One reason for denying that it does is this. If we want to pick out the class of pencils as what we are talking about, preparatory to going on to say something about it, the word 'pencil' will not serve our purpose. If, for example, we want to say that the class of pencils is very large, we will not succeed in doing so by uttering the sentence "Pencil is very large." The word 'pencil' simply will not do the job of referring to the class of pencils.[28]

It is to be pointed out that Alston has something quite specific in mind when he uses the term "refer" in this instance. He is concerned with referring as an act of naming. It is not clear that Hartshorne's notion of "reference" need be so restricted, for again, all he requires is that there be *some* connection between extra-linguistic reality and language. Yet, what is significant here is that, as Alston says, it is indubitable that "pencil" has *some* relation to the class of pencils. The word "pencil," then, is about *something,* it has some connection with extra-linguistic reality, even though we cannot say *exactly* how it has that connection. This is so since, if we suppose that the class of pencils is empty, we could not say that the word "pencil" has the same meaning that it has on the supposition that the class of pencils is non-empty, and the same meaning the word has in the usual pragmatic contexts, i.e., in those contexts where we are not seeking some special perlocutionary effect, for example, in a game where "pencil" is used as a code word for a certain kind of play.

We may well conclude with Keeling on the basis of Alston's analysis and other analyses of referring that reference is a *function* of word usage and not *vice versa.* However, it is a *non sequitur* to suppose that this conclusion shows that meaning and reference are absolutely disconnected. What Keeling must show in order to undermine Hartshorne's metaphysical and modal assumptions is that there can be meaningful expressions having, in the strictest sense, *no* connection to extra-linguistic reality. However, Keeling does not show this. He simply proceeds to show in greater detail that reference is a function of word usage.

What Keeling seems to get confused is this: When Hartshorne speaks of "meaning as such" and argues that some connection with extra-linguistic reality is necessary to "meaning as such,"[29] he is providing a theory about the "metaphysical" or "transcendental" conditions for meaningful expressions, not a "theory of meaning" in the sense of a theory which specifies the conditions for *differentia* of meaning. The *non sequitur* fallacy occurs because Keeling fails adequately to make or take account of the above distinction. This confusion is evident in the very language he uses to describe Hartshorne's "mistaken" theory of meaning: the meaning of a predicate word *is* that to which it refers. This is distinct from: meaningful expressions require connection with extra-linguistic reality.

Apropos of Keeling's thesis, it is interesting that Hartshorne has stated explicitly that he concurs with Wittgenstein that it is a confusion "to take every word as the name of some entity" (IO 296).

Wittgenstein's Contributions. While Hartshorne has been clear in rejecting the logical atomism and reductively "tautological and empty" view of necessary propositions found in the Tractarian Wittgenstein (CSPM 158, IO 298), he has recently written rather sympathetically of Wittgenstein's *Zettel* (IO 293-305). He applauds Wittgenstein for resisting a reduction of the mental to behavioristic and physiological notions, remarking that some seem to be misinterpreting Wittgenstein here. For, to point out as Wittgenstein does that *Erlebnisse* or experience cannot be understood in abstraction from the body and its environment is not thereby to *identify Erlebnisse* with the body, i.e., with our neural machinery. Further, Wittgenstein was quite correct in his arguments against the possibility of any merely private languages (IO 295), although this does not mean that there cannot be certain aspects of privacy in human experience, or indeed differences in the experience of the same objects between, say, human being and honey bee (IO 294, 304). Also, Wittgenstein was insightful in his discovery of nontautological yet logically necessary truths, e.g., it is logically necessary that orange is an intermediate of red and yellow, although there are no such intermediaries between, say, red and green (IO 304).

Finally, Hartshorne finds Wittgenstein's remark, "*theologie als grammatik*" (*Philosophical Investigations*, Sec. 373), an especially interesting one (CSPM 131, IO 298). Here Wittgenstein *seems* to be indicating that the task of theology is to delineate the kind of object theistic religion worships and speaks of, and it does this through the grammatical structures of its language. For the immediate context is: "*Welche Art von Gegenstand etwas ist, sagt die Grammatik*. Grammar tells what kind of object anything is" (Sec. 373). This seems not altogether removed from Hartshorne's notion that rational theology is concerned exclusively with meaning and consistency of meaning. As I argued in my dissertation,[30] to talk consistently and clearly about *what* God is, is for Hartshorne, tantamount to providing evidence that the concept of God is indispensable to any rational discourse, and hence God could not fail to exist. While surely the cryptic nature of Wittgenstein's remarks here prevent us from saying that he would have found such views tenable (his fideism makes this quite unlikely), he might nonetheless have at least understood why Hartshorne would find his remarks significant.

4. *Hartshorne, Quine, and Kripke*

The philosophy of W. V. O. Quine has exercised an enormous influence on recent "analytic" philosophy. Especially important has been his critique of the traditional distinctions between necessary and contingent, analytic and synthetic, *a priori* and *a posteriori* statements. In contrast, Hartshorne is deeply committed to such distinctions (or something like them), as well as to the related doctrine of the legitimacy of *de re* modality, which Quine has likewise notably challenged. However, as Hartshorne has noted recently in a brief essay on Quine, some work in logic and epistemology influenced by Saul Kripke is bringing the notion of real modal distinctions back to respectability

(CAP 247). Apropos of this remark, I want to argue in this section that Hartshorne stands aligned (*contra* Quine) with a number of Kripke's logical and epistemological notions in *Naming and Necessity*, and with a temporalistic interpretation of Kripke's possible worlds semantics. Further, I wish to argue that, irrespective of considerations of Kripke's thought, there is a case to be made against Quine's critique of (especially) the necessity/contingency distinction, upon which Hartshorne's whole metaphysical enterprise vitally depends. I will begin with considerations of Quine's critique of the necessity/contingency distinction.

Quine. Quine has argued that the distinction between necessary and contingent statements is untenable, largely on the grounds that no statement is immune from revision. In addition to the fact that this way of putting the matter seems to confuse the ontological and epistemological perspectives that can be cast upon statements (see below), it appears to me that a rather convincing argument in favor of the distinction is that we employ it willy-nilly, come what may, and even Quine himself provides an example. It is interesting and important that in, "On What There Is,"[31] Quine declares that there is at least one decision about "what there is" which is not an "ontic" one, namely, that we *must* admit some object or other into our universe of discourse. In other words, for Quine, *what* objects exist is relative to and thus contingent upon the theoretical or natural language we happen to speak, but *that* we speak of objects in speaking a theoretical or natural language is inescapable ("On What, etc.," p. 12). As students of Hartshorne will note, "something exists" is his prime example of a noncontingent metaphysical statement. In so far, Quine would seem to agree that language and logic commit us to *that much* ontology: we cannot sensibly speak of absolutely nothing at all. However, Quine seems not to have commented or reflected upon the sort of necessity that is involved in his insistence here upon the ontological commitment of language.

A connected reflection is presented in Ilham Dilman's recent book on Quine.[32] Quine argues against the notion that the claimed "necessity" of a so-called necessary truth resides solely in its analyticity. Analyticity is an undefined notion which involves a spurious circular appeal to synonymy, which likewise cannot be (or has not been) clearly defined. However, Dilman points out that, even if what Quine says here is true, it is no good reason for rejecting either the necessary/contingent or analytic/synthetic distinction. For there are many things in our language which cannot be set out in terms of independent, isolated, and clearly definable notions, yet it makes perfectly good sense to hold that the notions in question represent intelligible distinctions. For example, citing P. F. Strawson and H. H. Grice, Dilman observes that the notions of "not believing something" and "not understanding something" are such that:

> It would be rash to maintain that *this* distinction does not need clarification; but it would be absurd to maintain that it does not exist. (Dilman, *Quine on Ontology* etc., p. 82)

And so Quine's formal requirements for an "intelligible distinction" are inappropriately stringent. Dilman goes on to state (p. 82–83), in corroboration of the argument above concerning the indispensability of a notion of necessity, that we are *already* in possession of the distinction between necessary and contingent statements, and this is the very presupposition of our quest for an elucidation of such concepts. I think this much approaches Hartshorne's view that, if there is anything like an innate idea, it would be the idea of contingency and its contrast (CSPM 32).

Above, I mentioned that there are "ontological and epistemological perspectives" to be taken toward statements, and I hinted that this provides some argument against the doctrine of the untenability of the necessity/contingency distinction. It seems to me that Quine is right in thinking that such a distinction does collapse if one views statements only from an epistemological point of view. For, viewed epistemologically, any sentence is subject to revision, and hence for all we know "might be otherwise," and hence is *epistemically* contingent. However, while every sentence *might* well be epistemically contingent, it does not follow from this that *there are no* sentences which do not in fact represent states of affairs that cannot be otherwise. In effect, there may well be ontological necessities expressed in sentences which are, by virtue of the human epistemic condition, epistemically contingent. Moreover, it seems to me that Hartshorne has provided us with a clear criterion for the *submission* of such necessary metaphysical proposals: We have a warrant for *submitting* a sentence or set of sentences as necessarily true, if those sentences are somehow involved in our talk about any and all logically possible scenarios, made accessible to us by *Gedan kenexperimenten*. Such a criterion is suggested to us because of two facts: there *are* strong candidates for such necessary truths (e.g., "something always exists," "round squares never exist," "creative process always exists," "time always exists," "the *nihil absolutum* never exists"), and we know clearly what it is like for there *not* to be such truths, e.g., "George Shields III exists" is factual in 1986, but counter-factual in 1950. In fact, it is our possession of the power of

220

negating the very concept of a contingent truth, that allows us to conceptualize the notion that, *whatever our limitations of knowledge,* there may well *exist* truths which are necessary. Hence, there is absolutely nothing that Quine or Rorty or anyone else has ever shown, which could prevent Hartshorne from legitimately claiming that there *appear* to be ideas which are illustrated in every consistent, thought-experiment we undertake, and that such *appearance* is a reason for thinking that such ideas are metaphysical truths. By taking this philosophical formation of the matter, we are not committing ourselves to the apparently absurd notion that necessary truths simply cannot *exist*, while we are at the same time not insisting that *our* submitted notions of necessary truth are epistemically incorrigible.

Kripke. A study of Saul Kripke's "methodological" discussion in *Naming and Necessity* (pp. 34–42),[33] reveals much affinity for Hartshorne's views on these matters. Kripke agrees emphatically that "necessary" and "*a priori*" should not be understood as synonyms for the epistemic notion of "certainty" (NN 39, compare Hartshorne, CSPM 31). Like Hartshorne, Kripke points to the example of mathematics, where there are things which can be rationally believed *a priori*, yet without being certain in such belief. Secondly, he seems to agree fully that the distinction between necessity and contingency is legitimate as a metaphysical or ontological distinction (cf. NN 35f-36). Thirdly, as a negative variation on the above item, Kripke insists that modal distinctions are not merely linguistic or *de dicto*, but are *de re*. Here he appeals, like Hartshorne, to the ultimate arbitration of intuition (NN 41f-42). As Hartshorne once put this "intuitive argument":

> So then when an overtaken rabbit finds he cannot escape from but must go into the foxes jaws, this necessity derives from our way of talking about the world! Alas, I cannot make it out. I think there is physical necessity and it is also logical. (LP 175)

I wish to develop this third point concerning Hartshorne's and Kripke's affinity for the validity of *de re* modality more fully. It is the chief merit of George L. Goodwin's outstanding treatise on Hartshorne's ontological argument[34] that he shows how Hartshorne and Kripke complement one another in resolving Quine's objections to the intelligibility of *de re* modality. (Since Goodwin's work on this issue is still not sufficiently well-known, I take it to be worthwhile that I give a brief exposition of it at this relevant juncture.) Quine has objected to the idea of *de re* modality, since it involves quantification across modal operators, e.g., as in (Ex) (Necessarily, X is greater than seven), which he regards as logically illicit. Quine points out that we cannot existentially generalize from the "licit" *de dicto* formulation:

(a) Necessarily, nine is greater than seven

to

(b) (Ex) (Necessarily, X is greater than seven)

This is because "nine" in sentence (a) is referentially opaque, that is, it fails to denote in a *singular* way, and thus opens the door to counterexamples in the generalized sentence (b). For instance, Quine holds that "nine" can mean "the number of planets," but surely it is not a property of "the number of planets" that it is necessarily greater than seven. The thrust of this is that, because of referential opacity in quantified modal logic, we do not know what it *means* to introduce propositions of the form "(Ex) N (X > 7)." However, Hartshorne is clearly committed, in his ontological argument, to such forms as:

(c) (Ex) (Necessarily, X is perfect)

And, if Quine is right, we do not know what (c) means any more than we know what (b) means.

Consequently, an effective Hartshornean response to Quine's critique of *de re* modality requires an intelligible semantics for modal logic. Here is where Kripke's celebrated, "Semantical Considerations on Modal Logic,"[35] comes to bear effectively on the issue. On the terms of Kripke's semantics, we *can* get an intelligible notion of sentences having the form of "(Ex) N (X>7)." Such sentences say:

> that there is some object, x, in this world which has the property, greater-than-seven, in this world and in every possible world in which x exists. In other words, x exists in this world and at least some possible worlds accessible from this world, and x falls under the extension of the predicate, greater-than-seven, in every world in which it exists. (Goodwin, *Ontological Argument*, p. 100)

However, while Kripke semantics thus resolves the issue of providing a *formal* semantics for sentences involving quantification into modal contexts, the very terms of this semantics raise the further question of what it means for an individual to exist in various possible worlds. This problem has come to be known as the Problem of Transworld Identity. Quine has gone on to challenge Kripke further by arguing that his solution to the problem of referential opacity issues in a semantics involving the notoriously difficult idea of "essential properties." For instance, must C. S. Peirce be a philosopher in every possible world in which he exists in order to be C. S. Peirce in those possible worlds? Could he be a seventeenth century sea captain in some possible worlds, and yet still be C. S. Peirce? It is just here that Hartshorne's ontology of temporal process can be employed, providing Kripke with intelligible criteria for making "transworld" identifications. The Problem of Transworld Identity seems perplexing and insoluable when employing, to use Quine's phrase, "Aristotelian essentialism," in which essential properties inhere in substances and require no reference to temporality. Hartshorne's event ontology places the search for a criterion for transworld identity in the much wider matrix of successive and causally efficacious temporal units of becoming. "Temporal inheritance" becomes the *essential* factor in determining identity, and thus more readily settles the above questions: C. S. Peirce might well exist as a literary critic in some possible world, since he might have been one in this actual world, that is, since there was a time in the "history" of Peirce in which he was not a philosopher, and he could have been subjected at that time to different influences. But most certainly he could not be—in any possible world—a seventeenth century sea captain, since this would have *nothing* in common with his succession of temporal events. Thus, to put it cautiously, if Hartshorne's ontological criteria do not "resolve" the Problem of Transworld Identity, then it seems clear that they certainly simplify it.

One final point of affinity between Kripke and Hartshorne concerns the so-called "new theory of reference" sponsored by Kripke, Donnellan, Putnam and others. I see no reason intrinsic to neoclassicism why Hartshorne would not want to accept the thesis that names refer, at least very often, by attaching to "natural kinds," rather than to clusters of descriptive associations. To know whether or not we are talking about "water" is to know whether or not we are talking about hydrogen dioxide, or to speak in Hartshornean terms, sequences of molecular events answering to scientific tests for hydrogen dioxide. Kripke sees a problem here regarding the word "God" (NN 26-27)—is "God" a name or a description? But the problem can be resolved, I think, by taking up Stephen Schwartz' recommended distinction between "natural kind" and "nominal kind" words.[36] "God" cannot be a natural kind word with rigid designation, since God is not, on any one's theology, an object in the environment subject to scientific tests. In the case of "God," one provides postulates of meaning which give it content, in the same way we provide such for other nominal kind words, such as "love" or "power."

Conclusion

I conclude that, in a variety of ways, Hartshorne has had rather intimate working relationships with trends in the rich and diverse spectrum of analytic philosophy. Of course, my charting of these relationships has not been exhaustive by any means. For instance, I did not even mention Hartshorne's relationship to a number of important analytic philosophers about which he has been concerned, e.g., Wilfrid Sellars, C. J. Ducasse, or G. H. von Wright. Nor have I discussed Hartshorne's relationship to the critique of analysis taking place currently within the analytic tradition, such as in Rorty's deconstructionist program[37] or Stanley Rosen's arguments for the indespensability of intuition in his *The Limits of Analysis*. Rather, the main thrust of my discussion has been to explicate and document from a point of view sympathetic to Hartshorne, the extensiveness of his dialogue with the analytic tradition, and to argue, at least at a number of junctures, that there seems to be nothing sound in this tradition (insofar as reviewed here) which cannot be accommodated in some fashion by Hartshorne's philosophy. Hartshornean metaphysics seems to be an open issue, viable, and of interest to future philosophical inquiry.

Abbreviations of Works Cited

AD   Charles Hartshorne, *Anselm's Discovery*. Open Court, 1965.

AI   A. N. Whitehead, *Adventures of Ideas*. Free Press, 1961 reprint.

BH   Charles Hartshorne, *Beyond Humanism*. Peter Smith, 1975 reprint.

CAP   Charles Hartshorne, *Creativity in American Philosophy*. State University of New York Press, 1984.

CSPM   Charkes Hartshorne, *Creative Synthesis and Philosophic Method*. Open Court, 1970.

DR   Charles Hartshorne, *The Divine Relativity*. Yale University Press, 1948.

IO   Charles Hartshorne, *Insights and Oversights of Great Thinkers*. State University of New York Press, 1983.

LP   Charles Hartshorne, *The Logic of Perfection*. Open Court, 1962.

MMCH   Eugene Peters, "Methodology in the Metaphysics of Charles Hartshorne" in *Existence and Actuality*, ed. by J. Cobb and F. Gamwell. The University of Chicago Press, 1984.

MVG   Charles Hartshorne, *Man's Vision of God*. Archon Books, 1964 reprint.

NTOT   Charles Hartshorne, *A Natural Theology of Our Time*. Open Court, 1967.

OTM   Charles Hartshorne, *Omnipotence and Other Theological Mistakes*. State University of New York Press, 1984.

PPS   Charles Hartshorne, *The Philosophy and Psychology of Sensation*. The University of Chicago Press, 1934.

RSP   Charles Hartshorne, *Reality as Social Process*. Hafner Publishing, 1971 reprint.

WP   Charles Hartshorne, *Whitehead's Philosophy*. University of Nebraska Press, 1970

Notes

1. J. O. Urmson, *Philosophical Analysis: Its Development Between the Two World Wars*. Oxford University Press, 1967; Morris Weitz, "Analysis, Philosophical," in *The Encyclopedia of Philosophy*, Vol. 1. Macmillan, 1967.

2. Lewis Ford, "Hartshorne's Encounter with Whitehead: Introductory Remarks," in *Two Process Philosophers*. American Academy of Religion, 1973, p. 1.

3. "Strict and Genetic Identity: An Illustration of the Relations of Logic to Metaphysics," in *Structure, Method and Meaning: Essays in Honor of Henry M. Sheffer*. Liberal Arts Press, 1951.

4. "Bell's Theorem and Stapp's Revised View of Space-Time," *Process Studies*, Vol. 7., No. 4 (Winter, 1977).

5. See C. Gunton, *Becoming and Being*. Oxford University press, 1978, p. 104; and Donald W. Viney, *Charles Hartshorne and the Existence of God*. State University of New York Press, 1985, pp. 133–143.

6. See J. R. Lucas, *A Treatise on Time and Space*. Metheun, 1976.

7. See W. H. Newton-Smith, *The Structure of Time*. Kegan Paul, 1985, p. 110. Also see my article, "Is the Past Finite?" in *Process Studies*, Vol. 14, No. 1 (Winter, 1984).

8. Hilary Putnam, "The 'Corroboration' of Theories" in *The Philosophy of Karl Popper*, Bk. I, ed. by P. Schilpp. Open Court, 1974, pp. 221–239.

9. "Russell on Causality" in BH, Ch. XIII; "The Philosophy of Bertrand Russell (Review of the Schilpp *Festschrift*)," *The Journal of Religion*, Vol. 25, No. 4 (October, 1945); "Russell and Whitehead: A Comparison," in IO, Ch. 22.

10. E. D. Klemke, "Did G. E. Moore Refute Idealism," in *Studies in the Philosophy of G. E. Moore*. Quadrangle, 1969, pp. 3–24.

11. Bertrand Russell, *Outlines of Philosophy*. World Publishing, 1960, p. 293.

12. For an interesting discussion of Russell's views on time see R. M. Gale, *The Language of Time*. Humanities Press, 1968, esp. pp. 207–209.

13. S. M. Cahn sees this issue as far more complicated, and he disagrees with both Hartshorne's and A. N. Prior's (very similar) position, although he does not, in the last analysis, countenance fatalism. See his *Fate, Logic and Time*. Yale University Press, 1969, pp. 60–64. Also, see Hartshorne's comments on Cahn in CSPM 16-17.

14. R. M. Martin, "On the Logical Structure of the Ontological Argument" in his *Whitehead's Categoreal Scheme* (Martinus Nijhoff, 1974), Ch. VIII. Also my comments on Martin's contribution to *Existence and Actuality: Conversations with Charles Hartshorne* (University of Chicago Press, 1984) in my review of this work published in *The Journal of Religion*, Vol. 66, No. 3 (July, 1986), pp. 343–344.

15. B. Russell, "William James' Conception of Truth" in *Philosophical Essays* (Simon and Schuster), 1968, Ch. V.

16. See *Erkenntniss*, Vol. II, pp. 219–241.

17. Eugene Peters presents a masterful discussion of this point, providing interesting comparisons between Whitehead and Hegel, in CA 18-20.

18. A.G.N. Flew in *New Essays in Philosophical Theology*. MacMillan, 1964, pp. 96–99.

19. "Three Strata of Meaning in Theistic Discourse," in LP, Ch. 4, first appearing in part in *The Southern Philosopher*, Vol. III (1956).

20. "Reflections on Wittgenstein" in IO, Ch. 25; "Wittgenstein and Tillich: Reflection on Metaphysics and Language" in CSPM, Ch. 7 (parts of which appeared originally in *Foundations of Language*, Vol. 2 [1961], pp. 20–32; "Mind and Matter in Ryle, Ayer and Croce," in IO, Ch. 24; "The Structure of Metaphysics: A Criticism of Lazerowitz's Theory," *Philosophy and Phenomenological Research*, Vol. 19, No. 2 (December, 1958), pp. 226–240; "John Wisdom on God's: Two Views of the Logic of Theism," *Downside Review* (Winter, 1958–59), pp. 5–17 (reprinted in LP, Ch. 5).

21. Barry Gross makes a similar criticism of G. E. Moore's reliance on ordinary language and common sense on the issue of perception. Moore simply ignores scientific accounts of perception. See Gross, "G. E. Moore: Sense Data" in his *Analytic Philosophy: An Historical Introduction*. Pegasus Books, 1969, pp. 42–43.

22. Keeling, "God-Language and Metaphysics," p. 173.

23. Ibid., p. 13.

24. Ludwig Wittgenstein, *Philosophical Investigations*, trans. by G. E. M. Anscombe. Macmillan, 1967, p. 20. Keeling cites this passage in his dissertation on p. 180.

25. Keeling, "God, Language and Metaphysics," p. 181.

26. William P. Alston, *The Philosophy of Language*. Prentice-Hall, 1964, pp. 15–19.

27. Keeling, "God-Language and Metaphysics," p. 185.

28. William P. Alston, *Philosophy of Language*, p. 15. Cited by Keeling at p. 187.

29. "Extra-linguistic" is understood here in the broadest sense which includes meta-linguistic talk about object language expressions. Cf. C. Hartshorne, "Professor Hartshorne's Syllogism: A Rejoinder," *The Philosophical Review*, 54, No. 5 (1945): 507, and Hartshorne, "The Formal Validity and Real Significance of the Ontological Argument," *The Philosophical Review* 53, No. 3 (1944): 226.

30. George W. Shields, "The Semantics of Perfection." Ph.D. Dissertation, The University of Chicago, June 1981.

31. W. V. O. Quine, "On What There Is," in *From a Logical Point of View*. Harper & Row, 1961.

32. Ilham Dilman, *Quine on Ontology, Necessity and Experience*. Albany: State University of New York Press, 1984, pp. 81–83. While I found this work to be insightful in many respects, I also found its tone to be unnecessarily polemical.

33. Saul Kripke, *Naming and Necessity*. Harvard University Press, 1980. Hereafter: NN.

34. George L. Goodwin, *The Ontological Argument of Charles Hartshorne*. Missoula, Montana: Scholars Press, 1978, Ch. IV.

35. S. Kripke, "Semantical Considerations on Modal Logic" in *Reference and Modality*. Oxford University Press, 1971).

36. Stephen P. Swartz, *In Naming, Necessity, and Natural Kinds*. Ithaca: Cornell University Press, 1983, pp. 37–41.

37. However, see my "Natural Theology and Rorty's 'Philosophy Without Mirrors'" in *American Academy of Religion Abstracts* (Scholars Press, 1982). Also see CAP, Ch. 34.

Bibliography of Writings by Eugene H. Peters

compiled by Damaris Peters

BOOKS

The Creative Advance: An Introduction to Process Philosophy as A Context for Christian Faith. St. Louis, Missouri: The Bethany Press, 1966.

Hartshorne and Neoclassical Metaphysics: An Interpretation. Lincoln, Nebraska: The University of Nebraska Press, 1970.

ARTICLES

"The Isolated Ego in Modern Theology: Philosophical Sources of the Concept," *Encounter*, Vol. 20, No. 1 (Winter, 1959), pp. 26–32.

"The Revelation of God: An Informal Statement," *The Scroll*, Vol. LIII, No. 1 (Summer, 1962), pp. 19–23.

"Authority: Human and Divine—A Critique of Neo-Reformation Views," *Encounter*, Vol. 23, No. 3 (Summer, 1962), pp. 316–324. Also published in *The Reconstruction of Theology*, ed. Ralph G. Wilburn. The Bethany Press, 1973, pp. 227–238.

"Ruminations on a Conversation Concerning Value," *Journal of the Interseminary Movement of the Southwest*, Vol. 1, No. 1 (1962), pp. 73–76.

"Tillich's Doctrine of Essence, Existence, and the Christ," *The Journal of Religion*, Vol. XLIII, No. 4 (October, 1963), pp. 295–302.

"Some Reflections on the Thought of Paul Tillich," *Ohio Christian News: The Ecumenical Journal of Ohio*, Vol. 38, No. 10 (December, 1965), pp. 8–10.

"A Framework for Christian Thought," *The Journal of Religion*, Vol. XLVI, No. 3 (July, 1966), pp. 374–385.

"A Theological Typology," *Hiram College Broadcaster*, Vol. 38, No. 2 (July, 1967), pp. 9–12. An expanded version appears in the *Lexington Theological Quarterly*, Vol. III, No. 1 (January, 1968), pp. 20–28.

"A Conversation with Charles Hartshorne at Hiram College," *Eclectic*, Winter, 1972, pp. 1–18.

"Hartshorne on Actuality," *Process Studies*, Vol. 7, No. 3 (Fall, 1977), pp. 200–204.

"Philosophic Insights of Charles Hartshorne," *The Southwestern Journal of Philosophy*, Vol. 8 (February, 1977), pp. 157–170.

Comment on Charles Hartshorne, "Panpsychism: Mind as Sole Reality," *Encyclopedia for the Ultimate Reality and Meaning*, Vol. 1, pp. 115–129. In the *Encyclopedia*, Vol. 1 (Van Gorum, Holland, Winter, 1979), pp. 231–232.

"Education Isn't Always Practical," *The Disciple*, September 6, 1979, pp. 7–8.

"Divine Foreknowledge," *Encounter*, Vol. 40, No. 1 (Winter, 1979), pp. 31–34. (Contains discussion of Plantinga mentioned in the "Introduction.")

"Knowledge, Facts, and the Senses: A New Look at an Old Dialogue," *The Intercollegiate Review*, Vol. 15, No. 2 (Spring, 1980), pp. 87–93.

"Theology, Classical and Neo-Classical," *Encounter*, Vol. 44, No. 1 (Winter, 1983) pp. 7–15, (Lecture given at the Society of Christian Philosophers, 1982)

"Charles Hartshorne and the Ontological Argument," *Process Studies*, Vol. 14 (Spring, 1984), pp. 11–20.

"Methodology in the Metaphysics of Charles Hartshorne," with response by Charles Hartshorne, in *Existence and Actuality*, edited by John Cobb, Jr., and Franklin Gamwell. University of Chicago Press, 1984, pp. 1–15.

REVIEWS

Review of *Christian Social Ethics in a Changing World: An Ecumenical Theological Inquiry*, John C. Bennett, editor, New York: Association Press, and London: SCM Press, 1966. In *Journal for the Scientific Study of Religion*, Vol. VI, No. 2 (Fall, 1967), pp. 316–318.

Review of Norman Pittenger, *Process Thought and Christian Faith*, Macmillan. In *The Christian*, Vol. 107, No. 16 (April 20, 1969), p. 28.

Review of Eric C. Rust, *Evolutionary Philosophies and Contemporary Theology*, Westminster Press, 1969. In *Interpretation*, Vol. 24 (October, 1970), pp. 532–533.

Review of *Hartshorne and Neo-Classical Metaphysics* (Lincoln: University of Nebraska Press, 1970, p. 631. *In the Monist,* Vol. 56, 1972).

Critical Review of *Process Philosophy and Christian Thought*, edited by Delwin Brown, Ralph E. James, and Gene Reeves, Indianapolis: The Bobbs-Merrill Company, Inc., 1971. In *Process Studies*, Vol. 1 (Fall, 1971), pp. 218–227.

Review of William D. Dean, *Coming To: A Theology of Beauty*, Westminster Press, 1972. In *Encounter*, Vol. 37, No. 1 (Winter, 1976), pp. 116–119.

Review of *Religious Experience and Process Theology: The Pastoral Implications of a Major Modern Movement*, edited by Harry James Cargas and Bernard Lee, Paulist Press, 1976. In *Religious Education*, Vol. 72 (September–October, 1972), pp. 559–560.

Critical Review of George L. Goodwin, *The Ontological Argument of Charles Hartshorne* (American Academy of Religion Dissertation Series, No. 20, Missouls, Montana: Scholars Press, 1978). In *Process Studies*, Vol. 9 (Spring–Summer, 1979), pp. 45–49.

UNPUBLISHED PAPERS

Dating back to graduate school at the University of Chicago (1950–1957), part of the Eugene H. Peters Collection, these can be found at the Hiram College Library, Hiram, Ohio 44234. They include the following:

"The Logos Doctrine of Justin Martyr," 1950.

"An Inquiry into the Relation of Truth and Faith with Regard to the Problem of the Existence of God," 1950.

"Christian Faith and the Human Situation," 1950.

"Is the Gospel Faith True?," 1950–51.

"Josiah Royce" (with comments by Bernard Loomer), 1951.

"Richard Niebuhr," 1951.

"Constructive Theology Qualifying Examination" (with comments by Bernard Loomer), 1951.

"Form Criticism: Its Aim and Method," 1951.

"Religious Humanism" (with comments by Daniel Day Williams), 1951.

"The Crucifixion," 1952.

"Reflections on the Ideal Student of the History of Religions," 1952.

"The Problem of Confucianism," 1952.

"An Interpretation of Selfhood," 1952.

"Jesus' Farewell Discourses in the Fourth Gospel," 1952.

"Aristotle's Metaphysics," 1952.

"Thomas Aquinas on the Divine Unity," 1952

"On First Looking Into Whitehead's Adventures" (with extensive comments by Charles Hartshorne), 1953.

"An Essay on Christian Dramatic Tragedy" (with comments by Preston Roberts), 1953.

"Comments on Tillich's Theology," 1954.

"Weber and Aristotle" (with comments by James Luther Adams), 1955.

"Athanasius' Doctrine of the Incarnation" (with comments by Jaroslav Pelikan), 1955.

"Philosophy of Religion Doctoral Examination: Wieman, Whitehead, Plato, Augustine," 1955(?).

"Problems Concerning Tillich's Doctrine of God," 195?.

"The Concept of Self Transcendence in Reinhold Niebuhr" (with comments by Alvin Pitcher), 1955.

"An Interpretation of Augustine," 195?.

"The New Realism in Philosophy and Theology." 1956.

"Royce, Idealism, and a 'Pugnacious Proposition'" (with comments by Bernard Meland), 1956.

"Wieman, Whitehead, and the Problem of the Concrete" (with comments by Bernard Meland), 1956.

"Some Reflections on the Person of Jesus Christ," a statement submitted to the faculty of the Divinity School for the oral examination in Christian Theology, 1956.

"Science and Philosophical Idealism" and "Existentialism and Theological Naturalism," lectures delivered to the Christian Ministers' Institute, Little Rock, Arkansas, 1958.

"God and History," 1958.

"Sartre's *No Exit*," 196?.

"The Revelation of God: An Informal Statement," 1960.

"The Power of God," 1960.

"Form, Power and the Unity of the Individual," Ph.D. Dissertation, The University of Chicago, 1960.

"Man, Myth, and Meaning," undated paper.

"The Power of God, the Wisdom of God, the Love of God," a series of lectures for the Oklahoma Christiuan Ministers' Institute, 1961.

"Theology and Process Philosophy," a paper presented to the Association of Disciples for Theological Discussion, 1960.

"The Ontological Dimension of Existence," a paper read to the Association of Disciples for Theological Discussion, 1963.

"Process Philosophy and the Theological Enterprise," 196?.

"History, Eschatology, and Process Philosophy," a paper presented to the Association of Disciples for Theological Discussion, 1968.

"Racism," a lecture, 1969.

"Oedipus: A Few Reflections," 1974.

"Part and Whole in the Neoclassical Metaphysics of Charles Hartshorne," written at Hiram College, undated.

Untitled paper on Royce's discussion of Kant in *Lectures on Modern Idealism*, undated.

"Confucianism," undated lecture.

"Reflections on Griffin's 'Hartshorne's Differences from Whitehead,'" 197?.

"Your Money's Worth," lecture on the liberal arts delivered to a Phi Beta Kappa banquet, 1979.

"A New Look at the Ancient God: Process Theology and Process Ethics," lectures delivered to the annual conference of the Ohio-Meadville District, Unitarian-Universalists, April, 1980.

"A Word for the Liberal Arts," undated.

"Charles Hartshorne," undated.

"The Tree of Knowledge," a sermon delivered at Hiram College Baccalaureate, June 7, 1981.

"Job," 1982.

"Debate and Argumentation," 1982.

CORRESPONDENCE

Lengthy letters to and from Lewis Ford, Charles Hartshorne, Dallas M. High, Bernard Loomer, Schubert Ogden, and Alvin Plantinga.

Cassette tapes of conversations with Charles Hartshorne have been given to the Center for Process Studies, Claremont, California.

Notes on Contributers

John B. Cobb, Jr. received his Ph.D. degree from the University of Chicago. In addition to numerous articles in such journals as *The Journal of Religion* and *The Journal of the American Academy of Religion*, he has contributed to numerous books such as *Christian Theology and Civil Religion* and *Political Theology*. He is the author of *Living Options in Protestant Theology, A Christian Natural Theology, Christ in a Pluralistic Age* and *Beyond Dialogue: Toward a Mutual Transformation of Buddhism and Christianity*. Among other works, he is presently the Director of the Center for Process Studies at Claremont and the Ingraham Professor of Theology at the School of Theology at Claremont and Avery Professor of Religion, Claremont Graduate School.

Lewis S. Ford received his undergraduate and Ph.D. degrees from Yale University. He has written numerous articles in such journals as *The Thomist, The New Scholasticism* and *Process Studies*, the latter of which he edits. He edited *Two Process Philosophers* and co-edited *Explorations in Whitehead's Philosophy*. He has authored *The Lure of God: A Biblical Background for Process Theism* and most recently *The Emergence of Whitehead's Metaphysics*. He has taught at Pennsylvania State University and is presently Professor of Philosophy at Old Dominion University.

David Ray Griffin received his Ph.D. degree from the Claremont Graduate School. He has published numerous articles in such journals as the *International Journal of Philosophy, The Journal of Religion* and *Process Studies*. He is the author of *A Process Christology; God, Power and Evil: A Process Theodicy*, and co-author of *Process Theology: An Introductory Exposition* He introduced and is co-editor of *Physics and the Ultimate Significance of Time: Bohm, Prigogine, and Process Philosophy*. He serves as the Executive Director of the Center for Process Studies and founding director of the Center for a Post-Modern World. He is Professor of Philosophy of Religion at the School of Theology at Claremont and Claremont Graduate School.

235

Charles Hartshorne received his Ph.D. degree from Harvard University. He is one of the best known philosophers of the twentieth century for his vast contribution to metaphysics and philosophical theology. He has published hundreds of articles in such journals as *The Journal of Philosophy, The Review of Metaphysics*, and *The Monist*, among many others. He is co-editor of the papers of C. S. Peirce and author of *Whitehead's Philosophy,* and *Creative Synthesis and Philosophic Method*, among seventeen works. His distinguished contribution to ontological argument research can be found in numerous articles and two books, *The Logic of Perfection* and *Anselm's Discovery*. Recently he has published *Omnipotence and Other Theological Mistakes, Insights and Oversights of Great Thinkers*, and *Creativity in American Philosophy*. He has taught at Harverd, the University of Chicago, and Emory University and is presently the Ashbel Smith Professor Emeritus of Philosophy at the University of Texas at Austin.

George Nordgulen received his Ph.D. degree from the graduate school at Claremont. He has published articles in *The New Scholasticism, The Iqbal Review, The Thomist, Encounter*, and *The Journal of Dharma* and he writes abstracts for *Process Studies*. He is the author of *Perspectives in World Religions*. He edited and wrote an introduction to the articles on Classical and Neo-Classical Theism for Volume 44 of *Encounter*. He is Professor of Religion and University Chaplain at Eastern Kentucky University.

Schubert M. Ogden received his Ph.D. degree from the University of Chicago. His publications include numerous articles in such journals as the *Journal of Religion, Process Studies*, and *The Journal of the American Academy of Religion*. He is the author of several books including *Christ Without Myth, The Reality of God, Faith and Freedom, The Point of Christology*, and most recently *On Theology*. He has taught at Perkins School of Theology in Dallas, The University of Chicago, and presently is the University Distinguished Professor of Theology and Director of the Graduate Program in Religious Sudies at Southern Methodist University.

Damaris Peters received her BME degree at Texas Christian University and an MM degree from Kent State University. She is presently Associate Professor of Music at Hiram College, where she directs the college choir and Madrigal singers and teaches music history and studio voice. She has also served a term as department chairperson. A Danforth Associate, in 1985 she was the recipient of the T. A. Abbot Award for Faculty Excellence, given by the Division of Higher Education of The Christian Church (Disciples of Christ).

George W. Shields received the Ph. D. from the University of Chicago, where he was a Disciples House Scholar. He has done further study at Oxford University, England. He has published numerous articles and reviews in such journals as *International Journal for Philosophy of Religion, Process Studies, The Journal of Religion, Encounter*, and *Religious Studies Review*, among others. He has taught philosophy at the University of Louisville and Indiana University Southeast, and is currently Assistant Professor and Coordinator of the Philosophy Program at Kentucky State University in Frankfort, Kentucky.

Donald Wayne Viney received the Ph.D. from the University of Oklahoma. His revised doctoral thesis was published by The State University of New York Press in 1985 as *Charles Hartshorne and the Existence of God*. Having taught philosophy at the University of Oklahoma at Norman, he is currently Assistant Professor of Philosophy at Pittsburg State University in Pittsburg, Kansas.

Theodore Vitali received the Ph. D. from St. Louis University, where he wrote a doctoral thesis on the philosophy of Hartshorne. He has published numerous articles and reviews in such journals as *The Review of Metaphysics, Process Studies, The Modern Schoolman*, and *Transactions of the C. S. Pierce Society*. Currently, he is Associate Professor and Chair of the Department of Philosophy at Bellarmine College in Louisville, Kentucky.

Clark M. Williamson received the Ph. D. from the University of Chicago. He has published articles in *Process Studies, Journal of Religion, Encounter* (of which he is editor), *Impact*, and *Quarterly Review*. He is the author of *Has God Rejected His People?* and *God Is Never Absent*. Currently, he is Professor of Theology at the Christian Theological Seminary in Indianapolis.